CHINA
AND THE
WTO

RESHAPING THE WORLD ECONOMY

CHINA
AND THE
WTO

RESHAPING THE WORLD ECONOMY

Pradip Putatunda, Ph.D

STERLING PUBLISHERS PRIVATE LIMITED

STERLING PUBLISHERS PRIVATE LIMITED
A-59, Okhla Industrial Area, Phase-II, New Delhi-110020.
Tel: 26387070, 26386209; Fax: 91-11-26383788
e-mail: mail@sterlingpublishers.com
www.sterlingpublishers.com

China and the WTO – Reshaping the World Economy
Copyright © 2012, Pradip Putatunda
ISBN 978 81 207 6537 5

All rights are reserved. No part of this publication may be reproduced, stored in a retrieval system or transmitted, in any form or by any means, mechanical, photocopying, recording or otherwise, without prior written permission of the publisher.

PRINTED IN INDIA

Printed and Published by Sterling Publishers Pvt. Ltd., New Delhi-110020.

Preface

It has already been widely established that we live in an era in which the greater part of our social life is determined by the global process, and where national borders and distinct national economies are becoming increasingly blurred. Today's world economy is largely dominated by an ever-increasing and irresistible market forces. Transitional business appears to be the major economic factors that owe allegiance to no nation state but make its presence available everywhere in the global economic arena where market forces dictate the economy. Central to this situation is the rapid and recent phenomenon of globalization.

Over the years, the world economy has become global in its basic dynamics. International trade, fuelled by uncontrollable market forces, has been the main reason for this phenomenon. While the WTO represents the most dramatic advance in multilateralism since the 1940s, globalization and the WTO have been making the case for liberalizing trade. The WTO is the only global institution that has attempted, with reasonable success, to create a set of rules for trade that have reflected concern for the interest of the poor and developing nations – the rules reflecting the economic understanding of the time. Over the years, nations have come to realize that it is not governments that create wealth but global firms, small and medium sized enterprises and individuals participating in the markets. All play their part in translating the activities of the WTO into a better life for the many. However, a key for business is the transparency and predictabilities of the markets. While it is as a negotiating platform that the WTO can generate market access opportunities, it is as a rule based treaty institution that it can provide security and predictability. Traders, producers, and other market participants can rely on the binding rules. Where those rules are breached, complainants can go to their governments to seek redress under the WTO dispute settlement system. As risk lowering becomes more established and widespread, world economic activities become more productive and increasingly social welfare oriented.

Since early 1980s, while we noticed the rise of globalization, we also witnessed the emergence of China as an economic power, more precisely, as the leading trading nation of the world. Following the open-door policy since 1979, China has become second largest economy of the world in a span of thirty years. However, since its accession to WTO in 2001, China has also become both a challenge and an opportunity to almost all the trading nations of the world. Other member countries of the world trade body are steadily realizing that with the rise of China, they need to foster closer economic ties or co-operation in order to have a share in China's rampant growth. On the other-hand, China since joining the WTO, is gradually reclaiming a place on the world stage that it had lost in the last two centuries.

This book traces the perspectives – chronicles the important events relating to China's WTO accession – gives an account of the evolution of the economy, the major policy changes and the socio-economic implications of those changes in China's domestic, as well as its international trade and investment regime since its accession to WTO. This text also focuses on the key challenges for sustained growth in China as well as in the rest of the world.

Contents

Preface		v
Chapter - One	: An Introduction to WTO's long journey from Havana to Geneva	1
Chapter - Two	: China's long march to Geneva - joining the World Trade body	15
Chapter - Three	: China's accession to WTO: Impact on domestic and international trade	28
Chapter - Four	: An overview of the implications of China's WTO accession for the asian countries in particular	61
Chapter - Five	: Political, socio-economic and legal implications on China because of its accession to WTO	79
Chapter - Six	: China's WTO accession - development and trade-policy reforms in agriculture	116
Chapter - Seven	: China's state-owned enterprises and their reforms till date	141
Chapter - Eight	: China's accession to the WTO : A study of the developments in few selected sectors a) The banking sector reforms in China b) Civil service reforms in China c) China's stock-market reforms d) China's healthcare reforms	169
Chapter - Nine	: China's WTO accession and governance in taxation	234

Chapter - Ten : World financial and economic crisis,
2008 - learnings and remedies 258
Chapter - Eleven: Concluding observations 296

Economic and Financial Tables 304
Bibliography 332
Abbreviations 340

CHAPTER - ONE

An Introduction to WTO's long journey from Havana to Geneva

GATT (General Agreement on Tariffs and Trade) / WTO (World Trade Organization) had a long journey from Havana to Geneva in a period of around sixty-two years. While the WTO came into being only in 1995, the trading system over which it presides is more than six decades older. The formal foundation was laid in Havana in 1948. However, the international agreement which emerged as the General Agreement on Tariffs and Trade (GATT) came into existence in October, 1947. The International Conference on Trade and employment convened by the United Nations in Havana, also Known as Havana Conference, provided the Havana Charter in March 1948. It resolved the establishment of an International Trade Organization to cover various areas of international trade such as tariffs, economic development, restrictive business practices, commodity issues, employment and disciplines on import and export. Since the Charter was not finally ratified by the U.S. Congress, other countries found little benefit in bringing it into operation. Hence, the Havana Charter did not come into effect. But it is considered as an important landmark in the international initiatives in the field of trade.

Since the Havana Charter eventually did not become operative, the different provisions of the Charter did not come into effect, but the GATT became operative as an interim step and continued until 31 December, 1994. Thereafter, it continued as an annex to the Marrakesh Agreement that led to the creation of the World Trade Organization (WTO agreement) in January 1995.

The GATT presided over a succession of rounds of multilateral trade negotiations. The first five rounds, namely, the Geneva Round of 1947, the Annecy Round of 1949, the Torquay Round of 1951, the Geneva Round of 1956 and the Dillon Round of 1960-61 envisaged on the reform of import tariffs and quotas. Participation of the countries was limited. Twenty-five countries on average took part and sensitive areas of trade such as agriculture and textiles were excluded from the negotiations.

Subsequent Rounds of multilateral trade negotiations also covered tariffs and quotas, but progressively broadened the scope of negotiations. While the Kennedy Round (1964-'67) additionally covered anti-dumping codes, the Tokyo Round (1973-'79) covered a much wider range of issues, including non-tariff measures such as subsidies and countervailing measures, technical barriers to trade, import licensing, customs valuation, government procurement, and trade in civil aircraft. Not all the participating members formally endorsed to these agreements. However, they were informally considered as 'codes'.

The Uruguay Round (1986-'94) of trade negotiations went much further. That was the first 'most comprehensive' round of multilateral trade negotiations including agreements covering tariffs; non-tariff barriers; textiles and clothing; agriculture; trade-in services; trade related aspects of intellectual property rights (TRIPS); trade-related investment measures (TRIMS); the GATT system; GATT articles; subsidies; dispute settlement; anti-dumping; and the Tokyo Round Codes.

The GATT was only an intergovernmental agreement. It got the institutional support of the Interim Commission for the International Trade Organization (ICITO) which had been formally established by the governments and was hosted by the government of Switzerland in Geneva.

During April 12-15, 1994, government ministers from the 124 member countries of the GATT met in Marrakesh, Morocco to sign the agreements that embodied the results of the Uruguay Round. The most important was the Marrakesh Agreement, which established the World Trade Organization. The WTO was formally established on 1st January, 1995.

The preamble of the Marrakesh Agreement clearly established the principle that trade liberalization is not an end in itself but a means toward the larger objective of improving living standards in WTO member countries.

The main function of the WTO, like the GATT, is to ensure that member governments keep their trade policies within bilateral or multilateral agreed norms, and its members sign agreements to this effect as and when required, following a requisite process of negotiation. Once signed, the agreements provide the legal base or support for international trade within a multilateral framework. Those agreements are essentially binding contracts to which the related governments are expected to adhere to.

As of May, 2003, the WTO consisted of 146 member countries, while twenty-eight other nations had observer status. Normally observers, with the exception of Holy See (Vatican), must start negotiations for accession to the WTO within five years of becoming observers. Developing and emerging countries make up about four-fifths of the membership and have special provisions within the rules that are meant to deal with their special needs. By December 2005, the WTO's membership was officially heading for 150 as Tonga's accession talks had been finalized. By July 2008, the number of member countries of WTO was 153 and 31 more countries were having the observer status.

In the Marrakesh Round of trade negotiations, Ministers from the participating member countries took a decision that Least Developed Countries (LDC) in particular, are granted extra attention in the trade rules. The least developed countries that are net food importers would be eligible for aid. The World Bank and the International Monetary Fund were tasked with providing financial assistance to these countries to cushion them from the effects of possible increase of commodity prices as a result of agricultural subsidy reduction that were committed by the developed nations. However, in practice, the Marrakesh decision has never been implemented. In 1996, at the first WTO conference in Singapore - a plan of action was drawn up that formed the basis of the 1997 Integrated Framework for Technical Assistance to LDCs. However only a small number of LDCs have received such technical assistance under the said Framework.

More importantly, such assistance has been widely used as a 'carrot' in trade negotiations.

EVOLUTION:

Europe had been facing tremendous economic strain in 1920s and 1930s. Actually the problem started after the First World War (1914-18). The Western European countries who won the First World War insisted on reparations from the defeated countries. This resulted in severe economic strains on the defeated countries. On the other hand, USA also had been insisting for the quick repayment of loans by the Western European Countries. It was obvious that such an insistence on the part of the USA put a heavy burden on the economies of these Western European Countries. Besides, the stock market crash of 1929 across the Atlantic, dealt a severe blow to the US economy.

Amidst this all round gloomy picture, most of the countries became more inward-looking and tried to protect their respective economies without consideration for the impact on the economies of the other countries. High tariffs and direct import control became common as a tool of trade barrier. In 1927 in Geneva, the League of Nations convened a Diplomatic Conference to address the serious problems in connection with Trade barriers. A resolution for removing prohibitions on import and export was worked out, but it did not get enough signatures to become operative. In the following few years, the situation became worse because some actions of the two major powers, viz., the USA and UK, encouraged building up of trade barriers all around. In 1930, America enacted the Smoot-Hawley Act which raised its unweighted average tariff to 52 percent. The UK also gave up its free-trade policy and adopted for Imperial Preferences in 1932. Naturally, other countries of Europe and American Continent followed the trend and raised their tariffs. Some countries even introduced quantitative import restrictions.

However, soon the USA realized the urgent need of concrete and positive initiatives to address the problem. Firstly, it reduced its own tariffs and also encouraged or rather influenced many others to do so. During 1934-39, it entered into as many as 27 bilateral reciprocal trade agreements with various countries. Its

An Introduction to WTO's long journey from Havana to Geneva

own average tariff came down to around 30 percent. It also initiated multi-lateralisation of its reciprocal agreements. In the process, USA sowed the seeds of the most-favoured-nation (MFN) principle and that would become the most important pillar of the GATT.

The Second World-war (1939-45) brought the USA and the UK much closer through economic co-operation. Out of three main initiatives, the Atlantic Charter was the first resulting from the summit meeting between the two countries in August, 1941. As a subsequent initiative, a Lend-Lease (Mutual Aid) Agreement between the two countries was concluded to support the war effort. Thirdly, during 1943-45, intense bilateral negotiations were conducted between the two countries on the post-war multilateral trading framework. In the process of preparing for these negotiations, the US had prepared "A Multilateral Convention on Commercial Policy" and on the other hand the UK had its framework in "A Proposal for an International Commercial Union". "Proposals for Expansion of World Trade and Employment" was the final output of these negotiations.

The above changes and moves provided the whole world the main impetus for the convening of the Havana Conference by the United Nations. The prime idea was to multi-lateralise what had included into these bilateral moves. Almost all the important provisions agreed to by these countries at this stage and also of the earlier reciprocal bilateral agreements of the USA found their place into the various provisions of the GATT.

This was how GATT and today's World Trade Organization was evolved and was formally merged in October 1947 and became operational in January 1948. Since then, it has passed through many milestones.

WTO STRUCTURE AND DECISION-MAKING:

The Ministerial Conference is the highest decision-making body of the WTO. All WTO members can participate in all bodies except the appellate body, dispute settlement panels and pluri-lateral committees. WTO is continuing the practice of decision-making by consensus that was adopted by its predecessor GATT from its inception in 1947. If a decision cannot be arrived at by consensus, the matter shall be decided by voting unless specifically mentioned otherwise. Each member of the WTO enjoys one vote at the meetings of the Ministerial Conference and the General Council.

Trade or commerce Ministers make up the highest and most authoritative body at the WTO, making all major and crucial decisions primarily through ministerial conferences. Ministerial conference has to be convened at least once in two years to take decisions on all matters under any of the multilateral agreements.

A practice has currently emerged to hold mini-ministerial meetings by the influential members of WTO prior to the actual ministerial conference. These are informal meetings hosted by a member country inviting few selected countries to move matters along before the ministerial itself. These mini-ministerials can play a critical role in determining the outcome of formal ministerial conference though they do not form part of the WTO's formal decision-making processes, and also are not governed by its rules. The second most important body is the General Council which is composed of representatives of all the members. In the intervals between ministerial meetings, General Council meets as appropriate to carry out functions assigned to it by the agreements signed by ministers. It performs the day-to-day business of the organization in Geneva between ministerial meetings, and reports to the ministers on the status and progress of negotiations.

The General Council also requires to sit as the Dispute Settlement Body and the Trade Policy Review Body under different terms of reference and different Chairs. The Dispute Settlement Body governs and controls the process of settling trade disputes. It enjoys the sole authority to appoint panels of experts to consider a trade dispute between members, and also empowered to accept or reject each panel's findings. The Dispute Settlement Body also monitors the implementation of rulings and recommendations, and has the power to authorize one party to retaliate against the other when rulings have not been implemented.

The Trade Policy Review Body focuses on trade policies and practices of individual member. Those reviews are designed to provide feedback to the concerned country on its trade performance and also to provide information to remaining business community about its trade policies and circumstances. The USA, the EC, Japan and Canada are reviewed every two years; the next sixteen biggest trading nations in every four years; and the remaining countries in every six or more years.

Council for Trade-in-Goods, Council for Trade-in-services and Council for Trade-Related Intellectual Property Rights are also responsible to report to the General Council for day-to-day activities in a broad area of trade. Simultaneously, six committees whose functions are less broad also report to the General Council covering various issues such as trade and development, the environment etc. Working groups on investment, competition policy, transparency in government procurement and trade facilitation that were set up at the 1996 Singapore Ministerial Conference, also report to the General Council on the day-to-day progress. Two additional working groups on trade to look after debt and finance and transfer of technology were set up following the Doha Conference in 2001.

The decision-making structure of the WTO is summarized in the following figure (Figure 1).

Organizational Structure of the WTO

Ministerial Conference

General Council meeting as **Dispute Settlement Body**

General Council

General Council meeting as **Trade Policy Review Body**

Appellate Body
Dispute Settlement panels

Committees on
Trade and Environment
Trade and development
  Subcommittee on Least-Developed Countries
Regional Trade Agreements
Balance of Payments Restrictions
Budget, Finance and Administration

Working parties on
Accession

Working groups on
Trade, debt and finance
Trade and technology transfer

(Inactive:
Relationship between Trade and Investment
(Interaction between Trade and Competition Policy
Transparency in Government Procurement)

Plurilateral
Information Technology Agreement Committee

Council for Trade in Goods

Committees on
Market Access
Agriculture
Sanitary and Phytosanitary Measures
Technical Barriers to Trade
Subsidies and Countervailing Measures
Anti-Dumping Practices
Customs Valuation
Rules of Origin
Import Licensing
Trade-Related Investment Measures
Safeguards

Working Party on
State-Trading Enterprises

Council for Trade-Related Aspects of Intellectual Property Rights

Council for Trade in Services

Committees on
Trade in Financial Services
Specific Commitments

Working parties on
Domestic Regulation
GATS Rules

Plurilaterals
Trade in Civil Aircraft Committee
Government Procurement Committee

Doha Development Agenda: TNC and its bodies

Trade Negotiations Committee

Special Sessions of
Services Council/TRIPS Council/Dispute Settlement Body/Agriculture Committee amd Cotton Sub-Committee/Trade and Development Committee/ Trade and Environment Committee

Negotiating groups on
Market Access/ Rules/Trade Facilitation

Above Organizational Structure of the WTO is based on a Chart of the WTO Secretariat.

An Introduction to WTO's long journey from Havana to Geneva 9

MINISTERIAL CONFERENCES OF WTO: DEVELOPMENTS AND FEELINGS:

As mentioned earlier that the Ministerial Conference is the supreme decision-making body of the WTO; and it has to be convened normally once in two years. The first ministerial conference of World Trade Organization was held in Singapore in December 1996, the second in Geneva in May 1998, the third in Seattle in November-December 1999, the fourth in Doha in November 2001, the fifth in Cancun, Mexico, in September 2003, the sixth in Hong Kong in 2005, and the seventh in Geneva, Switzerland, in December 2009.

CHRONOLOGY OF WTO MINISTERIAL CONFERENCES:

Singapore Ministerial Conference:

Following the Uruguay Round – Which resulted in formation of World Trade Organization in 1995, the First WTO Ministerial Conference took place in Singapore from 9th December to 13th December 1996. Five new subjects, namely, investment, competition policy, government procurement, trade facilitation and social clauses, i.e., labour standards were being proposed by the major developed nations to be included within the ambit of WTO negotiations. A large number of members of the developing countries opposed such proposal. However, eventually the only subject i.e. social clauses (labour standards) was left out. And the other four issues were being included formally in a study process in the WTO. This was undoubtedly a significant expansion of the activities of the WTO. The implications are far reaching specially for the inclusion of 'investment' in the WTO ambit.

Another important decision of the Singapore Ministerial Conference was an agreement on zero duty on information technology goods. This issue was suddenly brought into the agenda of the meeting. The developing countries had hardly any opportunity or in other-words they were not equipped enough to examine the implications on the spot. The decision was taken and obviously it was final.

Since WTO emerged from GATT on 1st January 1995, the Singapore Ministerial Conference was the first meeting of its kind. One can observe four prominent features in that meeting. Firstly, pressures were exerted by the major developed countries to bring new issues onto the WTO agenda and they expected the developing nations to accept that; secondly, the major developed countries suddenly proposed an important matter, i.e., on zero duty on information technology goods forcing the developing nations to examine the implications on the spot and agree to it; thirdly, it was clearly observed that there were non-transparent negotiations in small groups which left a large number of the developing countries very much dissatisfied and unhappy; and fourthly, the absence of broad-base discussions as well as consensus after examining the foreseeable implications both on developing countries and developed countries before tabling the proposal.

Geneva Ministerial Conference:

The Second WTO Ministerial Conference was held in Geneva, Switzerland, during 18-20 May 1998. In the Geneva Ministerial conference, maintenance of status quo proposal was introduced in respect of electronic commerce. This proposal meant a commitment on the part of member nations to duty-free electronic commerce. A decision was taken to extend the status quo for eighteen months. In the subsequent conference, it was extended further.

Seattle Ministerial Conference:

The Third WTO Ministerial Conference of 1999, i.e., the Seattle Ministerial Conference ended in chaos. Not a single decision was taken. The major developed countries put up a strong plea for inclusion of labour standards in the WTO. However, there was no agreement on this issue in this meeting. It is to be noted that the same issue had been totally rejected by the developing countries in the Singapore Ministerial Conference in December 1996.

Seattle Ministerial Conference collapsed apparently because of various reasons. Firstly, this had been a unique case of an international conference where a majority number of the participating countries openly and formally criticized the organization and the manner of handling of the meeting. Secondly, as alleged that the large number of proposals of the developing nations did not get proper attention from the major developed countries although the developing countries had made serious preparations on their proposals unlike in the earlier conferences. Thirdly, a large number of non-governmental organizations had held demonstrations and disturbed the atmosphere of the conference. Fourthly, as reported that even in crucial point of time, the most countries did not play mediating roles. On the other-hand, it pressed for its own agenda at a very high level, which obviously frustrated the developing nations. Fifthly, there were serious differences among the major developed countries on important issues and those could not be resolved during the conference period. The final result was that the third WTO Ministerial Conference ended without even a formal closing ceremony.

Doha Ministerial Conference:

The Fourth WTO Ministerial Conference was held in Doha, Qatar, during 9-14 November, 2001. Nearly all the major subjects of the Uruguay Round including some additional had been included in the work Program of Doha Ministerial Conference. Comprehensive negotiations were envisaged in the areas of agriculture, services, subsidies, anti-dumping, regional trading arrangements, dispute settlements, industrial tariffs and even some aspects of intellectual property rights. Besides, there had been negotiations in the area of environment too. Intense work was focused on new issues, viz, investment, competition policy, government procurement, trade facilitation and electronic commerce. Developing countries identified a number of deficiencies and imbalances in the WTO agreements in the course of the implementation after WTO agreements had suggested specific correctives. Those were grouped under what has been called the 'implementation issues'. The Doha Ministerial Conference did not find solution to these problems. On the contrary, the conference intensified the work in the new areas which were of interest to the major developed countries. Thus there was a basic imbalance in the decisions of this conference.

Cancun Ministerial Conference:

Cancun Ministerial Conference was the Fifth WTO Ministerial Conference held in Cancun, Mexico, during 10-14 September 2003. Until the last day of the conference, the process was strikingly similar to the deeply flawed Doha process, except for the emergence of a new coalition of developing countries -- the G20 (then Comprising Argentina, Bolivia, Brazil, Chile, China, Columbia, Costa Rica, Cuba, Ecuador, El Salvador, Guatemala, India, Mexico, Pakistan, Paraguay, Peru, the Philippines, South Africa, Thailand and Venezuela)-and the re-emergence of the G90, comprising the LDCs (Least Developed Countries), the African, Caribbean and Pacific (ACP) group and the African Union (AU).

While most delegates were expecting a similar end-game, with the major players again prolonging the Ministerial conference and negotiating into the early hours, relying on last-minute brinkmanship to ram through their agenda, the Fifth WTO Ministerial conference came to an abrupt halt to the shock of developed and developing government delegates alike as Mexican Foreign Minister Luis Ernesto Derbez as conference chairman pulled the plug.

Hong Kong Ministerial Conference:

The Sixth Ministerial Conference was held in Hong Kong SAR, China during 13-18 December 2005. Initially, consultations on agriculture, non-agricultural market access (NAMA) and development issues showed that differences remained amongst the members on a number of issues. However, finally, after six days of intensive negotiations in Hong Kong, Ministers from the WTO's 149 member governments approved a declaration that many described as significant progress since the July 2004 'package'. The Conference agreed to ensure the parallel elimination of all forms of export subsidies and disciplines on all export measures with equivalent effect to be completed by the end of 2013, and that should be achieved in a progressive and parallel manner.

The Hong Kong Ministerial Conference recalled the mandate given by the Members in the decision adopted by the General Council on 1 August 2004 and reaffirmed commitment to ensure having an explicit decision on cotton within the agriculture negotiations and through the Sub-Committee on Cotton ambitiously, expeditiously and specifically as follows: (a) all forms of export subsidies for cotton would be eliminated by developed countries in 2006; (b) developed countries would give quota and duty free access for cotton exports from least-developed countries (LDCs) from the commencement of the implementation period; and (c) trade distorting domestic subsidies for cotton production be reduced more ambitiously than under whatever general formula was agreed and that it should be implemented over a shorter period of time than generally applicable.

The member countries participated in the conference reaffirmed their commitment to the mandate for negotiations on market access for non-agricultural products as set out in paragraph 16 of the Doha Ministerial Declaration. They also reaffirmed all the elements of the NAMA Framework adopted by the General Council on 1st August 2004.

Geneva Ministerial Conference:

In Geneva, Switzerland, the Seventh Session of the WTO Ministerial Conference took place from 30th November to 2nd December 2009. Instead of becoming a negotiating session, the Seventh Ministerial Conference became 'a platform for ministers to review the functioning of the house', including the Doha Round, and an occasion 'to send a number of strong signals to the world with respect to all the issues – from monitoring and surveillance to disputes, accessions, aid for trade, technical assistance and international governance'. Chile's Trade Minister Andres Velasco was already elected by the General Council as Chair of the Seventh WTO Ministerial Conference. For the conference, the general theme for discussion was 'The WTO, the Multilateral Trading System and the Current Global Economic Environment'. In parallel to the Plenary Session, there were also two Working Sessions in order to provide an interactive forum for Ministers for discussion under two broad sub-themes: 'Review of WTO activities, including the Doha Work Programme' for the first day; and 'The WTO's contribution to recovery, growth and development' for the second day.

On 2nd December, 2009, WTO ministers ended their two-and-a-half day Geneva conference having declared that they want to conclude the eight year old Doha Round negotiations quickly and also agreeing to extend 'moratoriums' on electronic commerce and intellectual property.

In conclusion, it can be mentioned that after nearly sixty-two years of the establishment of GATT/WTO, the World Trade Organization (WTO) has become the only global international organization dealing with the rules of trade between nations. In the core of it are the WTO agreements, negotiated and signed by the bulk of the world's trading nations as well as ratified in their parliaments. The ultimate goal is to help the producers of goods and services and the exporters and importers to conduct the business.

CHAPTER - TWO

China's long march to Geneva – joining the World Trade body

China, the world's most populous country, was officially admitted to the World Trade Organization on 11th November, 2001, after 15 years of negotiations. It was a moment the leaders in Beijing had been waiting for more than a decade. Kofi Annan, then United Nations Secretary General, described China's entry to the WTO as an event of historic proportions for the world trading system. In a ceremony lasting just a few minutes, the representatives of the 142 member countries of the World Trade Organization unanimously approved the accession of the world's largest country into membership. Hugs and loud applause between Mike Moore, the head of the WTO, and the Chinese delegation greeted the decision in the glittering conference hall in Doha, Qatar, where trade ministers of the member countries were meeting to try and launch a new trade round.

China, for its part, thanked the five heads of the WTO who have been in the post since it began its struggle for membership in 1986. China also pledged to work hard to ensure the success of the trade negotiations. However, it put the WTO on notice that a trade round could only succeed if it addressed the gap of standard of living between rich and poor nations, and ensured that all countries would gain from globalization, as it staked its claim to lead the group of developing countries. Chinese trade minister Shi Guangsheng expressed that it supported a new round of trade negotiations on the basis of full consideration of the interests and reasonable requests of developing countries.

United States Trade Representative Robert Zoellick was the first to congratulate China on its membership. He hailed the move as an historic step that would strengthen the WTO. He expressed his belief that as this century unfolds and people look back on this day, they will conclude that in admitting China to the WTO, world trade body took a decisive step in strengthening the global economic trading system. He also mentioned that everyone would benefit from the expanded access to markets and the expansion of a rules-based trading system.

For his part, Pascal Lamy, the European Union Trade Commissioner, said that it was the end of a long and arduous road and an enormous achievement. He also mentioned that just like every member of the WTO, China would require to deliver on its commitments and the EU would be watching that very carefully.

Industrial countries, who had, in the process, negotiated a wide range of deals of opening Chinese markets in agriculture, telecommunications and financial services, re-iterated their expectations that China would live up to its commitments.

China insisted that it would meet its obligations. It also hoped that WTO membership would cement its commitment to economic reform which had led to a rapid economic expansion in the past 20 years and an explosion of foreign investment.

'Of course China is going to be very competitive, but having China competitive under rules, under a binding dispute mechanism, is, I would have thought, in the whole world's interest". Mike More, then head of the WTO, said.

LONG MARCH TOWARDS JOINING THE WTO :

After 15 years of tortuous negotiations and vocal contestations, China signed the 900 page document on 11th November, 2001, and became a member of the World Trade Organisation (WTO). In common understanding, it shouldn't have taken so long. Usually, WTO accession is a two-step process. The applicant as its first step must negotiate bilateral concession agreements with each existing WTO member that requests such agreement. The final overall accession agreement must be drafted on the basis of those bilateral agreements to get it approved by the entire WTO membership, i.e., the General Council. As per the charter of WTO, one member country cannot be favored over another. In keeping with this principle, the most favorable offer made to one country must be offered to all member countries as part of the accession agreement. The bilateral agreement contains the mutual commitments of the applicant country as well as the individual member country with regard to market access for specific products. Agreement on tariffs is always an important and time-consuming issue. Sometimes there may be a general commitment to lower average tariffs to a certain level, binding tariff rates must then be assigned to individual products. It is an often tedious and time-consuming task because these are typically negotiated for thousands of items with dominant trading partners. However, although tariff negotiations can be time-consuming and contentious, it is usually considered as the easy part of the trade negotiations. Besides tariffs, in reality, trade is riddled with all sorts of non-tariff arrangements, ranging from quotas to health and safety standards. Agreement must be reached on the non-tariff barriers as well - such as quotas on the amount of a product that can be imported and/or exported, licensing requirements, permits or notification requirement. Some member countries can also hide behind pseudo-scientific trade barriers as well. One Japanese official famously contended in the 1980s that the Japanese people had different intestines from Westerners and, thus, that foreign beef imports should be restricted. To this end, the WTO adopted an agreement on technical barriers to trade (TBT). The TBT agreement encourages countries to accept internationally recognized tests in order to prevent the application of unilateral standards. Moreover, one country's standard can have a huge impact on the other member country. For example, if China decides to accept US food and drug administration approval for pharmaceutical drugs as sufficient to sell a product in China - it can have dramatic impact on pharmaceutical makers from other countries. There is certainly a growing trend for countries to accept each other's tests to reduce the cost and encourage trade. We can also refer to the mutual recognition pact between the US and the European Union in electronic equipment etc. in this regard. The terms of market entry for corporations, a services agreement, and other commitments in accordance with the Uruguay Round framework that governs trade talks are also considered to be parts of bilateral agreement.

During the process of China's accession to WTO, total 37 countries requested bilateral agreements. Those high numbers of bilateral negotiations reflected the concern on the part of the respective country that China, the emerging economic as well as trading giant, would have an unsettling impact on the world trading system. Each of the countries with which China conducted separate negotiations, wanted its specific concerns be met before it would agree to China's membership in the world trade body. Negotiations with the US were the most time-consuming, difficult and comprehensive. China also had tough talks and lengthy negotiations with the European Union. Like those with the United States, an initial agreement (in the case of the EU, in May 2000) was followed by continuing disputes which were finally resolved in mid-2001. However, even after the European Union and the United States had concluded bilateral agreements with China, Mexico remained a hold-out until just before final approval of China's accession to WTO. Mexico was concerned that its low-end manufacturing industries would be swamped by China. Indeed, this was a major concern that resonates throughout Latin America.

As an accession process, agreed bilateral protocols must be codified and synthesized into the protocol of accession. The arrangements made in the bilateral concession agreements become available to all members through the protocol, i.e., become multilateral. The bilateral agreements are incorporated into a schedule of commitments that is sent with the protocol, along with a report from the working party to the WTO General Council for approval. A two-thirds majority of the General Council must finally approve the application of a new member to WTO. Some applicants want to be identified by the protocol as a developing country to enable them to take advantage of the so-called special and differential treatment that allows developing countries some extra breathing space as they implement policies that make them fully compliant with WTO status. China also argued strongly for developing country status. The United States and some developing countries felt that letting China enjoy developing country status could seriously distort the WTO as well as the entire world trading system because China would have attracted additional trade benefits from other countries with developing-country status without having to reciprocate that. Thereby it could have turned preferential trade deals for China. Moreover, developing-country status would have allowed China to keep its existing non-tariff barriers on imports and to indulge protectionist policies towards the favored local industries. During the 1990s, China ceded on most of these points as negotiations proceeded. But China cited its 900 million strong rural population, more than one-third of whom are farmers, to refuse to give ground on agriculture.

The General Agreement on Tariffs and Trade (GATT) was originally signed by 23 member countries on October 30, 1947. The former Republic of China was one of those 23 countries. The spirit behind GATT inspired the establishment of the Bretton woods institutions, the International Monetary Fund and the World Bank, which came into existence after the Second World War as a way of building international co-operation and resisting the dangers of unilateral actions that had led to two world wars in less than 50 years.

China remained member in GATT, however, for short period. On October 1, 1949, after the proclamation of victory in his battle with the Kuomintang, Chinese Communist Party leader Mao-Zedong also declared the foundation of Peoples' Republic of China(PRC). Later on March 6, 1950, the Nationalist government of Chiang Kai-Shek in Taiwan withdrew from GATT. Taiwan requested observer status in GATT again in 1965, which was granted although there were protests from the communist world. In 1971, Taiwan was expelled from the United Nations and the seat was given to Peoples' Republic of China and at the same time it lost its GATT status.

Apparently, China could have sought GATT membership, at least as an observer, immediately in 1971 when it became a member of United Nations. That would have allowed China (PRC) to take part in two subsequent trade rounds, the Tokyo Round and the Uruguay Round. Also, China almost certainly could have gotten the membership of GATT very quickly. Because the threshold for membership was lower at that time and also because the GATT commitments weren't legally binding. But China was pre-occupied with different issues like rapid decline in health of Chairman Mao-Zedong, internal upheaval, and most importantly top level functional struggles that came hand-in-hand with the Cultural Revolution (1966-1976). China also remained resolutely anti-capitalist at that time and its trade volumes were discouragingly lower for China's self-motivation to enter into the world trade body.

In 1978, China started opening up its economy and accordingly its economic reform began from that time. China gradually started joining international economic-related organizations. China successfully applied to join the World Bank and the IMF in 1980. That same year, China opted to apply as a non-voting observer at GATT. However, GATT granted China observer status in November, 1982. Meanwhile, Chinese officials attended some GATT courses in Geneva designed for interested parties - member and non-members alike. By allowing observer status, GATT allowed Beijing to attend the GATT Ministerial Council meetings planning the terms of negotiation for subsequent trade rounds. As an observer, China participated in the Uruguay Round negotiations. In 1984, it became a permanent observer at the GATT Ministerial Council.

On July 11, 1986, China (PRC) formally applied to GATT for the restoration of its signatory state status. China hoped and desired to avoid the lengthy accession process by insisting GATT to give it back the membership that the erstwhile Nationalist regime had withdrawn in 1950. . But such hope of PRC did not materialize as it was evident from the subsequent 15-year negotiations for its accession to world trade body. GATT established a working party on China's status as a contracting party in March 1987 in response to China's request to rejoin the organization.

The powerful member countries of GATT were determined not to let China in on easy terms. Trade tensions increased during 1985-1989 as rich GATT members like United States and European Union countries sparred with the three fast-growing countries of East Asia - Japan, Taiwan and South Korea. These three rapidly growing economies were accused of following neo-mercantilist trade policies. They were also being blamed of stoking powerful export machines while keeping their domestic markets largely closed to imports. It was commonly apprehended that China might be the next biggest trading power. During that period, Hong Kong manufacturers were in the midst of setting up thousands of factories that would employ some six million workers in the Pearl River Delta by 1995 and would help make Southern China one of the most important low-end-manufacturing centers in the world. Not surprisingly, the unspoken fear was that more than a billion low-wage Chinese could decimate untold industries in the developed world. Some GATT member countries also feared that if China were permitted to enter the World Trade body on easy terms, it could undercut GATT's integrity as a trade-promoting body.

Since China was making a difficult transition from a planned economy to a mostly market-oriented economy, even agreeing on what would be included in the negotiations was complex and difficult, the following issues were included when formal negotiations with China began:

- Government subsidies provided by the Chinese Government to the State-owned enterprises that dominated the economy;
- Market access for foreign financial services companies, such as banks, insurance companies and securities houses;
- China's tariff barriers which at the time averaged 35%, far exceeded those of existing GATT members;
- China's non-tariff barriers such as the lack of transparency and the absence of uniformity in China's customs requirements and trade laws;
- Chinese labor standards;
- The lack of convertibility for China's currency;
- Enforcement of intellectual property laws which at the time was virtually non-existent.

Talks on China's accession to GATT progressed slowly. Initially, in the negotiation process, top Chinese policy makers showed little commitments to GATT membership. At that time, it seemed very often that the aim of GATT membership was more like a slogan than a serious policy commitment. Even in bilateral meeting between Chinese and Thai officials in the late 1980s, China's Minister for Foreign Trade and Economic Co-operation didn't even bring up the subject of GATT membership. Actually at that time, there was little obvious advantage for China in joining GATT because China had already been granted Most Favored Nation (MFN) Status by its major trading partners and also GATT had no binding way of settling trade disputes. Moreover, US was also clearly reluctant to use MFN treatment as a political tool. On the contrary, China would have required to make a number of concessions to GATT member countries and to overhaul its internal economy for its accession to world trade body.

One June 4, 1989, Tiananmen Square incident brought down the trade talks to a halt. The forceful suppression and crackdown of pro-democracy protests raised serious doubts in the developed world about China's sincere intention to reform towards integrating the country to the world economically, socially and diplomatically.

Much of the world put their economic and diplomatic ties with PRC on ice. China turned inward at least for the next two years. China also became more concerned with its domestic stability and keeping economic reforms at home on track rather than with major international initiatives.

However, from 1991 onwards, China's economic and diplomatic relationship with USA as well as western world started getting warmer because of its stance in the Security Council of U.N.O. on Gulf-War issue. Otherwise the negative effect of Tiananmen Square massacre on China would have been much stronger and forceful both politically and economically.

The United States of America and European Union were particularly alarmed at growing intellectual-property rights violations. Increasing textile shipments from China also added to tensions. The US Trade representative (USTR) initiated an investigation in October 1991 into Chinese Market barriers mainly because of the lack of transparency in China's trade laws and administrative rulings. In October1992, then USTR Ambassador Micky Kantor and Chinese Minister Wu Yi signed a memorandum of understanding on market access covering the issues such as quantitative restrictions on imports, import substitution, tariffs, export restrictions, transparency, standard and testing etc. The USA also agreed that it would "staunchly support" China's entry into GATT and formally agreed to drop a number of investigations into unfair trade practices. In the immediate subsequent years, additional Sino-US disputes emerged in areas ranging from allegations that child labor and prison labor were used to produce Chinese export products, trade issues like liberalization of financial services and telecommunications. Issue like whether or not China could enjoy developing-country status also remained unresolved.

In the subsequent years, as China's economic integration with the rest of the world gradually increased, and as China's exports played an ever-more important role in its economic growth, the benefits of GATT'S protections became more prominent and accordingly China's determination to join the World Trade body only grew stronger. Moreover, China started visualizing the potential cost of remaining outside of the GATT regime, particularly after the US Congress began to engage in an annual debate over revoking China's MFN trade status keeping in view of the human-rights violations. The debate over whether or not USA should revoke China's MFN trade status was initiated in response to the forceful suppression of Tiananmen Square protests, but it soon became the attempts to quantify China's abuses. All these factors and finally rivalry with Taiwan played important role in China's stepped-up interest in GATT entry. Incidentally, in September 1992, GATT set up a working group to consider Taiwan's application to rejoin GATT and granted observer status to Chinese Taipei. The GATT negotiations with China (PRC) at this time, occurred against the backdrop when China's exports were rising dramatically to USA and European Countries. USA was having large and persistent trade deficits with China as well as with other East Asian Countries. Chinese exports to the US surged from US$ 3.1 billion in 1984 to almost US$ 38 billion in 1994. During that period, US exports only increased from US$3 billion to US $ 8.8 billion.

In 1992, China and USA signed an agreement on intellectual property rights to ensure China's willingness to protect US intellectual-property rights (IPR). But that agreement had little effect. According to a US government report in 1994, as much as 94% of computer software in China was pirated. In many places of China, piracy rates hit nearly 100% for US CDs, video games, videos, books and movies. Even the pirate factories began to export on a large scale. Washington contended in 1994 that twenty-nine CD and laser disc factories in China had a production capacity of 75 million CDs that could absorb yearly only 5 million CDs. It was a particular source of concern to US authorities that despite repeated requests, PRC had not taken any significant step to stop infringement of Intellectual Property Rights (IPR) in those factories.

Citing China's inability to protect US computer software, pharmaceuticals, agricultural and chemical products, movies, books and trade marks from loosing heavily and also in retaliation against Chinese factories making pirated products, USTR Mickey Kantor imposed 100% tariffs on US$ 1.1 billion-worth of Chinese goods on and from February 4, 1995. Almost everything from answering machines to jewellery boxes to children's bi-cycles to surf board were included in the hit list. That was the largest trade retaliation ever announced by the US.

The threat of trade retaliation at last spurred Chinese action and initiated an intensive set of negotiations that continued until the sanctions were set to begin. Ultimately, the US and China wrapped up a round of intensive negotiations and finalized a landmark agreement on IPR on the very day the punitive tariffs were to take effect, i.e., February 26, 1995. As a clear demonstration of China's sincerity, on the previous night, Chinese authorities had raided the Sheafei Factory in Shenzhen as it was regarded by US as one of the most notorious pirate factories. China also vowed to take concrete steps to prohibit the export of pirated products and to implement a Special Enforcement Period during which the government would target large-scale manufacturers and distributors of pirated products. China also promised to make long-term structural changes to resist IPR violations by creating a Customs Service Enforcement system modeled on the US custom service, by establishing a special working groups at the central, local and provincial levels and by increasing import rights for US music and movies.

In June 1996, acting USTR Charlene Barshefsky declared that no sanction relating to IPR enforcement would be imposed against PRC. Ms. Barshefsky confirmed that PRC had closed 15 pirate CD factories with an estimated production capacity of 30-50 million units a year. It was obvious that the WTO membership issue of PRC took a back seat to the trade disputes during 1995-1996. In between, frosty Sino-US relations during the early years of the Clinton administration also acted to slow down the accession process. In 1993, the US Congress and the US Olympic Committee opposed Beijing's bid for the 2000 summer Olympics. Beijing lost narrowly to Sydney. US opposition angered many ordinary Chinese and marked the beginning of a subtle shift away from the pro-US sentiments that had prevailed among most Chinese since the early days of economic liberalization. In summer 1995, Taiwan President Lee Teng-hui's visit to the United States deteriorated the official relations between PRC and US badly. Although US had been re-iterating that it wouldn't allow the Taiwanese leader to speak at Cornell University, his alma mater, the foreign office changed its decision abruptly in favor of the visit and informed PRC authorities very late about the same. In March, 1996, on the eve of Taiwan's presidential election, PRC government retaliated with a series of live missile tests in the waters around Taiwan confirming the general consensus that Chinese leaders are extremely sensitive to any move that appears to legitimize Taiwan's government. The US sent two aircraft carrier battle ships to steam through the Taiwan strait as a show of force. During that time in 1996-97, different signals emanating from Beijing as well as different statements given by different Chinese leaders suggested that China was losing interest in WTO membership.

In October 1997, with a state visit that Jiang Zemin made to the United States, China's relations with US improved dramatically. During this visit of Jiang Zemin:

(i) China agreed to buy US$ 3 billion worth of Boeing Jets;

(ii) It announced that it would end the supply of nuclear technology to Iran, among other countries; and

(iii) Jiang also agreed that China would sign the Information Technology Agreement and would eliminate tariffs on a wide range of technology imports by 2005.

On the other hand, President Clinton lifted a 12-year ban on the sale of US nuclear-power-plant technology to China.

Besides above, there were also other signs of real progress in China's trade practices. For example, China agreed to phase in trading rights within three years of WTO entry, to eliminate export subsidies for agricultural products; to end a dual-pricing system; and to bring more transparency and fairness into the entire trading process. However, 'particular concern' still persisted from different quarters about the market access in the service sector including telecommunications, financial services, professional services and distribution services.

In November end, 1997, the two Presidents met again at the Vancouver APEC summit and showed their growing sincerity for serious talks before Clinton's impending 10-day state visit to China in June 1998. However, the Asian Financial Crisis which showed the dangers of a rapid opening of the financial services market and the consequential difficulties associated with reforming China's domestic economy created a good deal of skepticism during this period among the Chinese politicians about the China's rapid entry to WTO. Chinese leadership started thinking as if the dramatic opening that WTO entry demanded would be another shock and it seemed for a time as if conservatives in the leadership had won the argument to slow the pace of China's WTO accession.

Before Clinton's visit to China in June, 1998, the allegations of illegal campaign contributions by China-linked organizations and also the subsequent allegations of the Chinese theft of US nuclear secrets made it politically imperative that the Clinton regime be seen to be pursuing a tough bargain on China's entry to the WTO. In this backdrop, both the Presidents, during Clinton's visit to China, continued repairing what had often been a troubled (an apparently troubled) relationship. This was the first time that a US President had publicly affirmed US support for Chinese " Three Nos" policy – no support for Taiwan's independence, for Taiwan's entry into the United Nations or for its entry into international organizations. Clinton expressed his eagerness of constructive, strategic partnership between the two countries during an appearance at Beijing's Great Hall of the People. It was beyond doubt that Clinton's visit in China made the prospect of serious WTO negotiations better than at any time in several years,

It was against this background that Chinese Premier Zhu Rongji came to the US with his dramatic package. Zhu's offer far exceeded anything that had been offered previously, especially in areas like telecommunications. It was about as close as a trade negotiation ever gets to a knock-out bid. However, Chinese embassy bombing in Belgrade raised a further fear that negotiations would be knocked off track again for some time. This time, the WTO accession talks were not derailed again and the two sides were able to shake hands on a deal. As mentioned earlier, China also had tough talks and lengthy negotiations with the European Union and ultimately resolved by mid-2001. Finally, that historic day arrived and on 11th November 2001, China was officially admitted to the World Trade body.

CHAPTER – THREE

China's accession to WTO: Impact on domestic and international trade

China's accession to the World Trade Organization (WTO) was not an isolated event but rather was part of an ongoing process of integration into the global economy that China initiated in 1978. China's WTO membership did signify the beginning of a new era in China's economic restructuring. China's political leadership also re-iterated that the current policy of reform and opening up of the economy would continue and deepen. WTO membership indicated a broadening of trade reform in China from a policy that had been focused on special economic zones to a more comprehensive approach under which China would require to adhere to already agreed timetables on further reform and market opening. At the time of joining the WTO China had already agreed to change its laws, institutions, and politics so that it conforms to the norms of international trade. It was, therefore, almost certain that in the post WTO-accession period, China's reforms would increasingly be based on the rule of law, transparency, national treatment for foreign firms, and a closer adherence to global business practices.

Since WTO accession, China has seen rapid economic growth despite the unfavorable international economic environment. Increasing profitability for foreign affiliates operating in China, rising export, growth in import, and continuing increase in domestic consumer demand have, so far, positively affected regional growth rates, sustained prices for a wide range of industrial commodities, and benefited trading partners. These trends suggest that China's sustained growth will continue to have a significant impact on the global economy.

CHINA'S WTO COMMITMENTS AND COMPLIANCE THEREOF:

With its accession to the WTO what China had agreed to the changes in its trade and investment policies, was certainly going to have far-reaching implications for China's economic structure and social outlook. Tariff reductions, elimination of non-tariff barriers in industrial sectors, agricultural trade liberalization, and the opening up of major service sectors of the economy to foreign investment were the main terms of China's accession to WTO. The proportion of state-owned economy, in terms of industrial output, was more than three-fourths at the beginning of the reforms in 1978-'79. It has come down to about one-fourth in 2010. However, the proportion is likely to drop further as WTO accession brought a greater level of competition from foreign players to the domestic market. The WTO membership has also ensured greater access for China to the markets of industrialized countries, partially through the lifting of import quotas on Chinese textiles and clothing by North American and European countries.

To become the member of WTO, China's commitment on trade in services stood as a milestone. The overall breadth of trade reforms and market opening to which China had agreed represented a sharp contrast to the more limited reforms previously implemented by any other Asian countries. The commitments included the opening up of key service sectors where foreign participation was previously marginal or non-existent, especially in financial services, insurance and in telecommunications. Chinese leadership guaranteed that in these sectors, full access would eventually be provided to foreign providers through transparent and automatic licensing procedures. The reforms also encompassed sectors such as power, civil airlines, and the railways. In these sectors, Chinese government re-iterated their willingness and commitment to increase competition and also to establish modern regulatory systems. In addition, China had also agreed to remove restrictions on trading and domestic distribution for most products.

While China made remarkable commitments in the services sector, China's agreement on tariff reductions under the WTO agreement were the continuation of a long-standing trend. For example, there were substantial trade reforms in the 1990s, which included tariff reductions and the elimination of most non-tariff barriers. This trend accelerated sharply after 2000 as part of the accession process. To reciprocate this, the average MFN tariff rate was reduced from around 50 percent in the early 1980s to 15.6 percent in 2001 and to 9.5 percent in 2009. China also significantly reduced and removed non-tariff barriers such as licenses and quotas for imported products and other trading barriers.

China had also made significant concessions in the agricultural sector as part of the conditions to become member of WTO. It accepted to limit domestic agricultural subsidies to 8.5 percent of the value of production and that was less than the 10 percent limit allowed for developing countries under the WTO Agreement on Agriculture. China also agreed to eliminate all export subsidies upon WTO entry and that represented a sharp contrast with past commitments by other WTO members. As expected, there has been a major increase in imports of rice, wheat, corn and cotton as the average tariff on imports fell from 22 percent to 15 percent in trade-weighted terms.

Chinese government also agreed to establish intellectual property laws and enforcement procedures that would commensurate with the WTO's Trade related Aspects of Intellectual Property Rights (TRIPS) agreement. Through this agreement, Chinese government agreed to create a domestic IP regime that would live up to its WTO commitments. Moreover, China has already established a chamber of specialized IP courts throughout the country.

INCREASED MARKET ACCESS:

Increased market access in overseas has been one of the most major benefits of WTO accession for China. Other WTO members already granted China permanently most-favored nation (MFN) treatment which was a significant step in normalizing its international trade relations. However, the impact of this change appeared to be limited because most countries had granted China MFN treatment before its WTO accession. But investor confidence had improved significantly since MFN treatment to China by United States became no longer a subject for annual review. Additionally, upon China's accession to WTO, several of China's trading partners eliminated many of their trade restrictions on imports from China. As a whole, easier and smooth access to foreign markets already boosted significantly China's labor-oriented exports in a number of sectors.

China's clothing and textile exports still have some restrictions by countries in North America and Europe. China will be able to increase substantially its world export market in these areas as soon as those restrictions are removed. However, the timing of such a removal remains uncertain owing to safeguards that can be imposed by importing countries as part of China's accession protocol.

COMPLIANCE AND IMPACT:

China made remarkable progress on its WTO commitments during the nine years period following its entry to WTO and implemented them on schedule. It reduced its import tariffs on schedule and even lowered tariffs ahead of schedule for several products. As per WTO commitment, Chinese government opened up the sectors for increased foreign investment and also passed the requisite enactments allowing increased proportion of foreign shares in such service areas as banking, insurance, foreign trade, tourism, telecommunications, transportation, accounting, auditing, and legal affairs. Foreign securities and fund-management firms were also granted permission to enter once off-limit markets through joint ventures.

Since China's accession to WTO, its trade with almost all trading nations of the world has expanded rapidly, largely because of the reduction in tariffs and the high rate of Chinese economic growth. With average annual economic growth rate of over 9 percent, China has been transforming a market potential of its 1.3 billion consumers into market reality. It is now well accepted that China has one of the world's largest potential markets for a wide range of products. World business community are being proved to be rightfully hopeful about the growing market prospects resulting from China's accession to WTO and already undertaken and proposed liberalization measures. While China's exports are growing, its imports from almost every country of the world at all levels of development are also increasing rapidly. United States, European Union, Japan and other Asian countries have significantly increased their share of exports to China since WTO accession. Strong demand from China has also been supporting prices for a wide range of industrial products. China is now the second largest trading partner of the United States after Canada. Exports to China from the United States rose substantially on yearly basis since China's WTO accession. Agricultural exports from the United States to China also increased manifold during the same period. In contrast, exports from the United States to the rest of the world increased marginally during the same period. China has a huge trade surplus with the United States, and is also the largest foreign holder of US government bonds. The US trade deficit with China widened 9.2 percent in September 2009 to USD22.1 billion, the highest since November 2008, according to US data released in October 2009. In this context, Chinese Premier Wen Jiabao made the comments during a meeting with the US President in Beijing in November 2009 that China did not pursue a trade surplus and also added that Chinese government always wanted to encourage a steady balancing of bilateral trade. Chinese Premier also mentioned that vigorous global trade and investment would help to overcome the recent international financial crisis and accelerate global economic recovery and urged both countries to jointly oppose trade and investment protectionism. But Wen's comments did not mollify US industry groups and politicians who insisted that Beijing is stoking a US trade deficit with China and is worsening global economic imbalances by holding its currency so low against the US dollar. Despite all arguments, as a whole, in the nine years since China joined the World Trade Organization, it has become the world's second largest economy and holds more than USD2 trillion in its foreign reserves – the wealthiest country in this regard. It is the second largest trading nation and a beneficiary of decades of foreign investment. The economy became the largest contributor to global growth in 2008-2010, and this role will continue in the foreseeable future.

So far the legal reforms in China, initiated in conformity with WTO requirements, has made it possible for foreign firms to set up wholly-owned subsidiaries in China. The total number of companies wholly-owned by foreign investors in China in 2008 overtook the number of companies jointly owned by Chinese and foreign investors, and these firms accounted for the majority portion of the total capitalization of all companies with foreign investment. Because of increased investor confidence, net foreign direct investment inflows rose to USD 92.4 billion in 2008, up by 23.6 percent over 2007. However, in 2009, China's inward foreign direct investment amounted to USD90 billion, down by 2.6 percent from 2008. Investment growth was around 24 percent higher year on year basis since 2002 until 2008. As China increasingly opened up sectors of the economy and lowered trade barriers (including tariff and non-tariff), capital inflows have been surging,in the services sector and also in the manufacturing sector.Moreover, business conditions for the overseas companies had improved significantly since China's WTO accession and is expected to continue to improve in the coming days. Growing confidence in the Chinese market also shows the strength of the current leadership, its commitment to eradicate corruption and its sincere willingness to create a competitive market atmosphere over time.

Despite the above developments since China's accession to WTO, there are some criticisms. Those critics complain that China is not fulfilling commitments it made upon its WTO entry in 2001. The criticism, in other words, represents that the 'honeymoon' period of entering to WTO membership has already been over as China almost implemented all those reforms that are fundamentally changing the nature of its economic system. Critics say that China is leading to a loss of jobs in the United States and even in other developed countries. Soaring bilateral trade deficits of USA with China were made responsible for the lost manufacturing jobs in the United States. However, China's overall trade surplus actually declined during the last five years period, as China recorded growing deficits with other Asian countries. US imports from China have largely substituted for imports from other Asian countries. As a result, the US overall trade balance with Asia has not changed much in recent years.

Therefore, rising trade with China should not be viewed as a major reason to be responsible for job losses in US manufacturing.

There are also concerns about delays in the implementation of commitments on transparency and about enforcement issues in specific areas, such as agriculture, intellectual property rights, or the financial sector. Critics argue that although China had been reducing tariffs on agricultural products, it was also imposing unreasonable quarantine inspections on some agricultural imports. U.S. and European business groups have cited that barriers to agricultural imports are more prevalent in China now than they were before its WTO entry. Another criticism is high capital requirements for setting up bank branches, though foreign-owned insurance companies and banks are now authorized to operate in China. A key unresolved issue in the area of trading and distribution rights is the method of distribution of imported products in China. This is critically important for the foreign companies not only to widen the number of products that they can sell within China but also to permit majority foreign ownership in trade and distribution ventures.

CHALLENGES FOR CHINA:

In the context of the concessions China made as part of its WTO entry, we can address and examine the following specific issues that China faces as it tries to balance increasing global integration with the constraints at the domestic front. Firstly, the challenges China faces with regard to implementation and enforcement – challenges that come to the light from the strength of vested interests. Secondly, the implications for the agricultural sector from WTO accession, given the extensive opening of the agricultural sector and contentious trade relations in agriculture. Finally, apparently probable constraints on export growth resulting from the concessions to trading partners that China made in its accession agreement that go beyond the standard practices contained in the WTO agreement on safeguards. China was supposed to have some other challenges such as risks of social unrest caused by increased unemployment, industrial restructuring and agricultural and industrial policies. In reality, so far China has been able to manage these issues in a very sensible and capable manner.

The regulatory and legal framework at the central government level has been extensively upgraded. However, at the provincial levels, progress becomes comparatively difficult because the local governments, which exercise a great deal of autonomy, were not very cooperative in implementing these changes. One prominent instance of such conflicts between the national and provincial levels could be seen in the partially ineffective enforcement of intellectual property rights. Judicial and administrative capacity constraints at various levels of government automatically hamper implementation and enforcement. Moreover, protectionism on the part of the government bureaucrats to protect their powers and their own interests also appears to be growing. The Chinese government has been continuously focusing on institutional capacity building by running courses for government officials at various levels to equip them about WTO requirements and commitments and also to overcome the growing protectionism. The vested interests at various levels of provincial and municipal government, of state-run monopolies and industries, and of government bureaucrats at every level also play critical roles for the ambiguities in enforcing China's WTO commitments in certain areas. Chinese leadership expects that the requirements imposed by WTO membership will strengthen the hand of the central government in dealing with vested interests and other constraints at the local and provincial levels.

IMPLICATIONS DURING 2001-2005:

China's economy witnessed rapid growth and increased integration into the world economy since its accession to the WTO in 2001. Chinese economy registered GDP growth of 8.3 percent, 9.1 percent, 10 percent, 10.1 percent and 9.9 percent in 2001, 2002, 2003, 2004, and 2005 respectively. Thus, during the period 2001-2005, GDP growth averaged 9.48 percent per annum. The ratio of China's trade to its GDP rose more than seven-fold between 1978 and 2004, from less than 10 percent to 76.3 percent, with exports and imports of goods and services accounting for 39.7 percent and 36.7 percent respectively. As a result, by 2005, China became the world's third largest trader after the United States and the European Communities, and a major growth engine in the global economy. In 2005, total merchandise exports and imports amounted to some 63.9 percent of GDP. The main destinations for China's merchandise exports were the United States followed by the EC-25, Hong Kong, and Japan. Whereas Hong Kong's, Japan's, as well as Asia's shares of China's total exports had declined markedly, the shares of the United States, and the EC-25 had risen from 20.7 percent and 16.2 percent in 1998 to 21.4 percent and 18.9 percent in 2005. The main sources of China's imports in 2005 were Japan (15.2 percent), Korea (11.6 percent), Taiwan (11.3 percent), the EC-25 (11.1 percent), and the United States (7.4 percent). The merchandise trade surplus was USD101.9 billion in 2005, three times more than for 2004. China ran large trade surpluses in 2005 with the United States (USD114 billion), Hong Kong (USD112 billion), and the EC-25 (USD70 billion). However, it also ran large trade deficits with Taiwan (USD58 billion), Korea (USD42 billion), and Japan (USD16.5 billion). These trade deficits partly reflected outsourcing by these countries, whose companies invested in China. Those companies' operations, to a large extent, involved the importation of parts and components from their home bases for processing and assembly in China and subsequently exporting the finished products to other parts of the world, notably the United States and the EC. In the process, Taiwan, Korea, and Japan, in effect, exported their trade surpluses with the United States and the EC through China. In 2005, China's intra-industry trade with Taiwan (Chinese Taipei) accounted for more than half of China's intra-industry trade with the world. In the first half of 2005, services accounted for 9.2 percent of China's total exports and 11.8 percent of its imports. During the period, China's exports and imports of services nearly tripled, which means export and import of services grew more slowly than China's merchandise exports and imports. Transportation, business, and travel were the main services traded.

In 2004, manufactures accounted for 91.4 percent of China's total merchandise exports, up from 87.2 percent in 1998. The value of manufactured exports grew more than triple during 1998-2005. The value of exports of relatively high technology products, involving office machines, telecommunications, and transportation equipments and parts, which in 2005 accounted nearly half of manufactured exports, increased more than five fold during the period. Exports increased nearly two-fold in the case of textiles and clothing during 1998-2005. The share of processed exports in total exports remained high, 54.7 percent in 2005. In 2004, manufactures accounted for 76.3 percent of China's total merchandise imports. The value of these imports nearly quadrupled during 1998-2004. Nearly 41.5 percent of imports entered China under the processing trade regime in 2005.

During the period, China also became one of the largest recipients of FDI which had grown from virtually zero to approximately 4 percent of GDP annually over the past decade. Total accumulated FDI rose from USD1.8 billion in 1982 to USD562 billion in 2004. FDI in China increased from 3.8 percent of GDP in 2001 to 3.9 percent in 2002, but fell to 3.3 percent in 2003 and 2004. In 2005, FDI was USD60.3 billion, very slightly down from the previous year. Much of this involved the establishment of Foreign Invested Enterprises (FIEs), which tend to go to economic and technology development zones for having preferential treatment. In 2005, FIEs' exports amounted to USD444.2 billion, up by 31.2 percent from the previous year, and also accounted for 58.3 percent of total exports. On the other-hand, in 2005, FIEs' imports amounted to USD387.5 billion, up by 19.4 percent from the previous year, and accounted for 58.7 percent of total imports. Manufacturing attracted the most FDI to China, accounting for around 70 percent of newly established FIEs between 2002 and the first half of 2005. The share of services (excluding gas, electricity, water, and construction) in FDI inflows was around 23 percent during 2001-2005. FDI outflows, by contrast, had been relatively low, reaching only USD5.5 billion in 2004, with an accumulated total of USD44.8 billion. However, in the first half of 2005, the FDI outflow was USD3.9 billion, an increase of 284 percent from the same period in 2004. The increased outflow was largely driven by demand for natural resources, for example, oil, gas, and mining products. It is worth noting that during 2001-2005, many Chinese SOEs invested in the oil industry of many countries, such as Indonesia, Kazakhstan, Myanmar, The Sudan, and Yemen, and also in aluminum, steel, and coke industries in Brazil. In 2005, China's main sources of FDI were Hong Kong, which accounted for nearly one-third of the total, followed by the British Virgin

Islands (11 percent), South Korea (10 percent), Japan (9 percent), EC-15 (7 percent), the United States (6.5 percent), and Taiwan (5 percent).

China became a Member of WTO in 2001. China's commitments in the WTO provided a catalyst for further far-reaching economic reforms. During 2001-2005, these reforms were aimed at further perfecting the socialist market economy, where market-determined prices and private investors play a more important role in the allocation of resources and economic development. The gradual reduction in the simple applied average MFN tariff (from 35 percent in 1994 to under 10 percent in 2005) and the lowering of non-tariff barriers to trade, together with the opening of the economy to FDI, stimulated competition and thereby contributed to the improved competitiveness of domestic producers. According to the World Economic Forum's 2005 Growth Competitiveness Index and Business Competitive Index, China ranked 49th out of 117 countries and 57th out of 116 countries respectively. Among the factors contributing to this ranking were concerns over corruption, red tape, lack of judicial independence, and trade barriers. The accumulation of capital, financed for the most part by domestic savings, had also been vital during the period. Gross domestic investment and gross national saving amounted to nearly 40 percent and 43 percent respectively of GDP in 2004. Moreover, with capital growing much faster than labor, capital accumulation contributed 4.6 percentage points to the 7.4 percent growth in labor productivity, a key determinant of living standards. Growth in total factor productivity (TFP) as a key determinant of economic competitiveness, accounted for 2.8 percentage points of the growth in both GDP and labor productivity. Total factor productivity (TFP) reflected the efficiency with which factors of production were used and was thus a major determinant of the economy's performance. While the re-oriented parts of the economy including joint-ventures involving the state and foreign partners and the large flow of FDI associated with entrepreneurship, management skills and technology contributed to the emergence of the private sector whose growth in output and productivity had far outstripped SOEs, and also created alternative employment opportunities, the official urban registered unemployment rate had been gradually rising during 2001-2005 and reached to nearly 4.5 percent. Inflation, as measured by Consumer Price Index, had been fluctuating between −1.4 percent and 3.9 percent between 1998 and 2005.

The widening gap between China's gross national saving and gross domestic investment was reflected in the growing current account surplus, which increased from 1.3 percent of GDP in 2001 to 5.2 percent of GDP in 2005. By the end of 2005, the accumulated amount in official reserves was USD819 billion and the majority portion of this amount had been used to purchase government securities issued by G7 countries. However, China's rapid growth and reduction in absolute poverty levels had also been accompanied by a widening disparity in incomes and employment opportunities during the period. By 2005, income disparities reflected particularly in wage differentials owing to differences in labor productivity were especially wide between urban and rural areas. In 2005, labor productivity in non-agricultural activities was apparently more than four times than in agricultural activities. China's increased urbanization and rapid industrial growth during 2001-2005 had also had implications for its environment. Pollution control was improved under the government policies during 9th and 10th Five-Year Plans (1996-2000 and 2001-2005); and a balanced development approach under an environmentally friendly perspective has been stressed in the 11th Five Year Plan (2006-2010).

During 2001-2005, industry and services were the main economic activities in China. On the contrary, agriculture accounted for a declining share. In 2005, industry and services accounted for almost four-fifth of GDP, while agriculture's contribution declined to nearly 15 percent.

Monetary and exchange rate policies together with fiscal policy are especially important in shaping up a stable macroeconomic environment. In July 2005, a managed floating exchange regime was introduced. Until then monetary and exchange rate policies that maintained the stability of the Renminbi in nominal terms in relation to the U.S. dollar was through a currency peg, while allowing a certain volatility in inflation. The objective of China's monetary policy is to maintain the stability of the Renminbi and thereby promote economic growth. In the middle of 2001, ability to maintain a stable exchange rate against the dollar was strengthened by increasing the reserves from 14.8 percent of GDP at the end of 2001 to almost 43 percent of GDP at the end of 2005. Official reserves grew by a total of USD204 billion in 2005 alone, which was equivalent to 9.2 percent of that year's GDP. This action successfully stabilized the nominal exchange rate against the dollar. In 2005, with the authorization of the State Council, the PBOC announced a 2.1 percent revaluation of the RMB in relation to USD, and reform of the exchange rate regime. In connection with the latter, the PBOC announced a 'managed floating exchange rate regime' based on market supply and demand with reference to a 'basket of currencies' so that the currency would no longer be pegged to the USD. Since the revaluation of the RMB in July 2005, there had apparently been a significant drop in speculative inflows of capital into China; such a drop made it easier for the PBOC to conduct monetary policy.

In end-2005, China's fiscal position would seem to be sound. Government's total revenue had risen steadily, to 16.5 percent of GDP in 2004. Total expenditure rose between 1998 and 2004 to 17.8 percent of GDP. The obvious outcome was a fiscal deficit of 1.3 percent in 2004, considerably lower than in the intervening years. Gross government debt, in 2004, was 20.2 percent of GDP, out of which around 3.2 percentage points involved foreign debt. All debts were being owned by the Central Government, since local governments were required to balance their budgets annually. The State Council decided to adjust the orientation of fiscal policy towards a more neutral stance in 2005, aimed at bringing its fiscal deficit down to roughly 2 percent of GDP. In 2005, budgetary expenditure on education accounted for nearly 2.5 percent of GDP, while total government-financed capital spending had been over 9 percent of GDP in these years. Increased expenditure on health, education, and other public services both in rural areas and for migrants in urban areas required a subsequent adjustment of fiscal relations between the central and local governments in order to ensure that funds reach the level of government responsible for delivering these public services.

China was a moderately taxed economy. Its total tax revenue accounted for 15.1 percent of GDP in 2004. The main indirect taxes in end-2004, were the value-added tax, business tax, and the consumption (excise) tax which accounted for 37.3 percent, 14.8 percent and 6.2 percent of total tax revenues respectively. The business tax was assigned largely to local governments, the consumption tax revenues all went to the central government, and VAT revenues were shared between the central and local governments in the ratios 75 percent and 25 percent respectively.

IMPLICATIONS DURING 2006 - 2007:

China's economy continued its fast and steady growth during this period, with GDP growth of 12.7 percent and 14.2 percent in 2006 and 2007 respectively. Until 2007, for five consecutive years, the growth rate of China's economy reached 10 percent or above.

On employment, nearly 11.84 million and 12.4 million people were able to get newly employed in the urban areas in 2006 and 2007 respectively. The registered urban unemployment rate, in 2006 and 2007, was 4.1 percent and 4.0 percent respectively.

In 2007 the contribution of consumption to GDP growth exceeded that of investment for the first time in seven years. In turn, this actually changed the underlying mechanism for economic growth from mainly relying on investment and export to an approach that coordinates consumption, investment, and exports as an integrated force for growth.

As China continued to enjoy rapid economic growth during the period, the rise in prices exerted mounting pressure on the heavily-populated country. The increase in the overall level of consumer prices reached a record high of recent years, with the biggest jump in food prices. In this context, China was expected to continue to adopt a prudent fiscal policy and gradually tighten up its monetary policy. In terms of public finance, during 2006-2007, China's fiscal revenue continued to score rapid growth, increasing by 22.5 percent and 32.4 percent in 2006 and 2007 respectively. The Central Government's budget deficit declined year by year, from Y299.9 billion in 2005 down to Y274.9 billion in 2006, and further down to Y200 billion in 2007. Moreover, the issuance of Treasury bond for long-term construction projects also decreased year by year during the period, from Y80 billion in 2005 to Y60 billion in 2006, and further down to Y50 billion in 2007.

During the period under discussion, the Chinese Government adopted an integrated approach incorporating a variety of fiscal policy instruments in order to ensure structural optimization and promote system innovation so as to respond to the needs of social and economic upliftment as well as to achieve a well coordinated functioning of the economic and social sectors. During this period, China policy makers wanted the economic development approach – (i) to be responsive to the needs of social and economic uplift of its population and (ii) to facilitate well coordinated functioning of the economic and social sectors. Meeting these objectives requires structural optimization and system innovation. In order to achieve these goals the Chinese Government adopted an integrated approach incorporating a variety of fiscal policy instruments that included: to increase the investment for social causes such as education, science, public health, and social security so as to promote the coordinated development for both economic and social sectors; to increase the public finance to cover the three issues concerning 'agriculture, rural areas, and farmers' in order to balance the development of both urban and rural areas; to increase budget allocations with a view to promote resource conservation and environment protection; and to increase central government transfer payment earmarked to the interior regions of central and western China to achieve balanced development of different regions.

During this period, until mid-2008, the Chinese Government paid more attention to the transformation of economic development mode and followed a path of pro-innovation, resources saving, and environmental friendly industries and service sectors. The Chinese Government put in place: the policy incentives for the development of new and high-tech industries; restrictions on energy-intensive and high-emission industries; reinforcement of environmental protection measures; and more efforts on energy conservation as well as development of a circular economy. The '2007 Industrial Catalogue for the Guidance of Foreign Investment' encouraged foreign investment in the development of clean production, renewable energy, ecological protection, and comprehensive utilization of resources for multiple purposes. In 2006-2007, the Comprehensive Work Plan for Energy-saving and Emission Reduction was drafted and put on track of implementation. During this period, the Chinese government also established energy-consumption and environmental standards which require strict compliance. Since then, all new projects required energy consumption appraisal and environmental impact assessment. In terms of results of these policy incentives, the energy consumption per unit of GDP started to decrease from 2006.

The Ministry of Labor and Social Security (MOLSS) was established by the State Council in 1995, and mandated to oversee all social security measures. MOLSS was restructured afterwards as the Ministry of Human Resources and Social Security. During this period, the evolving social security system, covering both urban and rural residents, comprised of basic services such as social insurance, medical care and support as well as social welfare emphasizing mainly on provision of basic pension insurance, basic health insurance and subsistence allowance supplemented by charity and commercial insurance program. The social security fund was set up to reinforce the development of social security system. China's social insurance fund, as the most important component of the social security fund, mainly consists of basic pension fund for employees, unemployment insurance fund, and basic health insurance fund for urban workers, basic health insurance fund for urban residents, and insurance fund for work-related injury and maternity leaves. The accumulative national fiscal expenditure on social security amounted to Y1.92 trillion during the five years period of 2003 to 2007. The amount of cumulative national social security fund reached Y414 billion in 2007, Y298.8 billion more than that of 2002. In 2007, the subsistence allowance system was established in China's entire rural areas covering 34,519 million rural residents. By 2007, the number of participants in the basic medical insurance for urban workers had reached 180 million; the number of participants in the urban basic pension system had exceeded 200 million; the rural cooperative medicare system had covered 86 percent of the counties nationwide benefiting 730 million rural residents.

On 1st October 2007, the Real Right Law was implemented. It is a basic civil law governing property relationships which aims to regulate the civil relationships arising from ownership and appropriation. The Real Right Law made it clear for the first time that the real right of the state, collective, individual, or any other right holders should be protected by law, and should not be infringed by any organization or individual.

With regard to capital market development, China Securities Regulatory Commission launched the reform of the split share structure of listed companies in May 2005, aimed at realizing the circulation of non-tradable shares. A multi-level capital market system, since 2006, started to take its initial shape with the rapid development of China's main board and SMEs board markets, and with the further expansion of corporate bond market. With the establishment of a corporate bond issuance system based on information disclosure and market-orientation, the corporate bond market was further improved during the period.

In terms of financial sector reform, by 2007, Industrial and Commercial Bank of China, Bank of China, Construction Bank of China, and Bank of Communications completed their shareholding reform in succession, and were listed in domestic and/or overseas stock markets. Also during the period, profound changes took place in both corporate governance and managerial concept of these commercial banks. As a result, their asset quality, management skills, and, more rightfully, overall strength have been enhanced. During this period, the reform of China's Rural Credit Cooperatives also made steady progress. By the end of 2007, the pilot micro-credit enterprises cumulatively provided Y392.345 million of credit. Moreover, 32 new rural financial institutions had been approved to start operation by the end of 2007. Among these institutions, four are loan subsidiaries, eight are rural mutual cooperatives, and the remaining are rural commercial banks.

During the period under discussion, the Chinese Government continued to carry out with great care the reform of RMB exchange rate regime since it was inaugurated in July 2005. The flexibility of RMB exchange rate has increased markedly after several years of reform. From July 2005 to the end of 2007, RMB had appreciated by 13.3 percent against USD, and 14.06 percent against YEN. Systematic equilibrium management system of foreign exchange outflow and inflow has been gradually implemented during the period with the overall objective of achieving the basic balance of international payment. From 2007, individuals in China are entitled to purchase a maximum amount of USD 50,000 per person per year, largely satisfying the needs of individuals. Businesses are also entitled to retain the foreign exchange income from current transfers. The documents and procedures have also been simplified for sale and payment of foreign exchange for trade in services.

Towards changes in taxation policy, 'The Law of the People's Republic of China on Enterprise Income Tax' was promulgated in end-2007. The implementation of this law ended the co-existence of two separate tax systems, one applicable to foreign-invested enterprises and the other one to Chinese domestic enterprises,and promulgated an uniform enterprise income tax law. This new law unified the methods and standards of pre-tax deductions, consolidated tax policy incentives, and also lowered the statutory income tax rate from 33 percent to 25 percent. Besides Enterprise Income Tax law reform, the pilot program of reform on the transformation of VAT also made steady progress during this period. The Chinese Government also began to reform its consumption tax system on 1st April 2006 in order to promote both environmental protection and resource conservation, and to guide rational consumption and indirectly adjusting income distribution. Moreover, significant changes have also been made in recent years in personal tax policy keeping in view of the continued rapid economic growth. During the period, the income tax threshold was raised from Y800/person/month to Y2000/person/month after two rounds of changes. The personal income tax rate for deposit interest was also reduced from 20 percent to 5 percent. On 1st January 2006, China abolished the agricultural tax nationwide.

In the area of intellectual property right protection, China's State Council formulated the Outline of IPR Protection Actions (2006-2007) in 2006. During the period under discussion, China enacted a number of rules and regulations in order to further improve the legal system for IPR protection. The State Council promulgated in 2006 'the Regulations on the Protection of the Right of Communication through Information Network'. In 2007, Supreme People's Court and Supreme People's Procuratorate jointly issued 'Interpretation 2 of the Supreme People's Court and Supreme People's Procuratorate Concerning Some Issues on the Specific Application of Law for Handling Criminal Cases of Infringement upon Intellectual Property Right', which lowered substantially the criminal law enforcement threshold. In addition, Chinese Government also adopted various means to extend education and training programs to enhance the public awareness on IPR protection. China decided to join the WIPO Copyright Treaty and the WIPO Performances and Phonograms Treaty on December 2006. The two treaties formally came into force in China in June 2007. During the period, China also completed the domestic legal procedure for acceptance of the protocol on Revising the Agreement on Trade-related Aspects of Intellectual Property Rights.

During 2006-2007, China's merchandise trade continued to register reasonable growth. Total trade reached USD 1.7 trillion in 2006 and USD 2.1 trillion in 2007, representing an annual increase of 23.5 percent. Meanwhile, during 2005-2007, trade surplus also increased year by year, reaching USD 101.88 billion, USD 177.47 billion, and USD 262.21 billion in 2005, 2006, and 2007 respectively. During the same period, imports growth rates were 17.7 percent, 20.0 percent, and 20.7 percent respectively.

As of the end of 2007, China's top three trading partners were the EC, the United States, and Japan. China became the second largest trading partner of the United States and the EC, and the largest trading partner of Japan. Trade between China and ASEAN, Russia, India, Brazil, Korea, and Australia also registered rapid growth. Between 2005 and 2007, bilateral trade in goods between China and ASEAN reached USD130.37 billion, USD160.84 billion, and USD202.51 billion, a yearly increase of 23.1 percent, 23.3 percent, and 25.9 percent respectively. Trade between African countries and China recorded an even faster rate of growth. Between 2005 and 2007, the yearly growth rate of trade between China and African countries were 34.9 percent, 39.5 percent, and 32.1 percent respectively.

During this period, China also witnessed rapid growth in its services trade. China's services import and export amounted to USD191.75 billion in 2006, a growth of 22.1 percent over the previous year. In a breakdown, import was USD100.33 billion, and export was USD 91.42 billion, representing an increase of 20.6 percent and 23.7 percent over the previous year. Towards fulfilling the objective of the 11th Five-Year Program for National Economic and Social Development, China took several steps during the period to further develop a services export promotion system, including those to improve the statistics system of trade in services, to set up outsourcing bases for services and to encourage the participation of foreign investment in software development, the cross-border outsourcing and logistics industries.

During 2006 to 2007, China made a series of policy adjustments relating to processing trade. This was done in order to improve the structure of export commodities, discourage the excessive exports of low value-added and low technology content products, promote the transformation and upgradation of the processing trade, and encourage the relocation of the processing trade activities to the central and western parts of China. With a view to reducing the production, consumption and export of high energy-intensive, high emission and products of exhaustible resources, the Chinese Government adjusted the export VAT rebate policy in July 2007, covering 2,831 commodities, which accounted for 37 percent of the total number of export commodities. In specific terms, China lowered tax rebates for 2,268 commodities, and cancelled such rebates for 553 commodities.

During 2006-2007, China had been pushing forward reforms on regional customs regime of clearance and transit goods. Such reforms include measures to make better use of information technology, integrate the inland customs' management resources with those of the port customs, as well as simplifying the transit customs clearance.

In regard to standards and conformity assessment, the Chinese Government committed to reforming the relevant working mechanism, keeping existing standards and technical regulations up to date, in order to encourage the enterprises to participate more actively in the development and revision of standards and technical regulations. The Chinese Government, during the period, also established a unified conformity assessment system to promote compliance with standards and technical regulations. For certification and accreditation, the Chinese Government already established a unified and standard certification and accreditation system which applied equally to domestic and foreign enterprises, and effectively implemented the compulsory certification system, thus virtually eliminated the double authentication that existed prior to China's accession to the WTO.

Regarding participation in multilateral trade negotiations, the Chinese Government understands and believes that the multilateral trading system plays an irreplaceable role in maintaining world economic stability as well as promoting global trade liberalization. China, as a top priority in its trade policy, has committed to push forward the Doha Round negotiations to an early and successful conclusion. Since joining to WTO, China actively participated in all the negotiations under Doha Development Agenda and played a constructive role. China also submitted a large number of proposals on agriculture, Non-Agricultural Market Access (NAMA), services, rules, trade facilitation etc. in order to contribute to the development objectives of the negotiations. China already conveyed its strong believe that the multilateral trade negotiations should ensure an outcome benefiting all Members, particularly the developing ones. Therefore, the negotiations on specific issues should take into full consideration of the development level and capacity of developing countries, and enable them to gain tangible benefits through special and differential treatment. However, while multilateral trading system remains the priority, China also showed its strong believe that regional trade arrangements established on the basis of openness and non-discrimination can play a supplementary role to the multilateral trading system. Following this principle, China conducted bilateral and regional trade arrangement negotiations with a number of trading partners during this period. As of end-2007, the following regional trade arrangements involving 29 countries and regions have been either signed by China or in the process of negotiation. They were: Asia Pacific Trade Agreement (APTA) 2007 (still underway); Closer Economic Partnership Arrangement (CEPA)-Supplement3, 2006;

China-ASEAN Free Trade Agreement, 2007; China-Chile Free Trade agreement on Trade in Goods, 2006; China-Pakistan Free Trade Agreement on Trade in Goods, 2007; China-Pakistan Free Trade Agreement on Trade in Services; China-Gulf Cooperation Council Free Trade Agreement, 2007 (still underway); China-Australia Free Trade Agreement, 2005 (still underway); China-Singapore Free Trade Agreement, 2006 (still underway); China-Iceland Free Trade Agreement, 2006 (still underway); China-Peru Free Trade Agreement, 2007 (still underway).

China also actively participated in other regional cooperation mechanisms during 2006-2007. The 11th ASEAN and China, Japan, and Korea (10+3) Summit was held in Singapore in November 2007. The Summit adopted East Asia Cooperation and the ASEAN and China, Japan, and Korea (10+3) Cooperation Work Plan (2007-2017). China also actively participated in trade and investment liberalization under the framework of the APEC and Asia-Europe Meeting (ASEM) and fostered a pragmatic approach in cooperation. The Great Mekong Sub-regional Cooperation (GMS) was initiated in 1992 by six members, namely, China, Cambodia, Laos, Myanmar, Thailand, and Vietnam towards enhancing mutual economic cooperation, alleviating poverty, and promoting development. Forum on China-Africa Cooperation (FOCAC) has been a new mechanism between China and African countries to promote South-South cooperation. China and 48 African countries attended the FOCAC Beijing Summit and the Ministerial Conference in November 2006 and adopted the Declaration of the Beijing Summit of FOCAC and the Beijing Action Plan (2007-2009). China announced eight new measures for Sino-African cooperation including debt relief programs as well as duty-free market access for African LDCs. China also supports and actively participates in Aid for Trade initiative of the WTO. In this regard, China has been very active mostly on bilateral basis.

IMPLICATIONS DURING 2008-2009:

During the period, China encountered most serious difficulties in its economic growth due to the impact of the global financial crisis and unprecedented natural disasters. Towards balancing the short-term growth target and the long-term development goal, the Chinese Government had been working hard to boost domestic demand, advance reform, increase benefit and welfare of the people, and adjust economic structures.

In the latter half of 2008, the global financial crisis began to inflict increasing impact on China's economy and development. There had been a sharp decline in China's foreign trade, in particular in its exports as external demand contracted drastically. The fourth quarter of 2008 witnessed China's total value of imports and exports reverse to a negative growth of 1.6 percent year on year, compared with the increases of 24.7 percent, 26.9 percent and 24.3 percent registered respectively in the previous three quarters. China's total imports and exports dropped further by 24.9 percent, 22.0 percent and 16.6 percent in the first, second and third quarter of 2009 respectively.

China also suffered a series of unprecedented natural disasters in 2008 and 2009. The earthquake measuring 8.0 on the Richter scale in Sichuan Province on 12th May 2008 was particularly devastating. The earthquake left hundreds of thousands of people dead or injured, and caused severe damages to infrastructure, production facilities and the ecological environment. 51 counties covering 116,656 square kilometers in the three provinces of Sichuan, Gansu and Shaanxi were confirmed to be seriously stricken areas with a direct economic loss of nearly Y650 billion. In 2008 and 2009, China also suffered from heavy snow and ice storms in the south and severe drought in large areas of the north that had been rarely seen before. All these various types of natural disasters caused direct and indirect heavy economic losses for China in 2008 as well as in 2009.

China's GDP in 2008, despite the natural disasters and full-blown global financial crisis, still reached Y31.40 trillion, an increase of 9.6 percent over 2007. In 2009, China's GDP was Y33.54 trillion, an increase of 8.7 percent over 2008. Facing the unprecedented financial crisis, China contained the decline in growth in 2009 in a relatively short time, stabilized the national economy and witnessed an overall growth again. As a countermeasure to the global financial crisis, the Chinese Government relied primarily on expanding effective domestic demand to maintain a steady growth of the economy, and put forward a plan of stimulus package of 4 trillion Yuan to be implemented from the fourth quarter of 2008 to the end of 2010 reflecting both the short-term target of addressing the economic downturn and the long-term goal of promoting the transformation of the economic development pattern. Out of the total 4 trillion Yuan, 1.18 trillion Yuan would be direct investment from the central government. Of the total nearly 924 billion Yuan public investment by the Chinese central government for year 2009, 44 percent went to housing projects for low-income urban residents in order to improve the well-being of the residents and the infrastructure, and social programs; 23 percent to construction of major infrastructure; 16 percent to energy conservation, emission reduction, ecological improvement, and economic restructuring; and 14 percent to post-earthquake recovery and reconstruction. Since none of these investments translated into new large-scale production capacities, it is clear that the purpose of the stimulus package was to expand domestic demand through consolidation of the foundation for long-term economic development so that the economic downturn could be arrested and a steady growth be maintained. China's fiscal budget deficit for 2009, with the implementation of the proactive fiscal policy, was Y950 billion, or around 2.8 percent of the GDP.

The People's Bank of China, in its response to the impact of the global financial crisis, promptly adjusted policy orientation and began to implement a moderately easy monetary policy. It lowered the deposits reserve ratio four times between September and December 2008, adding up to a total reduction of 2-4 percentage points. During the same period, it also cut the benchmark deposit and lending rates of financial institutions five times, with the one-year bench-mark deposit and lending rates down by 1.89 and 2.16 percentage points respectively. Introduction of the moderately easy monetary policy in general was very effective, and the supplies of money and credit increased rapidly. Such policy played an important role in enhancing overall confidence, expanding demand and achieving turnaround in the development of the economy.

SMEs were the hardest hit by the global financial crisis. In 2009, the Chinese Government increased the fund for the development of SMEs from Y3.9 billion to Y9.6 billion to enhance the support to SMEs including in such areas as technological innovation and structural adjustment. In order to alleviate difficulties in obtaining financing and strengthening services system for SMEs, in September 2009, the State council issued Certain Opinions on Further Promoting the Development of SMEs. In December 2009, the State Council also established an inter-agency Leading Group on Promotion of the Development of SMEs to further strengthen policy coordination in this respect.

During 2008 and 2009, in order to expand the domestic demand, increasing consumer spending was a key element in the efforts of the Chinese Government. The Chinese Government, in 2008, increased the threshold for personal income tax, suspended personal income taxes on interest earnings from savings and stock account balance, and also reduced or exempted taxes related to the purchase or sale of homes for residential uses. In 2009, Y32 billion was provided by the Chinese Central Government for implementation of a series of consumption stimulus programs including those for rural residents. As a result, domestic consumer market saw relatively rapid expansion during 2008-2009. In 2009, retail sales of consumer goods in China totaled 12.53 trillion Yuan, up 15.5 percent from 2008. After adjustment for price changes, the increase in retail sales of consumer goods in real terms was nearly 16.9 percent. Even in rural areas, retail sales grew by 15.7 percent in 2009 over the previous year, 0.2 percent higher than that in urban areas. Also during 2008 and 2009, investment in infrastructure and social programs in rural areas as well as direct financial support to farmers increased significantly. During this period, financial support for poverty alleviation purposes was also increased. The new poverty line of annual per-capita income of Y 1,196 was adopted from 2008 onwards to cover all low-income rural population. Following the new standard, 40.07 million people become eligible to receive assistance under poverty-relief programs. During the period, the Chinese Government also continued pursuing the 'pay back' policies and strengthened further its support for agriculture, rural areas and farmers in a bid to steadily increase the farmers' income.

In 2008 and 2009, China formulated and amended a series of laws, regulations and rules concerning services sectors including insurance, securities, consumer credit, telecommunication, financial information service, legal service, postal service, tourism etc.

China also implemented institutional restructuring of the State Council in March 2008. Such reform focused on transforming government functions and streamlining responsibilities of different agencies and explored the establishment of larger departments with more integrated functions. Institutions concerning industry, information technology and transport were adjusted. Public administration and public service agencies were strengthened and integrated with more emphasis on the well-being of general masses. In this restructuring, 15 agencies were adjusted or changed and four ministerial-level agencies were removed. In addition, with the implementation of Regulations on Government Information Release since 1st May 2008, work on government information release has been further enhanced, and thereby the transparency of the public sectors further improved.

Regarding reform in taxation system, the Chinese Government further unified the real estate tax for Chinese and foreign-invested enterprises and individuals by introducing in 2008 of the new Law on Enterprise Income Tax and Interim Regulations on Tax for Farmland Occupation which are uniformly applicable to both domestic and foreign-invested enterprises. Furthermore, with the implementation of the amended Interim Regulations on Value-added Tax, Interim Regulations on Business Tax, and Interim Regulations on Consumption Tax in 2009, value-added tax has been transformed, and the systems of business tax and consumption tax have been further improved. With respect to price reform, in January 2009, the Chinese Government carried out reform of the prices, taxes, and charges of refined oil taking an important step forward in the reform of pricing mechanism of resource products. In January 2009, the prices of chemical fertilizers were also reformed with restrictions on the prices lifted. Instead of being guided by the government, the prices of fertilizers are now determined by market.

In 2008, the added value of the tertiary industry in China grew by 10.4 percent over 2007. In 2009, such added value of the tertiary industry reached Y14.29 trillion, registering year-on-year increase of 8.9 percent and 0.2 percentage points higher than the GDP growth rate. However, during the period, China encountered great difficulties in foreign trade and foreign direct investment as a result of the global financial crisis. China's merchandise export amounted to USD 1.2015 trillion in 2009, down by 16 percent over the previous year; and the import amounted to USD 1.0058 trillion, down by 11.2 percent over the previous year. On the other-hand, despite the growing impact of the financial crisis in the latter half of the year, China's export still reached USD1.4307 trillion in 2008, up by 17.3 percent over 2007, and the import reached USD1.1326 trillion, up by 18.4 percent over 2007. In this connection, it would be worth noting that the average annual growth rate in China's total import and export was 23.7 percent for 2005-2007. In 2009, China's inward foreign direct investment in non-financial sectors amounted to USD 90 billion, down by 2.6 percent from the previous year. In 2008, the figure was USD92.4 billion, up by 23.6 percent over 2007. With this backdrop, Measures for Administration of Establishment of Partnership Business in China by Foreign Enterprises or Individuals was promulgated on 25th November 2009 and came into effect as of 1st March 2010 as new vehicle and new field for foreign investment. The administrative regulation has provided foreign investors with a new form of business set-up in addition to wholly foreign-owned enterprise, equity joint venture and contractual joint venture. Moreover, the amended Catalogue of Advantaged Industries for Foreign Investment in Mid-West China (2008) came into force in 2009. In addition, central and western regions of China have also opened up more fields to foreign investment on larger scales.

Alongside the economic globalization and the global redeployment of the manufacturing sectors, China has also become one of the most important production bases in the world with its firm commitment to the policy of opening up and that is one of the main reasons why the recent global financial crisis has had severe impact on China. Out of China's total export of USD1.4307 trillion in 2008 and USD1.2015 trillion in 2009, processing trade represented USD675.1 billion (47.2 percent) and USD586.9 billion (48.8 percent) respectively. Exports of foreign-invested enterprises amounted to USD 790.5 billion in 2008 and USD672.1 billion in

2009, or 55.3 percent and 55.9 percent of the total export of the respective years. Of China's total import of USD 1.1326 trillion in 2008 and USD1.0058 trillion in 2009, processing trade represented USD378.4 billion (33.4 percent) and USD322.3 billion (32 percent) respectively. Imports of the foreign-invested enterprises amounted to USD619.4 billion and USD545.3 billion, or 54.7 percent and 54.2 percent of the total import in 2008 and 2009 respectively. China's main exports are currently concentrated in those of middle and lower end manufacturing industries with low added value, and at the same time a large amount of capital, technologies, designs, management, and even raw materials, components and parts come from abroad. As a result, China maintains large trade surplus with some WTO members and large trade deficits with some others. Such a characteristic of China's foreign trade appears as a manifestation of the international division of labor brought about as economic globalization further deepens. It has benefited both China, and also foreign investors and consumers of Chinese products all around the world.

During this period, it has been evident that the global financial crisis increased the risk of protectionism against China. Exports from China including the products of many foreign-invested enterprises, has been facing increasing number of protectionist measures and thereby adversely affecting the growth of the trade volume. There has also been a clear tendency of rising trade frictions between China and some of the major developed countries. In 2008, WTO members initiated a total of 71 antidumping investigations against China, accounting for 33.7 percent of the total in that year. In addition, in 2008, the number of countervailing investigations against China was 11, accounting for 68.8 percent of the total. In 2009, the number of trade remedy investigations against China reached 116, involving a total trade volume of USD12.7 billion. In the face of such precarious foreign trade situation, the Chinese Government had been working hard during 2008 and 2009 to pursue the goal of boosting domestic demand and stabilizing external demand in order to maintain a stable and rapid economic growth.

In terms of trade financing, in 2009, China Export Credit insurance Company expanded its coverage of short-term export credit insurance to USD90.3 billion. As a measure to the international co-operation towards trade financing, in 2009, China bought bonds of USD1.5 billion from International Finance Corporation of the World Bank group; the People's Bank of China signed bilateral currency swap agreements totaling Y650 billion with central banks or currency authorities of Argentina, Belarus, Indonesia, Malaysia, Hong Kong SAR, and South Korea; China also signed the Chiang Mai Initiative Multilateralization (CMIM) Agreement valued at a total of USD120 billion together with the 10 ASEAN countries, Japan, South Korea, and Hong Kong SAR. During this period, China also announced the program of giving loans worth USD15 billion to ASEAN countries, loans worth USD10 billion to African countries and other member countries of Shanghai Co-operation Organization (SCO), and also to establish China-ASEAN Investment Co-operation Fund with an amount of USD10 billion. In addition, in 2009, China EXIM bank launched a series of international cooperation programs in trade financing. It provided trade financing of up to USD 3 billion to banks in Russia, Turkey, India, and Chile as well as to multinational financial institutions such as the Afri-Exim Bank.

During 2008-2009, China was committed to balanced development of import and export. In 2009, the Chinese Government organized 13 trade and investment promotion missions to purchase goods and expand investment cooperation in over 30 countries and regions. While there was a substantial decline in both Chinese imports and exports due to the global financial crisis, the year-on-year decrease in import (11.2 percent) was much lower than that in export (16 percent). Export to China from many countries performed much better than the overall export of these countries. For example, while the overall export of the United States in 2009 decreased year-on-year by 18.1 percent, its export to China decreased by merely 0.2 percent. The same year saw a 20.6 percent year-on-year decrease in the overall export of the European Union, while its export to China decreased by 1.5 percent only. Among China's neighboring countries, while the export of Thailand, Indonesia and Malaysia to China in 2009 remained stable, their overall export in the same year decreased by 14.6 percent, 15.0 percent and 21.1 percent respectively. Australia and New Zealand experienced overall export decrease of 17.3 percent and 18.3 percent in 2009, while their export to China during the same period increased by 21.7 percent and 29.2 percent respectively. During the period, China also imported a great amount of products from least-developed countries and regions, which obviously contributed to the economic development of these countries and regions. The WTO Secretariat circulated a document in February 2010 titled Market Access for Products and Services of Export Interest to Least-developed Countries, noting that China became the largest export market for LDCs in 2008, purchasing 23 percent of the LDCs' export. It is also worth noting that the share of China's market for LDCs has been increasing.

With regard to strengthening and enhancing the multilateral trading system, China remains a staunch supporter of WTO which is playing a key role in regulating trade policies and measures among various countries in the world and in laying foundation for maintaining stable international trade environment. However, confronted with the severe challenges posed by the global financial crisis, the multilateral trading system is facing two very important tasks. One is to conclude the Doha Round negotiations at an early date and the other is to fight hard against protectionism. The Chinese leaders attach great importance to the Doha Round Negotiation and accordingly on numerous occasions during various World Summits they have called for joint efforts of all members to push for the conclusion of negotiation at an early date with balanced and comprehensive outcome to achieve the targeted development. China, at the Ministerial meeting in July 2008, tried its best to bridge the differences among members and spared no efforts in pushing forward the negotiation to reach a consensus. China, at the 7th WTO Ministerial Meeting at the end of 2009, also called for improvement and strengthening of the multilateral trading system and encouraged all members to send collectively a positive signal to the world. In order to oppose protectionism in any form, Chinese President Hu Jintao, in a meeting with G20 members in 2009, expressed China's commitment to refrain from raising new barriers to investment or to trade in goods and services, imposing new export restrictions, or implementing any WTO inconsistent measures to stimulate exports. The Chinese Government also ensures to promptly rectify any such measures.

During this period, China continued to develop its economic and trade relations with other countries and regions under both bilateral and regional frameworks. China and New Zealand signed the China-New Zealand Free Trade Agreement in April 2008, which entered into force in October 2008. The Supplementary Agreement on Trade in Services for the China-Chile Free Trade Agreement was also signed in April 2008; and the negotiation of the agreement on the investment in the China-Chile Free Trade Agreement started in January 2009 and six rounds of negotiations have taken place by April 2010. In July 2008, China signed CEPA Supplementary Agreement V with Hong Kong SAR and Macao SAR. China and Singapore signed the China-Singapore Free Trade Agreement in October 2008, which entered into force in January 2009. The Agreement on Trade in Services under the China-Pakistan Free Trade Agreement was signed in February 2009, which became effective in October 2009. China and Peru signed the China-Peru Free Trade Agreement in April 2009, which took effect in March 2010. On 9th and 11th May 2009, China signed the CEPA supplementary agreement VI with Hong Kong SAR and Macao SAR respectively. China and ASEAN signed the Investment Agreement of the China-ASEAN Free Trade Agreement in August 2009. The China-ASEAN Free Trade Area was fully established in January 2010. China and Costa Rica signed the China-Costa Rica Free Trade Agreement in April 2010.

In order to strengthen the trade relationship with different countries and regions, China also continued to attach great importance to the Aid for Trade initiative of the WTO. China actively participated in the three regional reviews held in Zambia, Jamaica and Cambodia in 2009. During this period, under Aid for Trade framework, China also made financial contributions to the DDA Global Trust Fund in order to help other developing members, specially the less developed countries, so that they can be benefited from the multilateral trading system and also can be integrated into the global economy in a useful manner. Under bilateral, regional and global cooperation framework, China's assistance in the areas of infrastructure, agriculture, and human resource development and granting of debt exemption as well as the duty-free treatment to specially less developed countries played a positive role in improving the trade capabilities of those countries. At the UN High-Level Meeting in September 2008 on Millennium development Goals as well as at the Fourth Ministerial Conference of the Forum on China-Africa Cooperation in November 2009, Chinese Premier Wen Jiabao announced a series of measures to support other developing member countries in their pursuit of economic and social development. Accordingly, China is assumed to continue to grant duty-free treatment to products exported to China from LDCs. The phased implementation plan will start in 2010 for duty-free treatment covering up to 95 percent products of these countries. China will also exempt LDCs and heavily indebted poor countries interest-free loans due from them. By April 2010, debt exemption agreements have been signed with 50 countries with 380 overdue debts exempted. China has been already helping developing countries in Africa and Asia to build agricultural technology demonstration centers by providing agricultural experts and technical personnel to those countries. China has also planned to help other developing countries to build more than 100 small clean energy projects, such as small hydropower, solar power and biogas projects, by 2013 in order to assist those recipient countries to develop renewable energy as well as to improve their production and living conditions and also to promote their sustainable development. Under the framework of the FAO (Food and Agriculture Organization) Special Program of the United Nations for Food Security and human resources training, China signed an agreement in March 2009 to establish a trust fund and also paid the first installment of USD10 million in 2009.

Finally, after more than eight years of China's accession to WTO, it is apparent that the Chinese Government is sincere and will continue to strengthen bilateral, regional, and multilateral economic and trade cooperation in pursuance of its opening-up policy to achieve a mutually beneficial outcome. However, given the amount of uncertainties in the world economy, China's economy has also become complicated with interweaving of the short-term and long-term issues and interaction of domestic and international factors. Under these circumstances, the Chinese Government will apparently require to continue to implement proactive fiscal policy and moderately easy monetary policy. But at the same time, China also needs to properly balance the relations between achieving steady and faster economic development, adjusting economic structure, and managing the inflation pressures while keeping the continuity and stability of such policies, fine-tuning the specificity and flexibility of these policies under changing situations and conditions and finally keeping the pace, steps and priorities in the implementation of these policies.

CHAPTER – FOUR

An overview of the implications of China's WTO accession for the asian countries in particular

China's market opening process, which began in 1979, is moving towards full-fledged integration with the global economy at an accelerated pace because of its membership to the World Trade Organization (WTO). It is evident that developing countries, including China, are increasingly getting much more influential in the world trade order while United States, European Union, Japan, Canada and other developed nations have been leading the multilateral trading system.

China is on the right track to become an advanced economy with its new approach of 'reform and open door' policy. As a member of WTO, China has already undertaken big initiatives to remove the barriers to trade and investment, and to provide market access for foreign capital and commodities. Consequently, China's market has been steadily expanding and foreign enterprises are becoming increasingly more interested to enter into it. While some domestic industries apparently suffer from restructuring in the process, the overall Chinese economy continues to become more competitive. Moreover, as the market expands in size and the market-function works effectively, Chinese products are increasingly becoming more competitive internationally, both in terms of price and non-price factors. Thus, Chinese high quality products will continue to make inroads in the world market.

So far China's accession to WTO has been proved to have affected sensibly its trading with other countries, especially with the developing nations. The latter have been able to improve their trade balances with China, as China accelerated its market opening. Similarly, Chinese products are also increasingly penetrating in the markets of its trad'ng partners. Since the labor-intensive products of Asia-Pacific developing economies have been competing with Chinese commodities, they would have been affected the most. However, by fostering innovative reforms, those countries have contained the decline of their exports in competition with China and also the deterioration of their economic growth.

Exports by other member countries to China are gradually growing, as China promotes reform and globalization under the new regime of its WTO membership. Competition among countries and firms to enter the huge Chinese market is creating further trade and thereby making positive contribution to the world economy. By reforming its domestic institutions in a way that is consistent with international norms, China has groomed itself to play an important role in strengthening the efficiency of world trade system.

Since China became a WTO member, it has granted itself the period until 2010 as a strategic period in its march towards becoming an advanced economy. China's economic policies have been oriented towards industrial restructuring since 1989 when it promulgated its first explicit industrial policy. China has been promoting the development of pillar industries like machinery, electronics, petroleum, raw-chemicals, automobiles and construction in parallel to its development efforts in agriculture. Foreign trade has always been related to industrial restructuring. China's foreign trade policy has, so far, encouraged exports of mainly home electronic appliances, some high value-added products and also agricultural products with comparative advantages. Importing of equipment, technologies and crucial parts are also encouraged by the authorities. As a consequence, China has become a very major trading nation in the world. Additionally, as a WTO member, China has been successfully transforming its economy from a centrally planned autarky into a market-linked system. One can observe that by end-2009,

China has become fairly open to trade and investment. China has systematically reduced its tariff rate since the early 1990s from above 40 percent to current average of about 9.4 percent level. China also promulgated the landmark Law of Foreign Trade of the People's Republic of China in 1994 and took the necessary steps to accelerate the elimination of license requirements and of most import quotas, and introduced an automatic import licensing system. Since it's joining of WTO, China has made comprehensive liberalization in its trade and investment. Foreign enterprises in China have started enjoying equal treatment. Many trade barriers have already been removed. Most of the remaining few trade barriers are also expected to be lowered or removed in the near future. China has accelerated its plan towards comprehensive market opening since its accession to the WTO. Quantitative growth mode that was previously adopted is also getting changed to a qualitative growth mode driven by increasing efficiency and productivity.

ASIA PACIFIC DEVELOPING ECONOMIES AND WORLD TRADE :

Asian Trade in 1990-2009 grew faster than world trade as a whole including both advanced and developing economies. Machinery and transport equipment is the only sector in which trade by the advanced economies recorded the highest growth. Chemicals and chemical products sector recorded second highest growth by both advanced economies and Asian economies. In all the remaining products, Asian economies were the most active traders. World trade, in brief, is getting more and more concentrated in the advanced and Asian economies. This suggests that international trade tends to become influenced by theories based on technological aspects and economies of scale than by factor-endowment theory alone.

It is evident that developing economies have great stakes in the trade in manufactures. However, it is also true that their shares fall very short of the average for the developed economies. The traditional view that the liberalization of trade in manufactures is just in the interest of the developed countries, is getting contradicted by the above observation. In reality, exports of manufactures account for almost three-quarters of all developing countries' exports. Such a scenario in the structure of merchandise exports has important implications for Asia Pacific developing economies following China's accession to WTO.

The export structure of middle-income Asian economies is significantly different from other Asia Pacific economies. For example, South Korea's exports are concentrated in machinery and transport equipment and the total share of manufacture exports is above 90 percent. During the last decade, while the share of export of heavy industrial products gained 10.7 percentage points, South Korea's share of export of light industrial products shrank considerably.

The most striking difference between the manufacturing industry in China and other developing economies is the sheer difference in size. Manufacturing Value Added (MVA) in China in 2009 is approximately half that in the rest of Southeast Asia combined. During last ten years period that ended in 2009, the average Chinese growth rate has been around 2.5 times higher than the region, which itself is the most dynamic part of the world economy. As of 2009, China is not only the largest industrial economy in the developing world; it is also the fastest growing one. This combination may have significant implications for its competitiveness. The relatively rapid growth of Chinese industry is surely to complement its size advantages. It is evident that China's enterprises are investing more in newer equipment and technology than its competitors. China's WTO accession has strengthened such advantages in China, as infrastructure and services are opened up to foreign entry and industry leaders are increasingly attracted to the giant, growing market.

The Chinese industrial structure had been relatively slow to upgrade despite its rapid growth, particularly in comparison with most Asian Tigers (Asian nations which lead the Asian economy) during 1990-2000 period. In case of most of the Asian Tigers, the upgrading has been largely driven by export activities, but mostly with different agents involved like affiliates of Transnational Corporations (TNCs). However, in Republic of Korea and Taiwan and to a small extent in Singapore, local high-tech firms have also developed sufficient independent capabilities to set up their own global production chains. Since China's accession to WTO, while China has been exploiting its advantage in low-cost labor, it has also been moving up the technology ladder within and across products. As of today, what is possible to quantify is the changes in the technological structure of exports across categories.

IMPLICATIONS DURING 2001- 2005:

China acceded to the WTO on 11th December 2001. Since then China's overall trade policy objective has been to accelerate its opening to the outside world, develop foreign trade, and promote sound economic development. China has shown its sincere wishes to achieve these objectives by further strengthening the multilateral trading system as embodied in the WTO. China has provided at least MFN treatment for all WTO Members except El Salvador and some territories of EC Member States. By end-2005, 99.99 percent of China's total imports were subject to applied MFN tariffs, or more favorable rates. China also progressively lowered its MFN tariff and reduced non-tariff barriers to trade during this period. In 2005, the overall average MFN tariff was 9.7 percent; the averages for agricultural and non-agricultural products were 15.3 percent and 8.8 percent, respectively. Slightly lower average tariff rates, ranging from 8.2 percent to 9.5 percent were levied under its bilateral agreements, while unilateral preferences for some products were offered to 39 least developed countries. During the period, as a member of WTO, China also reduced other barriers to imports, notably import prohibitions and restrictions. China's import licensing regime was also being simplified.

The average applied MFN rate in 2005 was 9.7 percent, (9.8 percent including the *ad valorem* equivalents (AVEs) down from 17.6 percent in 1997, 15.6 percent in 2001 before China became a member of the WTO, and 12.2 percent in 2002 just after it acceded to the WTO. The tariff for agricultural products had declined from 23.1 percent in 2001 to 18.2 percent in 2002. The average tariff for non-agricultural products was 8.8 percent (8.9 percent including AVEs) in 2005, declining from 14.4 percent in 2001 and 11.2 percent in 2002. Despite the gradual decline in tariffs, their dispersion, indicated by the coefficient of variation, had remained relatively unchanged (0.8) since 2002 till 2005. The coefficient of variation is defined as the standard deviation divided by the overall tariff average. The overall standard deviation of tariff rates declined gradually, from 12.2 percent in 2001 to 9.1 percent in 2002 and to 7.6 percent in 2005.

Tariff escalation occurs when import tariffs on products increase as they undergo processing or add value. Tariff escalation results in a bias against imports of more processed goods and therefore gives an effective rate of tariff protection to the processed goods that is higher than the nominal rate. The effective rate of protection (ERP) measures the protection provided by the entire structure of tariffs, taking into account those levied on inputs as well as those on final products. China's overall tariff was subject to negative escalation between unprocessed and semi-processed products and escalation between semi-processed and fully processed products, suggesting that imports of semi-processed products would face lower tariff barriers than raw materials and fully processed goods. The average tariff for unprocessed products also remained consistently higher than for semi-processed products; the degree of negative escalation between the two stages increased marginally during this period (14.5 percent and 12.4 percent respectively in 2001, and 9.6 percent and 7.3 percent respectively in 2005). Negative escalation, in 2005, was especially pronounced between semi-processed and processed products in food, beverages and tobacco, and between unprocessed and semi-processed products in textiles and clothing.

In March 1996, the first Asia-Europe Meeting (ASEM) was held in Bangkok, with China, Japan, South Korea, and seven ASEAN countries (Brunei, Indonesia, Malaysia, the Philippines, Singapore, Thailand, and Vietnam), 15 EC member states, and the European Commission. The second ASEM Summit was held in London in April 1998, the third in Seoul in October 2000, the fourth in Copenhagen in September 2002, and the fifth in Hanoi in October 2004. The objective always remained to create a new Asia and Europe partnership and strengthen dialogue in political, economic, cultural, and other issues on an equal basis and in a spirit of co-operation between the two continents. ASEM also established a Trade Facilitation Action Plan (TFAP) with a view to reducing non-tariff barriers, increasing transparency, and promoting trade opportunities between Asia and Europe. China participated actively in the process. In addition, China, along with Japan and the Republic of Korea, holds regular meetings with the Association of South-East Asian Nations (ASEAN) under the ASEAN+3 framework for cooperation. On 4th November 2002, a Framework Agreement on Comprehensive Economic Cooperation between China and ASEAN was signed, and entered into force on 1st July 2003. The objectives included: facilitating more effective economic integration of the newer ASEAN member states and bridging the development gap among the parties to the agreement; strengthening and enhancing economic, trade, and investment cooperation; increasingly liberalizing and promoting trade in goods and services; creating a transparent, liberal and facilitative investment regime; and exploring new areas and developing appropriate measures for closer economic cooperation. ASEAN and China agreed to strengthen economic cooperation by building upon existing activities and developing new programs in five major sectors i.e. agriculture, human resources development, information and communication technology, investment and Mekong River basin development. ASEAN and China also agreed to negotiate the establishment of an ASEAN-China Free Trade Area (ACTFA) within ten years towards establishing an open and competitive investment regime to facilitate and promote investment among partners to the ACTFA and also simplifying customs procedures and developing mutual recognition arrangements. In order to accelerate the establishment of the ACTFA, an 'early harvest program' was established, which specified that the tariffs on all products in HS Chapters 1-8 and a limited number of products outside these chapters would be eliminated over a period of three years beginning 1st January 2004. However, a longer time-frame i.e. no latter than 2010, was accorded to Cambodia, Laos, Myanmar and Vietnam. The ACTFA involving the original six nations, namely, Brunei, Indonesia, Malaysia, the Philippines, Singapore, and Thailand, is to be established by 2010. For Cambodia, Laos, Myanmar, and Vietnam, a flexible time-frame up to 2015 has been provided.

An Agreement on Trade in Goods and an Agreement on the Dispute Settlement Mechanism of the Framework Agreement on comprehensive Economic Cooperation between ASEAN and China entered into force on 1st January 2005. The Agreement on Trade in Goods specified that tariff reductions and eliminations should apply to all tariff lines not covered by the Early Harvest Program under Article 6 of the Framework Agreement. The Agreement explicitly adopted GATT 1994 provisions on national treatment in respect of internal taxation and regulation, transparency, balance of payment safeguard measures. Both China and ASEAN committed to abide by the provisions of WTO disciplines on, *inter alia*, non-tariff measures, technical barriers to trade, sanitary and phytosanitary measures, subsidies and countervailing measures, anti-dumping measures, and intellectual property rights.

The Bangkok Agreement, a preferential trading arrangement between developing countries in the Asia-Pacific region, entered into force in 1976. China acceded to the agreement on 12th April 2001, and started implementing concessions from 1st January 2002. As per WTO document WT/ COMTD/ N19 dated 29th July 2004, the other members were Bangladesh, India, the Lao People's Democratic Republic, the Republic of Korea, and Sri Lanka. In 2005, under the Bangkok Agreement, 749 tariff lines carried rates that were lower than the MFN rates. More specifically, in 2005, the overall average tariff applied to parties to the Bangkok Agreement was 9.5 percent compared with an MFN rate of 9.7 percent.

On 29th June 2003, China signed Closer Economic Partnership Arrangements with Hong Kong, SAR of China. China also signed a similar agreement with Macao, China on 17th October 2003. Under these agreements China began phased elimination of tariffs on imports originating in Hong Kong and Macao, China from 1st January 2004. China was to fully eliminate tariffs on imports originating in Hong Kong and Macao no later than 1st January 2006. Under both CEPAs, China opened 18 service sectors to service providers from Hong Kong and Macao from 1st January 2005. Those service sectors were management consulting, convention and exhibition, advertising, accounting, real estate and construction, medical and dental services, audiovisual, logistics, freight forwarding agencies, storage and warehousing, transport, tourism, distribution, legal, banking, securities, insurance, and telecommunications. Moreover, from 1st January 2005, market access restrictions were relaxed for additional services for patent agencies, trade-mark agencies, airport services, cultural entertainment, information technology, job referral agencies, job intermediary, and professional and technician qualification examinations.

In November 2003, China signed a preferential trade agreement (PTA) with Pakistan. It was China's first PTA with a foreign country. China's overall average tariff on imports from Pakistan was 9.5 percent in 2005, compared with the overall MFN average of 9.7 percent. China and Pakistan signed an FTA Early Harvest Agreement on 5th April 2005 under which bilateral tariffs on certain products were to be eliminated gradually between 1st January 2006 and 1st January 2008. Pakistan recognizes China as a market economy.

On 24th October 2003, China and Australia signed a Trade and Economic Framework Agreement in order to promote strategic cooperation in energy and mining, textiles, clothing and footwear, agriculture, mechanical and electronic products, tourism, education, inspection and quarantine, customs cooperation, environmental protection, investment, information and communications technology, biotechnology, public health, food safety, and intellectual property rights. The agreement also stated that Australia would participate in China's central and western development initiatives. Meanwhile, China and Australia undertook a joint feasibility study into a possible bilateral free-trade agreement (FTA). The study was completed in March 2005 and concluded that the FTA would bring mutual benefits to both countries. Accordingly, the two countries agreed on 18th April 2005 to commence negotiations on such an agreement. Since April 2005, Australia recognizes China as a market economy.

On 28th May 2004, China and New Zealand signed a Trade and Economic Cooperation Framework Agreement and agreed to promote cooperation in agriculture; animal husbandry; forestry; wool; services including education, tourism, air services, and labor and professional services; science and technology; environmental protection; information and communication technology; and investment. In addition, areas of cooperation also included: human, plant, and animal health and food safety; technical regulations and standards; conformity assessment; customs administration; intellectual property; and the facilitation of business travel and of links between business groups and industry. China and New Zealand also jointly undertook a feasibility study on a possible bilateral free-trade agreement (FTA) and concluded that both China and New Zealand would benefit from a FTA. Accordingly, in December 2004, FTA negotiations started between the two countries and by December 2005, four rounds of talks had been held. New Zealand was the first country to recognize China as a market economy in April 2004.

In February 2003, China and India concluded bilateral tariff-reduction negotiations and signed the bi-lateral agreement on adopting the Bangkok agreement. In June 2003, China and India also agreed to form a joint study group in order to explore the potential for expanded bilateral trade and cooperation. The Group first met in March 2004. Simultaneously, a feasibility study on a China-India FTA was also started in April 2005. China offered preferences to Bangladesh, India, Korea, Lao PDR, and Sri Lanka under the Bangkok Agreement. In addition, Bangladesh was also offered special preferential rates on some products. Compared with an overall MFN average of 9.7 percent, the overall average tariff under the Bangkok Agreement in 2005 was 9.5 percent. Similarly, in 2005, the rates for agricultural products (WTO definition) and non-agricultural products were slightly lower than the corresponding MFN rates (8.5 percent compared to 8.8 percent for non-agriculture, and 15.1 percent compared to 15.3 percent for agriculture).

The Gulf Cooperation Council (UAE, Bahrain, Kuwait, Oman, Qatar, and Saudi Arabia) and China announced in July 2004 that they had signed a Framework Agreement on Economic, Trade, Investment and Technology Cooperation. They also formed a joint committee for cooperation in order to implement the agreement and to create a consultation mechanism; and also agreed to launch FTA negotiations. By June 2005, two rounds of negotiations took place.

China also offered unilateral special preferential tariffs to least developed countries for some products. In September 2005, the number of countries receiving such unilateral preferences was increased to 39.

IMPLICATIONS DURING 2006-2007:

In terms of Asia-Pacific Economic Cooperation, in 2006, 73.6 percent of China's merchandise imports were from APEC members compared to 67.8 percent in 2004, and 66.6 percent of its merchandise exports were to APEC members compared to 70.2 percent in 2004. In 2006, APEC members accounted for 60.6 percent of China's FDI which was 69.8 percent in 2004. In line with its policy of supporting multilateral trade and investment liberalization, China supported APEC's open regionalism goals. China, like other members, used to submit an annual Individual Action Plan (IAP) which provided a roadmap of its intended actions in various policy areas in order to realizing APEC's liberalization goals. In November 2006, at the fourteenth APEC Leaders' meeting, leaders of APEC economies reaffirmed their support for the Doha Development Agenda as a top priority. In September 2007, at the fifteenth APEC Leaders' meeting, leaders agreed that the Doha Round negotiation was at a critical juncture. Therefore, the Leaders issued a statement setting out the urgent need for progress and pledged their commitment to work to deliver an ambitious and balanced result. During the period, China also joined in the APEC Business Travel Card (ABTC) scheme.

In connection with ASEM, in September 2006, the sixth ASEM Summit was held in Helsinki. Leaders commemorated the first ten years of the ASEM, and agreed to commence the second decade by focusing on key policy areas such as strengthening multilateral trade and addressing issues like globalization, competitiveness and structural change in the global economy, science and technology, and sustainable development.

In regard to Association of Southeast Asian Nations, China, Japan, and the Republic of Korea hold regular meetings with ASEAN under the ASEAN+3 framework of cooperation. High level meetings are held annually. In November 2007, the third East Asia Summit meeting involving members to the ASEAN+3 as well as Australia, India and New Zealand, and the eleventh ASEAN+3 summit were held in Singapore. In January 2007, the Agreement on Trade in Services of the China-ASEAN Free Trade Area was signed. However, the agreement entered into force on

1st July 2007. During the period, academics from China, Japan, and the Republic of Korea had been conducting a feasibility study in order to explore the possibility for a trilateral free-trade agreement covering trade and investment, information and communication technology industries, environmental protection, and financial cooperation. Government officials from all the three countries participated in the study as observers.

From 1st November 2005, the Bangkok agreement was re-named as the Asia-Pacific Trade Agreement (APTA) – a preferential trading arrangement between developing countries in the Asia Pacific region. Members were China, Bangladesh, India, The Lao People's Democratic Republic, the Republic of Korea, and Sri Lanka. In 2007, under the agreement, 1652 tariff lines carried rates that were lower than the MFN rates, resulting the overall average tariff applied to members to the APTA was 9.1 percent, compared with an MFN rate of 9.7 percent.

Under the Closer Economic Partnership Arrangements (CEPAs), tariffs on merchandise imports originating in the SARs of Hong Kong and Macao were fully eliminated since 1st January 2006. In its attempt to gradually liberalize markets in various services sectors, China, on 1st January 2006, further relaxed restrictions in legal services, accounting, construction, audio-visual services, distribution, banking, securities, tourism, and transportation. China also relaxed equity restrictions and thresholds on registered capital, qualification requirements, geographical limitation, limitations on business scope and the movement of natural persons applicable to individual business owners that are permanent residents (with Chinese citizenship) of the Hong Kong and Macao SARs. In June 2006, the Third Supplemental Agreements to the Mainland and Hong Kong/Macao Closer Economic Partnership Arrangements (CEPA III) was signed and the same entered into force on 1st January 2007. China further reduced the market access threshold in certain service sectors including legal, accounting, information technology, conventions and exhibitions, audiovisual, distribution, tourism, transport, and certain individually owned stores. Conventions and exhibitions as well as protection of intellectual property rights were added to the scope of trade facilitation under the two CEPAs. During June and July 2007, the Fourth Supplemental

Agreements of CEPA were signed. The Mainland further relaxed the market access conditions on 28 areas on 1st January 2008. Those areas were legal, medical, computer and related services, real estate, market research, services related to management consulting, public utility, job intermediary, building cleaning, photographic, printing, translation and interpretation, conventions and exhibitions, telecommunications, audiovisual, distribution, environmental, insurance, banking, securities, social services, tourism, cultural, sporting, maritime transport, air transport, road transport, and individually owned stores.

On 24th November 2006, the China-Pakistan Free Trade Agreement covering trade in goods and investments was signed and the same entered into force on 1st July 2007. As a result, compared with the overall MFN average of 9.7 percent, China's overall average tariff on imports from Pakistan was 7.9 percent in 2007.

China and Australia, following the completion of a joint study, agreed to commence FTA negotiations in 18th April 2005. In June 2006, a sixth round of talks was concluded in that regard. Similarly, China and New Zealand, following a joint feasibility study, started FTA negotiations in December 2004. In December 2007, a fifteenth round of negotiation was held accordingly.

China and Gulf Cooperation Council established a joint committee for cooperation to implement the agreement and to create a consultation mechanism, and agreed to launch FTA negotiations. By December 2007, four rounds of negotiations took place between them.

In November 2006, the Official business and Academic Joint Study of China and Korea were launched after the completion of its FTA study. In 2007, three rounds of meetings were held covering issues including trade in goods, trade in services and investment.

IMPLICATIONS DURING 2008-2009:

China's overall trade policy objective, during this period, remained largely same as before: to accelerate its opening to the outside world with a view to introducing foreign technology and know-how, develop foreign trade, and promote sound economic development. China also continued to intensify its pursuit of bilateral/regional arrangements involving free-trade agreements. However, China's share of trade involving its trading partners with which it has adopted bilateral/regional free trade agreements still accounted for a minor share of its total trade. In 2009, China's imports from these trading partners accounted for 24.7 percent of its overall imports, down from 26.4 percent in 2006. Similarly, China's exports to these partners accounted for 31.3 percent of its overall exports, up slightly from 31.1 percent in 2006. It would be relevant to mention that these trading partners are Chile, Hong Kong SAR, Macao SAR, Pakistan, New Zealand, ASEAN countries, and member countries of APTA.

China has been a member of Asia-Pacific Economic Cooperation (APEC) since 1991. China's merchandise imports from APEC members accounted for 69 percent of its total merchandise imports in 2009, down from 73.6 percent in 2006. Merchandise exports of China to APEC members in 2009 accounted for 61.6 percent of its total merchandise exports, down from 66.6 percent in 2006. During this period, there has been a faster growth of China's trade than before with Middle East and Africa.

China has been a party to the Asia Pacific Trade Agreement (APTA). Under the Agreement in 2009, 1,662 tariff lines carried rates below the MFN rates; the overall average tariff applied to parties to the APTA was 8.9 percent, compared with an MFN rate of 9.5 percent. In the 31st Standing Committee Meeting of APTA held in Bangkok in February 2009, the authorities reached a consensus on such issues as trade in services, investment, framework agreements on trade facilitation, and rules of origin. In the third session of the Ministerial Council of the Asia-Pacific Trade Agreement held in Seoul in December 2009, the Framework Agreements on trade facilitation and promotion, and protection and liberalization of investment were signed. In addition, the Framework Agreement on promotion and liberalization of trade in services was also finalized. The Ministers of the participating countries declared that the fourth round of negotiations under the APTA had reached its final stage.

In October 2009, the seventh ASEM (Asia-Europe Meeting) summit, chaired by China, was held in Beijing; leaders, *inter alia*, reaffirmed the importance of an open, fair, rule-based and stable multilateral trading system under the WTO in order to achieve economic growth and development, as well as to reduce global disparities and trade imbalances.

In October 2009, the 12th ASEAN+3 Summit was held in Thailand to exchange views on issues including the global financial crisis. Participated leaders reconfirmed to stand firm against protectionism and to refrain from introducing and raising new barriers. They also supported the need to reach an ambitious and balanced conclusion of the Doha Development Agenda.

Under the Framework Agreement on Comprehensive Economic Cooperation between China and ASEAN, which entered into force on 1st July 2003, China – ASEAN Free Trade Area (CAFTA), involving the original six ASEAN nations (Brunei, Indonesia, Malaysia, the Philippines, Singapore, and Thailand), is to be established by 2010; flexibility up to 2015 has been provided for Cambodia, Laos, Myanmar, and Vietnam. As mentioned earlier, China and ASEAN agreed to strengthen economic cooperation by building upon existing activities and developing new programs in five priority sectors, namely, agriculture, human resources development, information and communication technology, investment, and Mekong River basin development. As per CAFTA Agreement on Trade in Goods, two rounds of tariff reduction took place on 1st January 2009 and on 1st January 2010. The Agreement on Trade in services of the China-ASEAN Free Trade Area entered into force on 1st July 2007. In 2009, the share of duty-free tariff lines applicable to China's imports from individual ASEAN countries ranged from 14.4 percent to 60.5 percent.

In terms of bilateral arrangements, by end-2009, China concluded several bilateral FTAs and has also been negotiating or seeking negotiations on free-trade agreements with some other trading partners. In end-2009, the share of China's trade with its current bilateral FTA partners (i.e. Hong Kong SAR, Macao SAR, Chile, New Zealand, Pakistan, and Singapore) accounted for small and declining shares of its total trade. Imports from these partners decreased from 4.6 percent in 2006 to 4.3 percent in 2009; and exports to these partners decreased from 19.6 percent in 2006 to 17.5 percent in 2009.

Under the Closer Economic Partnership arrangements (CEPAs) with the Special Administrative Regions (SARs) of Hong Kong and Macao, in 2009, the simple average applied rates for imports originating in Hong Kong and Macao SARs were 7.2 percent and 8.3 percent respectively compared with the simple average MFN applied rate of 9.5 percent. The fourth, fifth, and sixth Supplemental Agreements of the Closer Economic Partnership Arrangements were signed separately with the Hong Kong and Macao SARs between 2007 and 2009. In 2009, the Shares of China's imports from the Hong Kong and Macao SARs in its total imports were 0.9 percent and 0.0 percent respectively (1.4 percent and 0.0 percent respectively in 2006); the shares of China's exports to the Hong Kong and Macao SARs in its total exports were 13.8 percent and 0.2 percent respectively (16 percent and 0.2 percent respectively in 2006).

The China- Pakistan Free Trade Agreement which entered into force on 1st July 2007, was reviewed by the WTO Committee on Regional Trade Agreements on 20th April 2009, with several members expressing disappointment on the relatively low tariff line and bilateral trade coverage in the Agreement. In 2009, China's overall average tariff on imports from Pakistan was 6.9 percent (overall MFN average was 9.5 percent). The share of duty-free tariff lines applicable to China's imports from Pakistan was 19.2 percent in 2009. The agreement on Trade in Services of the China-Pakistan FTA was signed on 21st February 2009 and entered into force 10th October 2009. Under this Agreement, China has committed to further open its market to Pakistan in 28 sub-sectors, including transportation, tourism, sports, and health-care. In 2009, the share of China's imports from Pakistan in its total imports was 0.1 percent, unchanged since 2006. The share of China's exports to Pakistan in its total exports was 0.5 percent in 2009, up from 0.4 percent in 2006.

On 23rd October 2008, the Sino-Singaporean Free Trade Agreement on goods and services was signed, and the same entered into force on 1st January 2009. From January 2009 itself,

Singapore eliminated all tariffs on imports from China. However, Chinese authorities maintained that in terms of tariff lines, China undertook reduced tariffs to zero on 97.1 percent of all imports from Singapore from 1st January 2010. Under the FTA, the share of duty-free tariff lines applicable to China's imports from Singapore was 19.2 percent in 2009. China and Singapore have also made commitments in health, education, and accounting. The two countries also extended commitments on certain sub-sectors such as hospital services, sports promotion services, and facility operation services, in which there is no WTO commitment. In 2009, the share of China's imports from Singapore in its total imports was 1.8 percent, down from 2.2 percent in 2006. The share of China's exports to Singapore out of its total exports was 2.5 percent in 2009, up from 2.4 percent in 2006.

The China-New Zealand FTA was signed on 24th July 2008, and entered into force on 1st October 2008. On trade in goods, in terms of tariff lines, China is to eliminate the tariffs on 97.2 percent of imports from New Zealand by 1st January 2019. The share of duty-free tariff lines applicable to China's imports from New Zealand was 24.7 percent in 2009. The share of China's imports from New Zealand out of its total imports in 2009 was 0.2 percent, unchanged since 2006. On the other-hand, in 2009, the share of China's exports to New Zealand out of its total exports was 0.2 percent, unchanged since 2006. From 1st January 2009, preferential TRQs started to be applied to some wool and wool top originating from New Zealand under the FTA. As of 1st January 2009, China reserved the right to apply special safeguard measures to 11 agricultural products imported from New Zealand. On services, China made commitments in 15 sub-sectors of 4 main services sectors i.e. business, environment, sports and entertainment, and transportation. The two countries also made commitments on the movement of natural persons. The China-New Zealand FTA contains provisions for the promotion and protection of investment and co-operation in customs, SPS, and IPR.

With regard to other agreements, a 13th round of talks on China-Australia FTA negotiations was concluded in December 2008. Also after signing a Framework Agreement on Economic,

Trade, Investment and Technology Co-operation and agreeing to launch FTA negotiations in July 2004, China and the Gulf Cooperation council (Bahrain, Kuwait, Oman, Qatar, Saudi Arabia, and the UAE) completed five rounds of negotiations by December 2009.

Finally, we observe that with the globalization of world economy, with the integration of Chinese economy into the multilateral trading system, and with the liberalization of trade and investment, Asian developing countries are given opportunities to benefit from their comparative advantages in natural resources and cheap labor. In return, Asian developing countries are also making sincere efforts to strengthen their international competitiveness in sectors where they have comparative advantage. With China's entry to the WTO, Asian developing countries have been greatly enticed to engage more actively in the multilateral trading system. In addition, they are now prepared to comply with the international norms related to trade and investment liberalization and are willing to carry out domestic regulatory reforms that are necessary for such compliance. They are also participating actively in regional economic cooperation programs which are designed to promote trade and investment liberalization. In the past, free trade agreements were made mainly either among developed or among developing countries. In recent years, however, free trade agreements between developed and Asian developing countries are prevailing. Thus, it seems that the stage of development of a nation is not a key consideration in reaching such agreements. Though there are controversies over the relationship between regionalism and multilateral system, the consensus is growing that regionalism is not necessarily detrimental, but can be complimentary to multilateral trading system towards achieving trade liberalization.

CHAPTER – FIVE

Political, socio-economic and legal implications on China because of its accession to WTO

WTO Accession and Political Reforms:

What does WTO accession mean for China's political system? Some political analysts and some world political leaders placed great hopes that China's WTO accession would be an instrument to put the country's political system on a more liberal and democratic path. Remarkably, Mr. Bill Clinton – the former President of United States also expressed similar hopes in his speech to Democrats in New York on May 21, 2000. However, one may argue that Clinton administration had to highlight the prospective benefits of China's WTO accession in a sufficiently stark manner to justify their China policy in the domestic front and to win over Congress. Moreover, Clinton was able to pass such remarks because he knew that he would be able to convince Chinese leaders that such statement was a necessary tactical maneuver to secure a positive vote on the trade bill in the House of Representatives as well as in the Senate. This statement from President Clinton, despite their tactical nature, triggered the academic endeavor of analyzing the political implications of China's accession to WTO. Will WTO accession really pose acute challenges to Communist Party rule in China? Will WTO accession lead finally to the demise of the one-party state in China? Or will WTO accession rather give impetus to a re-centralization of political power? Or will it cause any change in the political arena at all?

For the past three decades of economic reforms, we witnessed a gradual erosion of monolithic power structure with a clear-cut and efficient top-down command hierarchy of the Chinese Communist Party. The Central Party leadership still formulates the political guidelines and also dominates the decision-making process at the top and supervises the activities of the government organs at different levels. However, economic decentralization and the devolution of administrative power have certainly invigorated entrepreneurs, different social groups and local agents. They have already learned to pursue their respective interests and if situation warrants, also to defend them against the interests of the Central-party state.

For China, WTO accession is a strong driving force toward globalization. The word 'globalization' has been referred to as growing interdependence among countries and accelerated integration into the world market. Conventionally, the dynamics of 'globalization' are supposed to erode the capacities of the nation-states to regulate their domestic economies and to govern their countries. Therefore, it can be argued that China's WTO accession should gradually restructure, if not weaken, the grip on power of the central-party state.

From a functional perspective, however, the outcome appears to be somewhat different as a result of China's WTO accession. While individual decision making powers are being increased on the one hand because of WTO accession, it has also on the other hand increased the leverage of central-state agencies vis-à-vis local interests. The complex regulatory tasks needed for the management of international financial transactions, technological innovations and the maintenance of currency-rating, have become critical and crucial factors of governance of the globalization which is supposed to be the outcome of WTO accession as mentioned earlier. Regional actors as well as local agents are unable to manage sufficiently well the complex tasks mentioned above and therefore they are increasingly relying upon the Central government to undertake those tasks. Thus the central government will still be in regulatory role of the overall economic framework, implementing international and national standards and overlooking local interests as well as the interests of the different sectors.

During the negotiation period for China's entry to the WTO, the Central authorities felt it easier to push through reforms which seemed to have reached an impasse. The central leadership used even the constrains of international negotiations and WTO rules as a weapon and had been able to break crucial deadlocks especially in three areas of domestic reforms which had been entangled in a close web of vested interests. Those three areas are state-owned enterprises, financial markets and the ownership system. A thorough reform of the tax system has been made in order to curb the wide-spread smuggling, tax evasion and related corruption activities. Reforming the tax system is another example of improving policy co-ordination at the central level which was intensified in the light of China's accession to WTO. As a consequence the share of fiscal revenues of Central government is on the rise again. Central government's share of fiscal revenues had been declining steadily since the early 1980s till 1995. However, during 1996-2000 period, China's total tax revenue topped around Y4.7 trillion which was 3.2 times the amount of the period 1991-1995. In terms of GDP, tax revenue was accounted for 14 percent of GDP in the year 2000 compared to 10.2 percent in 1995. In 2006, total tax revenue as a percentage of GDP was at around 16.5 percent, up from 15.7 percent in 2005. By 2008, such share of fiscal revenues of central government had further increased. From the foregoing examples and statistics, it is evident that the role of the central government in regulating the overall economic framework, controlling the local interests and also the interests of different sectors as well as implementing national and international standards are gradually getting enhanced. Moreover, the central government is also already playing a greater role in redistributing benefits and costs resulting from WTO accession. The Central government is now equipped from inside as well as from outside to step up its efforts to compensate the adversely affected persons through redistribution schemes.

Observance of uniform administration, i.e., the elimination of protectionist barriers by uniform application of WTO rules across provinces and sectors is a requisite factor to continue the membership of the WTO. However, WTO rules do indeed allow for limited protection. It is needless to mention that Chinese leadership, even in the coming days, will not be whole-heartedly committed to wiping out protectionism. On the other-hand, with the menace of the WTO dispute settlement mechanism readily at hand, they will continue to determine the degree of protection various industries will enjoy. Thus, after eight years of China's WTO accession, we can predict that there will not be an absolute end to protectionism in China because of its WTO membership, but that the discretion on how much protection is to be granted will mostly and gradually be shifted to the Central authorities.

The main factor for the stability of the political system in China considerably hinges on the moral standing and the social acceptance of state-power. It is rightfully observed that China's WTO membership has enhanced not only the capacity but also the legitimacy of the central party-state to rule and therefore it has also automatically enhanced the abilities of the central authorities to handle potential conflicts which are already there or might arise in the future.

It is evident that China's central leadership in the recent past, have been able to create an aura of international prestige and responsibility which should be taken into consideration while assessing the Chinese peoples' understanding about themselves. China's WTO membership as an equal partner with global standing has already increased the acceptance of thorough measures taken by the central leadership within bureaucracy and the populace. Chinese people are increasingly prepared, although temporarily, to suffer some economic and social hardship, if at all, with a hope that they will be able to catch up with the world's most developed economies in the near future. This proves that the Chinese Communist Party has successfully and rightfully projected itself as an advocate of social welfare and they have been able to gain the confidence of the masses that they are in full control of the social risks in a more modern sense. Initially, there were some voices in China who accused the leadership of betraying and selling out the country to foreign imperialists. However, as of 2010 after eight years of WTO accession, those voices have not been able to drown the general pro-accession consensus.

To sum up, it can be argued that China's WTO membership is surely not going to bring about the demise of its one-party state in the imaginable future. On the contrary, it might enhance the central party-state's capacity and legitimacy to rule. If there has been at all a gradual decay of one-party rule over the reform period since 1978, China's WTO membership will reverse that downward trend and enhance the support for one-party rule.

During the last three decades, there has been media boom all over the world. Most of the countries of the world are now not only allowing a larger inflow of external information and the introduction of new media, but also encouraging competition at home among traditional media. Similarly, in case of China also, its information borders have become more porous than before. More rapid and efficient flows of information from different media groups have put pressure on the Chinese government to open up, consult with the related group of people in case the situation demands, and also react more speedily and sincerely on different issues. Thus it is pushing the task of policy making of the government to be more transparent. Additionally, as the access to information in China has increased considerably over the last thirty years, a gradual pluralization of values, interests and lifestyles, as a whole, has taken place. The spread of the internet and the availability of information of different products and services of different markets all-over the world has intensified these trends. China's integration with the world trading nations because of its WTO membership has been accelerating the process.

Chinese leaders are fully aware of the above and they have not tried, so far, to go against the tide of above mentioned pluralization. However, instruments of firm control are still being used quite efficiently and effectively where the leadership deems them useful to prevent party-rule from being challenged. As for example, in November 2000, the Chinese government had listed cable TV networks as a prohibited sector for foreign investment and that a national cable TV group would be formed.

We observed that the Chinese Communist Party as well as State agencies have also used cyberspace very efficiently to monitor and maneuver public opinion. While it is suspected that China used the internet to deface Taiwan government web sites during cross-strait tensions and also to launch attacks on Falung Gong, they also found the internet useful for spreading important official messages and channeling public sentiments as a means of inflamed patriotism serving national interests.

In a more clear sense, the Chinese government can be found to be making active use of the new medium for its own purposes. The government wants to use the internet as a device to regain information control which they partially lost during last three decades of economic liberalization. One of the earliest internet projects was designed to connect government leaders and to give them access to data held by various organizations under the jurisdiction of the Communist Party.

In this backdrop, it will be too simplistic to draw a direct link between the internet and the evolution of democracy in China. Also, the internet has not yet been proved an effective forum for transforming and organizing individual voices into committed civic activities where there is not a pre-set organizational agenda of some kind. Therefore, the prospects for the formation of a virtual civil society through internet seem rather dim in the medium term. In other words, it is difficult to foresee how a 'virtual' civil society could emerge independently from 'real world' civic organizations to become a hotbed for political democratization in China while until now the Chinese authorities have quite successfully prevented the emergence of autonomous civic organizations.

China's accession to WTO has already been creating and will continue to create a real and strong demand for professional information and expertise in various fields. Since WTO accession requires the adaptation of national laws to WTO rules, the demand for legal expertise is extremely strong. Anti-dumping laws, anti-subsidy rules, joint venture, copyright and trade-mark laws, foreign trade, laws relating to import and export commodities inspections and regulations on anti-trust etc. are under the process of either redrafting or revising by the National Peoples' Congress (NPC). But being a committed member of NPC simply does not provide the expertise to cope with these complex tasks. There will also be increasing demand for legal experts outside the field of legislation. To meet this growing demand, China has already welcomed significantly larger numbers of foreign lawyers to work in China and to expand their services even in the matters relating to China's national law. More cities, of course including major cities, have already been opened to many international law firms. The result will be that the intensified competition should help to breed a new generation of highly skilled Chinese lawyers within the next few years. Central and provincial government agencies have also made significant efforts during the last eight years to train more personnel about WTO rules, procedures and practices. Central as well as provincial level state agencies have also started to send substantial numbers of civil servants abroad to make them acquainted with international practices in fields relating to WTO. Even the renowned and top grade universities have been offering training courses on WTO rules, free-trade mechanism, anti-dumping export principles etc. and these training courses are being taught by Chinese as well as international scholars, experts and business people.

Thus, China's WTO accession might gradually lead to empowering new group of experts who are not party cadres. The evolution of these new experts might eventually produce a bias toward more liberalization of China's political system. However, this will certainly not imply or confirm the democratic participation of the broader populace in the political system. On the contrary, it appears that rather than following the traditional international democratic ideas and principles, the communist party will not only continue to play a dominant role in the political liberalization process, but will also steadily become more powerful and influential during this process.

WTO ACCESSION AND CONSEQUENCIAL EFFECTS IN SOCIO-ECONOMIC FIELDS:

China's accession to the World Trade Organization has raised high expectations both in the economic as well as in the social fields. The impact of China's WTO accession on its social stability largely depends on the effects of the gradual changes in China's political economy on social transition and also on to what extent the foreign trade and investment practices are influenced by the changed situation.

In the long run, the social effects of China's WTO membership will depend on how it helps China's reform policies and also how the political leadership is able to mediate the problems that may arise as it moves further along the reform process. Chinese economists, social and political scientists and high officials seem to agree that China's WTO accession was an inevitable and an integral part of its socialist economy at that point of reform process. WTO membership is fully compatible with China's socio-economic reform. Economists are also convinced that the China's remaining problems can only be solved by pursuing its reform policies, which has been made easier through its integration into the neo-liberal international socio-economic order as a WTO member.

SOCIO-ECONOMIC ENVIRONMENT DURING 2001-2005:

China's economic reforms and 'open door' policy, which began in 1978, have allowed the emergence of a private sector alongside the public sector and gradually opened up the economy to international trade and inbound foreign direct investment (FDI). These reforms and resulting growth enabled China to raise GDP per head from USD148 in 1978 to USD1700 in 2005. The associated income growth also lifted about 400 million people out of poverty (defined as USD1.00 a day of expenditure) during this period. The proportion of people in China living below the USD2.00 per day poverty line fell from 72.6 percent in 1990 to 32 percent in 2004. During 1998-2005, real GDP growth averaged 8.9 percent per annum. Since 2001, this growth appeared to have been driven largely by exports and investment. Especially since China's accession to the WTO in 2001, rapid economic growth and increased integration into the world economy had increased China's share of world trade to 6.7 percent in 2004. Thus, by the end of 2004, China became the third largest trader (after the European Union with 14.5 percent and United States with 13.6 percent) and a major engine of growth in the global economy. Total merchandise exports and imports amounted to 63.9 percent of GDP in 2005, compared with less than 10 percent in 1978. Indicators of health and education also showed great improvement during the period.

The 10th National People's Congress, in its second session in March 2004, emphasized the importance of a more balanced approach to development and the need to push ahead with structural reforms. China became a member of the WTO in 2001. China's commitments in the WTO provided a catalyst for further far-reaching economic reforms. During this period, the key structural reforms, which were inter-related, included the continued re-organization of state-ownership and measures to develop a smooth-functioning capital market that would eventually meet the financing needs of the emerging dynamic private sector as well as the government. Progress in this regard had been such that, by end of 2005, the private sector accounted for well over half of China's GDP and three-quarters of its exports, the bulk of which were produced by foreign-controlled companies. To a great extent, private firms had been able to improve productivity and profitability in the whole economy and became the main source of new jobs. But with the gradual reduction of the role of SOEs in the economy and the resulting job loss of 16 million workers by state-owned industrial companies during 1998-2003, a need arose to establish a smooth functioning labour market that would not only provide a social safety net hitherto largely provided by the SOEs but also would provide alternative employment opportunities for displaced workers, new entrants to the labor force and migrants from rural areas. Trade and inbound FDI also played a major role in the growth of China's economy. The gradual reduction in the simple applied average MFN tariff (from 35 percent in 1994 to under 10 percent in 2005), the lowering of non-tariff barriers to trade and the opening of the economy to FDI, stimulated competition and thereby improved the competitiveness of domestic producers. As per the World Economic Forum's 2005 Growth Competitiveness Index and Business Competitive Index, China ranked 49th (out of 117 countries) and 57th (out of 116 countries) respectively. Among the factors contributing to this ranking were concerns over red tape, corruption, judicial independence and trade barriers. During this period, the large inflow of FDI and associated entrepreneurship, management skills and technology greatly contributed to the export orientation of the Chinese economy by providing the required platform that enabled China to manufacture products that meet world-market expectations with regard to quality, design, and technological content.

The accumulation of capital, financed mostly by the domestic savings, had also been vital. In 2004, gross national saving and gross domestic investment amounted to 42.9 percent and 39.3 percent of GDP respectively. During the period 1998-2003, growth in the capital stock accounted for 4.9 percent of the average 8 percent annual growth rate of GDP. In addition, with capital growing much faster than labor, capital accumulation contributed 4.6 percent to the 7.4 percent growth in labor productivity, a key determinant of living standards. Moreover, growth in total factor productivity (TFP), a key determinant of economic competitiveness, accounted for 2.8 percent of the growth in both GDP and labor productivity. The re-allocation of labor from agriculture and the improved quality of the labor force through the increased average level of education accounted for 0.5 percent and 1.1 percent of the growth in TFP respectively. However, capital productivity fell by an average of 1.2 percent annually during 1998-2003. Such decline in capital productivity might be partly due to over investment in aggregate, and also perhaps because of misallocation of investment as reflected in the banks' Non-Performing Loans (NPLs). Similarly, during 2001-2004, the marginal productivity of capital also experienced a sustained fall, suggesting that the efficiency of investment was increasingly declining. Notwithstanding the restructuring of the economy resulting from reforms, the official urban registered unemployment rate during the period under discussion had been gradually rising from 3.1 percent in 2000 to 4.2 percent in 2004. However, the effective unemployment rate might be higher than the official rate. Inflation, as measured by the consumer price index, remained relatively low, albeit rather volatile, fluctuating between (–) 1.4 percent and 3.9 percent between 1998 and 2005.

China's growing current account surplus, which increased from 1.3 percent of GDP in 2001 to 5.2 percent in 2005, was the reflection of the widening gap between its gross national saving and gross domestic investment. During 2001-2004, FDI was relatively stable, at around 3 percent of GDP per annum. Portfolio capital inflows were heavily restricted by the government during that period. The overall total inflow of foreign currency owing to the surplus in the balance of payments amounted to 12.5 percent of GDP in 2004, up from 4 percent in 2001. This had put upward pressure on the monetary base, complicating the operation of monetary policy and limiting the ability to ensure stable inflation. Central bank's efforts to stabilize such inflow of foreign currency resulted in the accumulation of USD819 billion in official reserves by the end of 2005 (equivalent to more than 14 months of import cover), much of which had been used to purchase government securities issued by G7 countries.

China's increased urbanization and rapid growth has also had implications for the environment. Under the 9th and 10th Five Year Plans, Chinese Government policies had improved pollution control. For example, the quantity of sulphur emissions rose by only 5 percent between 1993 and 2003, despite GDP increase by 136 percent. During 2001-2005, industry and services were the main economic activities in China. In 2004, industry and services accounted for almost 78 percent of GDP, while agriculture's contribution declined from 18.6 percent in 1998 to 15.2 percent. However, agriculture made the biggest contribution to employment with nearly 44 percent in 2002, in contrast to its declining share of GDP. Between 1998 and 2004, services and industry had been the most rapidly growing sectors of the Chinese economy. Growth in industry was particularly rapid, at an average of almost 11 percent annually. It was also suggested by different studies that over 90 percent of the industry's growth during the period under discussion was due to labor productivity growth, led by mainly large-scale investment and the resulting increase in the capital-output ratio.

Table 5.1:

BASIC ECONOMIC AND SOCIAL INDICATORS, 1998-2005:

	1998	1999	2000	2001	2002	2003	2004	2005
Nominal GDP (Yuan billion)	8,440	8,967	9,921	10,965	12,033	13,582	15,988	18,232
Nominal GDP (USD billion)	1,019	1,083	1,198	1,325	1,454	1,641	1,932	2,226
GDP per capita (Yuan)	6,765	7,129	7,828	8,592	9,368	10,510	12,299	13,926
GDP per capita (USD)	817	861	946	1,038	1,132	1,270	1,486	1,700

Note: Data correspond to adjusted GDP figures, as announced on 10th January 2006 by the National Bureau of Statistics. Source: Statistical Yearbook, National Bureau of Statistics.

A stable macroeconomic environment is a pre-requisite for a smooth functioning market economy. Fiscal policy together with monetary and exchange rate policies are basically crucial in shaping such an environment. In July 2005, a managed floating exchange regime of RMB was introduced in China. Until then, monetary and exchange rate policies through a currency peg had maintained the stability of the RMB in nominal terms in relation to the U.S. dollar, allowing a certain volatility in inflation. Fiscal policy also operated in a stable manner during the period. The overall fiscal situation was seemingly sound with rapid growth of tax revenues and tight control over expenditure bringing the overall budget deficit down to around 1.3 percent of GDP and keeping public debt stable at around 20 percent of GDP at end-December 2004.

China's multiple exchange rate regimes was abolished in 1994 and since then China has had a managed floating exchange rate regime. However, the currency was *de facto* fixed to the U.S. dollar from 1997 until July 2005 after a mild appreciation during 1994-1997. Until July 2005, the authorities used to purchase or sell foreign currency according to market demand to keep the exchange rate almost constant at Y 8.28 to the USD. During that period, the daily variation was kept within a very narrow range of 20 basis points. In 1996, the RMB was made fully convertible for current account transactions. However, such full convertibility did not extend to capital account transactions. In the middle of 2001, intervention to maintain a stable exchange rate against the dollar was strengthened, with reserves rising from 14.8 percent of GDP at the end of 2001 to almost 43 percent of GDP at the end of 2005. Official reserves grew by a total of USD204 billion in 2005 alone, which was equivalent to 9.2 percent of that year's GDP. Such intervention successfully stabilized the nominal exchange rate against the dollar. However, the real effective exchange rate of the RMB had depreciated in line with the weakening of the U.S. dollar during 2002-2005. In November 2005, it was about 13 percent below its previous peak in February 2002.

Since 2003, instead of relying on market-based instruments of monetary policy, Chinese authorities attempted to curtail credit growth through 'window guidance'. Such 'guidance' involved monthly meetings with commercial banks in order to urge these banks to avoid excessive credit expansion without placing a hard brake on lending. At the same time, some sectors were subject to administrative controls over their investment in order to reduce their demand for credit. However, the banking system continued to accumulate excess reserves despite these administrative controls. Therefore, the PBOC decided to raise the central bank benchmark interest rates for deposits and lending in October 2004 (for the first time since July 1995), allowing financial institutions to lower RMB deposit rates and broadening the range of lending rates. The central bank benchmark rates for one-year deposits and loans were both raised from 1.98 percent to 2.25 percent and from 5.31 percent to 5.58 percent respectively. The PBOC also scrapped a rule that forbade commercial banks from charging more than 1.7 times that rate, allowing them more freedom to take on riskier loans. However, rural and urban credit co-operatives, which finance SMEs and micro-credits, and have higher overheads, were still subject to a ceiling of 2.5 times the benchmark interest rate. Such rise in interest rates constituted an important step in moving away from administrative control of monetary policy to indirect control involving price mechanisms, such as the interest rate, which could pave the way for an increasingly efficient transmission of monetary policy to the real economy through the capital market.

The PBOC with the authorization of the State Council announced, in July 2005, a 2.1 percent revaluation of the RMB in relation to the US dollar, and also reformed the exchange rate regime. The PBOC announced that it was moving into a 'managed floating exchange rate regime' based on market supply and demand with reference to ' basket of currencies' so that the currency would no longer be pegged to the US dollar. The PBOC also added that whereas the daily trading price of the RMB in relation to the US dollar would continue to be allowed to float within a narrow range of 0.3 percent of the central parity, the trading prices of non-US dollar currencies would be allowed to move within a certain range announced by the PBOC. Because of this revaluation and also for the move towards a more flexible exchange rate regime, the nominal effective exchange rate was appreciated by roughly 5 percent as of November 2005.

In terms of fiscal policy, China's fiscal position would seem to be sound. During the period under discussion, tax revenue grew steadily, while public spending used to stimulate demand and thus continuously maintained growth even during economic downturns. Fiscal deficits had been moderate and therefore government debt was low. In 1998, in the wake of the Asian financial crisis, China embarked on a pro-active fiscal policy which included, among others, increased expenditure on infrastructure and issuance of national construction bonds. As a result, since 1998, Chinese government's total revenue rose steadily to 16.5 percent of GDP in 2004. Total expenditure also rose between 1998 and 2002 to 18.3 percent of GDP, before dropping slightly to 17.8 percent in 2004. The fiscal deficit was of 1.3 percent in 2004, slightly up from 1.1 percent in 1998, but reasonably lower than in the intervening years. Gross government debt was 20.2 percent of GDP in 2004, which involved 3.2 percent of foreign debt. All debt was owed by the Central Government, since local governments were required to balance their budgets annually.

Since 2000, the government adopted series of major reforms in order to increase budget transparency. Such reforms included the introduction of departmental budgets in order to assign all spending to a specific ministry or agency; bringing off-budget items into the budget; establishing the government procurement system; abolishing unauthorized local fees and charges, such as those levied on farmers; introducing a new budgetary classification system; and bringing the definition of figures more in line with international standards. The gradual re-allocation of public expenditures from areas where social returns were low, to those having high returns, such as health and education, would improve the efficiency of public spending and improve the growth prospects of the economy. Budgetary expenditure on education accounted for 2.46 percent of GDP in 2004. A reallocation of government spending from physical capital to human capital could raise total factor productivity in China's economy, so long the social returns on investment in latter exceed those in the former.

SOCIO-ECONOMIC ENVIRONMENT DURING 2006-2007:

In 2006-2007, China's economy continued its steady growth, with GDP increasing by 11.1 percent and 11.4 percent respectively. Until 2007, before the severe economic and financial crisis hit the world, for five consecutive years, the growth rate of China's economy reached 10 percent or above. The per capita disposable income of urban residents, adjusted by price factors, grew by 10.4 percent and 12.2 percent in 2006 and 2007 respectively. The per capita disposable income of rural residents, also adjusted by price factors, grew by 7.4 percent and 9.5 percent respectively during the same period. The net income increase of both urban and rural residents during the period accelerated markedly. On employment, while the registered urban unemployment rate was 4.1 percent in 2006 and 4.0 in 2007, 11.84 million and 12.04 million people were able to get newly employed in the urban areas respectively. In 2007, the contribution of net exports, investment and consumption to GDP growth was 2.5 percent, 4.4 percent and 4.5 percent respectively. Since 2000, it was the first time that the contribution of consumption to GDP growth exceeded that of investment. In fact, it had changed the underlying mechanism for economic growth from mainly relying on investment and export to an approach that co-ordinates consumption, investment and exports as an integrated force for growth.

During the period under discussion, as China continued to enjoy rapid economic growth, the rise in prices visibly exerted mounting pressure on the heavily populated country. Consumer price index (CPI) rose by 1.5 percent in 2006 and 4.8 percent in 2007. The increase in the overall level of consumer prices reached a record high in recent years, especially with the biggest jump in food prices. Since July 2007, in response to China's macroeconomic performance, the People's Bank of China had begun to strengthen liquidity management in order to maintain aggregate balance. The PBOC also intensified regulatory measures on credit policies and optimized credit structure, so as to guide the rational growth of money supply and investment as well as credit. Since the beginning of 2007, China's economy had been facing heightened pressure of CPI increase. As a result, until the end of 3rd quarter of 2008, the People's Bank of China adopted a moderately tighter monetary policy; further strengthened liquidity management; continued to consolidate open market operations; raised the RMB deposit reserve ratios for 10 times successively; raised saving and loan interest rates of financial institutions for 6 times; and further strengthened the credit risk warning system and provided guidance to over-heating industries such as the real estate.

In terms of public finance, China's fiscal revenue continued to score rapid growth during 2006-2007, increasing by 22.5 percent in 2006 and 32.4 percent in 2007. The ratio of fiscal revenue to GDP rose from 18.4 percent in 2006 to 20.8 percent in 2007. Accordingly, the Central Government's budget deficit also declined year by year, from Y299.9 billion in 2005 down to Y274.9 billion in 2006, and further down to Y 200 billion in 2007. Alongside the decline in budget deficit year by year, the issuance of treasury bond for long-term construction projects also decreased year by year, from Y 80 billion in 2005 to Y60 billion in 2006, and further down to Y50 billion in 2007. In order to respond to the needs of social and economic development as well as to achieve a well coordinated functioning of the economic and social sectors during this period, the Chinese Government adopted an integrated approach incorporating a variety of fiscal policy instruments to ensure structural optimization and also to promote system innovation. These policies included: expansion of the public finance to cover 'agriculture, rural areas, and farmers' with a view to balancing the development of both urban and rural areas; increasing the investment for social commitments such as education, science, public health and social security in order to promote the coordinated development for both economic and social sectors; to promote resource conservation and environment protection through increased budget allocations; and increasing central government transfer payment earmarked for the interior regions of central and western China in order to achieve coordinated development of different regions..

So far manufacturing in China had grown much faster than services and agriculture because of the Government's effort to promote investment in manufacturing through tax and non-tax measures. The share of industry (including mining, electricity generation, and manufacturing) in GDP (43.3 percent) was higher than that of services (39.3 percent) and agriculture (11.7 percent) in 2007. In 2000, the share of industry, services, and agriculture to GDP was 40.3 percent, 39.4 percent, and 14.8 percent respectively. Moreover, in 2007, about 40 percent of China's labor force was employed in agriculture which accounted for nearly 11.7 percent of GDP, labor productivity in agriculture was only one-fifth of that in the rest of the economy. In effect, wage differentials between manufacturing and non-manufacturing became wider.

In terms of external sector, China's current account surplus increased to about USD361 billion in 2007 from USD160.8 billion in 2005, representing 11.1 percent and 7.1 percent of GDP respectively. The increasing surplus reflected a widening gap between gross national savings and gross domestic investment. Gross national savings had been consistently higher in China. It appeared that a large portion of household saving use to be precautionary, aimed especially at the provision of education, healthcare, and retirement income. In addition, corporate savings also remained high. The surpluses on both the current and capital accounts were reflected in China's foreign exchange reserves, which increased to USD1,530 billion in 2007 from USD819 billion in 2005, equivalent to 19 months of import cover.

SOCIO-ECONOMIC ENVIRONMENT DURING 2008-2009:

Global economic and financial meltdown of 2008 started to make increasing impact on China's economy and development in the latter half of 2008. During this period, the whole world witnessed that the crisis brought the world economy into deep recession. In case of China, external demand contracted drastically, resulting in a sharp decline in its foreign trade, particularly in its exports. China's total value of imports and exports in November 2008 declined by 9.3% - the first such monthly decline year-on-year since March 2002. The decline continued in December 2008 by 11.2 percent. China's total exports and imports dropped further by 24.9 percent in the first quarter of 2009. In the second and third quarter of 2009 year-on-year quarterly decline were 22 and 16.6 percent respectively - though not as the first quarter decline, but quite significant.

China's year-on-year GDP growth in the first three quarters of 2008 were 10.6, 10.1 and 9.0 percent respectively. But it dropped to 6.8 percent in the fourth quarter. This went down further to 6.1 percent in the first quarter of 2009, the lowest quarterly figure since 1992 when such quarterly statistics first became available.

During 2008-2009, China also encountered catastrophic natural disasters. The Wenchuan earthquake measuring 8.0 on the Richter scale that occurred on 12 May 2008 in Sichuan Province was particularly devastating. Fifty-one counties covering 116,656 square kilometers in the three Provinces of Sichuan, Gansu and Shaanxi were confirmed to be seriously or extremely seriously stricken areas with a direct economic loss of about Y651 billion. The earthquake left hundreds of thousands of people dead or injured, and also caused massive damage to infrastructure, production capacity and the ecological environment. Between 1990 and 2008 the average direct economic loss in China due to various types of natural disasters was over Y200 billion annually. In 2009 alone the loss was estimated to be around Y252 billion.

Despite unprecedented natural disasters as well as worst global economic crisis in seven decades, China's GDP still reached Y31.40 trillion in 2008, an increase of 9.6 percent over 2007; and Y33.54 trillion in 2009, an increase of 8.7 percent over 2008. However, China's per-capita GDP still ranks behind more than 100 countries (calculated by the World Bank's poverty standard of USD1.25 per person per day). China still had some 150 million people living in poverty by the end of 2008.

Addressing the severe challenges posed by the global financial crisis, the Chinese Government initiated a stimulus package, i.e., a plan of additional investment of Y4 trillion to be implemented from the fourth quarter of 2008 to the end of 2010. The purpose was to expand domestic demand through consolidation of the resources of long-term economic development so that the economic downturn could be arrested as well as a steady growth could be maintained. In the stimulus package, direct investment from the Central Government would be Y1.18 trillion. In 2009, of the total public investment of Y924.3 billion by the Central Government, 44 percent went to housing projects for low-income urban residents as well as to projects for improving the well-being of rural residents and rural infrastructure; 23 percent to major infrastructure construction; 16 percent to economic restructuring, energy conservation, emission reduction and ecological improvement; and 14 percent to post-earthquake recovery and reconstruction.

The transformation of the value-added tax system from production-oriented to consumption-oriented on and from 1st January 2009 was the most significant tax reduction. Other tax reductions included - reform of the taxes, fees and the prices of refined oil products; purchase tax reduction by half on small automobiles; and suspension or abolition of administrative fees for at least 100 items. In addition, in 2008, the Chinese Government increased the threshold for personal income tax, suspended personal income taxes on interest earnings from savings and stock account balance, and exempted or reduced taxes related to the purchase or sale of homes for residential uses. In 2009, the Chinese central government provided Y32 billion for implementation of a series of consumption stimulus programs including those for rural residents to purchase home appliances, motor vehicles and motorbikes, and others for people to trade-in old motor vehicles and home appliances for new ones. In effect, throughout 2009, 13.64 million motor vehicles were sold, which was an increase of 46.2 percent over 2008; and also commodity housing sales were up by 42.1 percent. However, for 2009, with the implementation of the proactive fiscal policy, China's fiscal budget deficit was Y950 billion, or around 2.8 percent of the GDP. In September 2008, the People's Bank of China promptly adjusted policy orientation and began to implement a moderately easy monetary policy. Such relatively easy monetary policy coupled with proactive fiscal policy played an important role in enhancing confidence, expanding demand and achieving turnaround in the development of the economy. While addressing the impact of the global financial crisis, the Chinese Government adopted measures to stabilize and promote employment, particularly for the university graduates and migrant workers. They also increased the pension for enterprise retirees; expanded the coverage of medical insurance and increased the funding and the level of remuneration; raised the level of basic living allowances for low income groups in both urban and rural areas; and also increased investment on the construction of housing for low-income families.

The stimulus package started showing positive results from the second quarter of 2009. Reversing the trend of continuous decline since the first quarter of 2008, China's GDP registered a 7.9 percent year on year growth in the second quarter of 2009. The GDP growth pace further picked up, achieving a 9.1 and 10.7 percent increases for the last two quarters of 2009. In the fourth quarter of 2009, government revenue, corporate profits, and personal income all increased rapidly. At the end of 2009, the Consumer Price Index (CPI) also came back to growth from a nine-month drop. Domestic consumer market also witnessed relatively rapid expansion. In 2009, retail sales of consumer goods in China totaled Y12.53 trillion, up 15.5 percent from 2008.

During 2008-2009, investment in infrastructure and social programs in rural areas as well as direct financial support to farmers increased significantly. In addition, financial support for poverty alleviation purposes was also increased. The new poverty line of annual per-capita income of Y1,196 was adopted from 2008 to cover all low-income rural population. During 2008-2009, in addition to measures in the stimulus package, the Chinese Government also enforced the minimum wage system, expanded the coverage of all social security schemes and raised remuneration levels, increased further investment in education and implemented free compulsory education both in urban and rural areas, increased investment in the medical and health care system, and above all accelerated its reform process.

Finally, how China's WTO membership has been affecting the country's social stability? In literal sense, WTO accession has limited direct effects on social development and the labor market. However, in practical terms, China's WTO accession does have an indirect impact on the country's social stability by guiding the behavior of enterprises and redefining the economic outlook and interest. More precisely, the imposition of equal treatment of domestic and foreign business activities in China, the lowering of tariffs, and the incorporation of universal norms in market practice and in administration have been showing positive effects since accession. Moreover, WTO framework and rules are designed to provide a moral justification and legal atmosphere for undermining corruption, infringement on intellectual rights, and smuggling. These are already happening. Chinese companies and individuals, whose copyrights and trademarks are infringed, have been initiating legal action against the perpetrators. Legal importers and competitors are now enjoying a stronger case under WTO rules against the smugglers. Simplified customs procedures and lowering tariffs are bound to reduce incentives to smuggle. Finally, the evolution of a market culture based on legitimate economic interests will undoubtedly lead to more fair employment conditions by adopting a practice giving more importance to the merit and economic rationality.

The market success of some non-Chinese enterprises due to their reliability and high technical quality of products, flexibility and good management indicates that the competitive advantage in the near future may not be the price, but quality. The sharpening of foreign competition on the Chinese market after China's WTO accession has certainly introduced a culture of low transaction costs, i.e., reliability and predictability, which are getting reflected already in a higher level of trust. Chinese consumers are already enjoying and will certainly continue to enjoy the benefits. They have already observed that competition in some of the new economic sectors has led to great improvements in service provision and product quality. In terms of reality as a consequence of China's WTO accession, a culture of trust, fairness and legitimate economic dealings may promote better social relationship and also influence, in a positive way, the practices of the authorities.

China's reforms have, so far, aimed both at preventing social hardship and at creating a level playing field by establishing and promoting a market economy. China's WTO accession has empowered both domestic and foreign players in the Chinese market to remove vestiges of political market interference.

LEGAL IMPLICATIONS ON PRC DUE TO WTO ACCESSION:

There have been already significant changes on the establishment of a system of rule of law in China since its entry to WTO. We have been observing that changes in the legal framework are already taking place since 1978 as a result of China's pursuit of liberal economic reform, modernization and open door policy. It has been proved so far that China's WTO accession is certainly acting as an impetus to continue or even speed up reforms that are already taking place.

RULE OF LAW IN CHINA:

The meaning of the term 'rule of law' has been contested in China since December1978 when the Central Committee of the Chinese Communist Party (CCP) took decision to re-establish the legal system. In the west, the impact or the consequences of rule of law includes the idea that the power of government is constrained by the operation of an autonomous legal order. Rule of law also means and includes a requirement that the law protect certain individual rights against incursion by the state.

It would not be correct as a whole to assert that the legal system in China is autonomous, or that law can or is even intended to constrain the power of the state or the CCP. Although, there is a clear provision in the constitution that all organs and individuals are subject to the constitution and law, the relationship of the CCP to law remains fluid. The Preamble to the constitution itself spells out the fundamental requirement for leadership of the CCP. Law has been used instrumentally by the CCP not only to entrench and ensure the continuation of the current political system and to ensure the social stability and order, but also to structure and carry out the massive institutional and economic reforms of the past thirty years. Critics frequently remark that the CCP seeks to use law and the establishment of a comprehensive legal system as a method to legitimize its own rule.

It is evident that despite the massive increase in the volume of laws, regulations and rules and the existence of legislation requiring their publication, significant problems remain with the internal consistency and coherence of the body of the laws and rules that comprise the legal system. This influences the confidence level of the individuals and groups that their actions, even with the assistance of lawyers, fall within the legal parameters.

Under the Chinese constitution, unified power including legislative power rests in the National Peoples' Congress (NPC). The NPC Standing Committee exercises this power on a day to day basis. The State Council as the executive organ of State has power to pass administrative regulations. The State Council can also receive specific delegations of law making power from the NPC. Ministers and Commissions established under the State Council are empowered to pass ministerial rules, both within their spheres of functional competence and in order to implement particular legislation. The local Peoples' Congress and governments at the local level are empowered to pass regional regulations which are applicable within that local area. Some special economic zones (SEZs) have received delegations of power from the Standing Committee to pass laws relating to economic matters within the SEZ.

The decentralization of rule-making power to the local authorities makes them responsible for local economic development. Therefore, to achieve the desired level of economic development, the local governments and congresses are having major incentives to pass a large volume of local regulations. However, those local regulations and rules are gradually becoming the source of a complex, multi-tiered and in many cases incoherent body of laws and rules which overlap and in many cases conflict. Problems have cropped up as a result of overlap between rules and regulations, partial or total conflicts between them and passage of implementing rules that either extend or limit the scope of the primary legislative instrument. Sometimes, some rules are being superseded in whole or in part by other rules. These problems have been mostly prominent in respect of ministerial rules and local level rules.

Legislations passed by the National Peoples' Congress and its Standing Committee have tended to be drafted in accordance with the principles of generality and flexibility. Detailed regulations that are required to make these laws operational are passed by the State Council or the respective Ministry or Ministries responsible for their implementation or enforcement. This form of legislation also facilitates implementation of local government regulation that is formulated to take account of the specific local situation. State Council or ministerial regulation tends to fill the gaps in the legislative regime.

At the third session of the Ninth NPC on 15th March, 2000, an attempt had been made in the legislative law to impose greater order and certainty over law making. This law set out a list of matters about which the NPC and its Standing Committee have exclusive legislative power. Article 8 provides that the NPC and its Standing Committee have exclusive jurisdiction to pass legislation in relation to matters relating to state sovereignty, establishment, organizational structure and authority of peoples' congresses, governments, courts and procurators, the system of autonomy for minority areas, special administrative regions and grass root levels, crime and punishment, deprivation of political rights and coercive measures and punishments for the deprivation of personal freedom, exportation of non-state assets, fundamental civil rights, etc. However, it failed to specify more clearly the limits of rule-making powers of different state organs in other respects. The drafters of this law hoped that this law would be able to establish a detailed, workable mechanism for resolution of conflicts between rules passed by central level ministries and commissions and those passed by local governments and congresses. So far, such hope has been fulfilled to a limited extent. As the legal system develops, an additional requirement is being imposed that, for an administrative action to be valid, it must be based on a published and publicly available law or rule.

Chinese administrative agencies have always been particularly empowered in all aspects of governance. Politically, the State Council has always been the strongest arm of the state. One of the results of the establishment of a legislative framework has been to concentrate the power to make, interpret and enforce rules and regulations in the hands of the State's administrative organs, thus giving them broad powers. This explains the need for the development of rules seeking to better define the scope of powers of administrative agencies, the procedures and principles for exercising those powers and to constrain their discretionary usage. Such a body of rules is of fundamental importance to the realization of any degree of transparency in governance.

There are currently several systems in place for externally generated supervision of administrative action. The best known is review of the legality of an administrative decision by the courts under Administrative Litigation Law (ALL). The ALL initially represented a major reform in the legal system and still constitutes an important development in establishing forms of legal accountability of government officials for their actions. The ALL enables courts to review the lawfulness of an administrative act. In administrative litigation, the administrative agency is required to prove that the act was lawful and must supply the documents and rules upon which the particular decision was based. If it refuses to do so, the court is entitled to find that the act was unlawful and quash it. However, the effectiveness of this legislation in establishing mechanisms for scrutinizing administrative conduct, and thereby making administrative agencies accountable for their actions, is constrained in a number of legal and other ways. The first is that the courts are not empowered to examine the lawfulness of a rule upon which a particular decision was based. The second is that only comparatively few cases are brought under this law because people may be reluctant to commence an action, either because of fear of retribution from officials with whom they will be forced to have ongoing contact, or because of lack of confidence in the courts and also because of traditional attitudes of not to fall or attract troubles by going against the officials. The third is the comparative institutional weaknesses of the courts and reluctance in some cases to handle difficult cases where the defendant is the local government, or a local government department.

The other main form for externally generated supervision of administrative action is administrative review under the Administrative Review Law. The administrative review apparently constitutes an independent review mechanism of the type required by the Protocol of WTO Accession. Under the Administrative Review Law, a citizen or entity may seek review of any administrative act that he or she believes infringes upon his or her lawful rights and interests. Administrative review under the Administrative Review Law is a process of internal bureaucratic review, not judicial review. The review agency is required to examine not only the lawfulness, but also the appropriateness of the act in question. The review agency can change the administrative decision and may also amend or overturn the rule on which the decision was based to the extent of its functional power. If the review agency does not have the power to change the rule itself, it may refer the question to a state organ that does have the power to do so. Administrative Review Law (ARL) provided significantly broader scope of powers to the review agency than those exercised by the courts under Administrative Litigation Law (ALL).

The Protocol of WTO accession requires that laws, regulations, decisions and rulings be administered in a uniform, impartial and reasonable manner. A minimum requirement for compliance with these principles is that laws be applied consistently in similar situations. However, at the local level, law enforcement and implementation often fails to maintain consistency and impartiality. Because there are practical problems which, among others, include extremely broad discretionary powers coupled with policies which encourage uneven enforcement of laws and local protectionism.

One of the major problems in ensuring uniform implementation of law throughout China is local protectionism. The problem arose largely out of decentralization of financial control and tax collection. Now the local governments have much more power to attract foreign investment and to undertake a wide range of activities independent of the center. It is evident that there is fierce competition between provinces and localities for markets and to attract and retain investment. The Ministry of Foreign Trade and Economic Co-operation (MOFTEC) and other Central agencies find it very hard to control such competitions. Moreover, the authority of central agencies is reduced because of the formation of strong alliances between local business interests, either domestic or foreign, and local government. Additionally, the power of local governments and peoples' congresses to make laws and rules which are appropriate for the local level is fully exercised and often exceeded. Although the legislation law seeks to address these problems by instituting a system of supervision over local-level rule-making, it is still to be seen in the long or short term whether such effective control is really happening and giving the desired result. Local protectionism also creates a particular problem for law enforcement. Local governments exercise a very high degree of power over local organs of state, including courts, because they fund their operation. Local courts are often unwilling to make a finding adverse to a local company, entity, or government agency for this reason. In practice, courts lack effective coercive powers to enforce their judgments.

Under the above backdrop, since China's accession to WTO in 2001, the changes in China's institutional and legal framework including institutional structure, legal structure and legislative process, law enforcement, and transparency; as well as the formulation, administration, and implementation of trade policy could be outlined as follows:

DURING 2001- 2005:

Since China's accession to WTO in 2001, it has been working to change its institutional and legal structure in accord with its role as a leading Member of the multilateral trading system. The institutional structure of trade policy-making has been changed several times. Such changes include restructuring of China's State Council, the executive authority responsible for policy formulation, and also of key trade policy-making bodies such as the Ministry of Commerce. In order to ensure better implementation of trade and related policy objectives as well as to introduce greater transparency in policy-making and implementation, coordination among different agencies has also been improved during the period. Moreover, China had also reviewed legislation and revised and issued a considerable number of new laws in connection with its membership of the WTO. The current constitution, which was adopted on 4th December 1982, had been revised several times in order to adapt to the needs of economic reform and the evolution of the economy. The amendment of the constitution on 14th March 2004 revised several articles. Among them, the protection of private property rights was specified explicitly as 'citizen's lawful private property is inviolable'. The amendments also included the protection of non-public sectors of the economy, such as the individual and private sectors, specifying a new clause that 'the State encourages, supports and guides the development of the non-public sectors of the economy'. The revision also included the addition of the 'Thought of the Three Represents' to the constitution, indicating that private entrepreneurs are also encouraged to join the Communist Party, thus increasing the influence of the private sector on the formulation of policy. The 'Three Represents' stated that the Communist Party of China (CPC) must always represent 'the development trend of China's advanced productive forces, the orientation of China's advanced culture and the fundamental interests of the overwhelming majority of the Chinese people'.

In terms of institutional structure, under the constitution, the National People's Congress (NPC) is the highest organ of state power, and its permanent body is its Standing Committee. The NPC is composed of the deputies from provinces, autonomous regions, the special administrative regions, municipalities directly under the Central Government, and also from the armed forces. The NPC, which has a term of five years, meets in session once a year and is convened by its Standing Committee. The Communist Party of China exerts considerable influence on the NPC's legislative and law enforcement activities through its Central Committee headed by the Politburo and its Standing Committee. In addition, the CPC also makes proposals concerning national economic and social development plans. Accordingly, in October 2005, the CPC Central Committee's 'Proposal on the Eleventh Five-Year Program on National Economy and Social Development' was adopted at the Fifth Session of the 16th CPC Central Committee. The proposed program was further reviewed at the National People's Congress in March 2006.

The WTO agreement, under the Constitution and the 'Law on the Procedures of Conclusion of Treaties', falls within the category of 'important international agreements', subject to ratification by the Standing Committee of The NPC. China's Protocol of WTO Accession as well as WTO Agreement is implemented domestically through enabling legislation. China has been enacting new laws and revising the existing laws, regulations, and administrative measures relating to trade of goods, services, and trade-related aspects of intellectual property rights with a view to ensuring that they are aligned with the Accession Protocol and the WTO Agreement. Efforts in this regard, so far, included: the 'Legislation Law', 'Regulations on

Procedures for the Formulation of administrative regulations', and 'regulations on procedures for the Formulation of rules', to ensure the consistency of newly-issued regulations or rules with the WTO Agreement and the Accession Protocol; the 'Regulations on Submission of Regulations and Rules for the Record', to streamline the formulation and promulgation procedures for different types of legislation, and also to deal with contradictions between regulations. Article 90 of the Legislation Law stipulates that individuals, enterprises, or organizations may submit to the Standing Committee of the NPC written suggestions, if they consider that regulations or rules contradict the Constitution or laws; the Standing committee of the NPC will accordingly conduct studies of these suggestions. Similarly, Article 9 of the 'Regulations on Submission of Regulations and Rules for the record' stipulates that any individual or organization may submit written suggestions to the State Council for regulations or rules that they consider inconsistent with the Constitution or Laws; The State Council will accordingly conduct examination of these suggestions. Additionally, at the time of China's accession to the WTO, a program was launched to review national legislation. The authorities notified that, between 1999 and 2003, 17 laws were revised; 63 administrative regulations were issued, amended or abolished; and 34 State Council decrees were abolished. Since September 2001, local governments have also been conducting a review of local regulations, rules, and administrative measures in line with the principles of transparency, uniform application, and non-discrimination. Accordingly, 196,453 pieces of local legislation, rules, and other policies were revised or abolished in the provinces, autonomous regions, municipalities and comparatively larger cities during September 2001 to July 2003.

In regard to legal structure and the legislative process, under Articles 12 to 41 of the Legislation Law, legislative bills may be submitted to the NPC or its Standing Committee, by any of the following: the State Council, the Central Military Commission, the Supreme People's court, the Supreme People's Procuratorate, a special committee of the NPC, a delegation or a group of thirty or more deputies, or ten or more of the Standing Committee members. The Law Committee under the NPC, for a draft bill on the NPC's agenda, organizes discussions and also conducts a review, based on the opinions of delegates and special committees. Similarly, for a draft bill on the agenda of the Standing Committee, opinions are sought from various sources through seminars, hearings etc. For example, the first hearing of the NPC's Standing Committee regarding the revision of the Income Tax Law for individuals was conducted on 27th September 2005 in Beijing.

In terms of Law enforcement, there have been a number of significant changes to legislation, but the implementation as well as the enforcement of laws require similar changes to the law-enforcement infrastructure. In China, traditionally law enforcement has been based on intermediation rather than recourse to the courts, although this appears to be changing gradually. Under its WTO Protocol of Accession, China committed to establishing a judicial review process for administrative actions related to the implementation of laws, regulations, judicial decisions, etc. for trade of goods and services, and for intellectual property rights. By end 2005, Chinese authorities emphasized that China's current laws and regulations had met the requirements of that commitment. According to the authorities, China also issued 'anti-dumping Regulations' and 'Regulations on Countervailing Measures'. Moreover, the Supreme People's Court abolished around 20 legal interpretations that were not consistent with the China's WTO Agreement. In 2002, in an effort to further clarify the court's jurisdiction over international trade-related 'administrative litigations', the Supreme People's Court issued the 'Rules of the Supreme People's Court on Certain Issues on Handling of International Trade-related Administrative Cases', 'Rules of the Supreme People's Court on the Legal Application of Anti-Dumping Administrative Cases', and 'Rules of the Supreme People's Court on the Legal Application of Anti-Subsidy Administrative Cases'.

The 'Administrative Permission Law', effective from 1st July 2004, is a notable example of the efforts made to improve transparency. 'Administrative Permission Law', also known as the Administrative Licensing Law, was enacted in accordance with the constitution to standardize the procedure for, and the granting of, administrative permission, to ensure and supervise the effective exercise of administration by administrative departments. Administrative permission connotes approval given to the citizens, legal persons, and other organizations for engaging in special activities by administrative departments, on the basis of, and upon lawful examination of, their applications.

Since China's accession to WTO, public participation in the legislative process and its transparency appeared to have been improved. In general laws, regulations and rules take effect some time after being promulgated. All foreign trade-related laws, regulations, and rules are published in the China Foreign Trade and Economic Cooperation Gazette. Enquiry websites are set up under the MOFCOM and the AQSIQ. English translations of laws are compiled and published by the Legislative Affairs Commission of the standing Committee of the NPC, while trade-related laws and regulations are compiled and published by the Legislative Affairs Office of the State Council. The national Audit office and the Procuratorates took several measures since China's accession to WTO, to increase transparency as well as to counteract corruption. In 2004, for example, investigations carried out by the Procuratorates found more than 2900 officials across the country, at or above county level, guilty of corruption. Similarly, the 2003 Annual Audit Report, released on 23rd June 2004, identified budget management problems related to the previous State Planning Commission, the State Forestry Administration, the General Administration of Sport, and others. The Chinese Government also signed the UN Convention against Corruption. Since China's accession to WTO, the Government has also been promoting the use of the Internet to enhance transparency. More than 16000 official websites of different ministries, commissions, and other departments under the State Council as well as of local governments had been launched by the end of 2004. In addition, as authorities confirmed in end-2004, central and local government legislations and administrative measures are all available on the Internet; public comment on draft legislation is also often solicited through the Internet.

In terms of formulation, administration, and implementation of trade policy, as a consequence of accession to the WTO, China had enacted, until end-2005, several new trade related laws and regulations and also amended existing ones in order to meet its WTO commitments. The Foreign Trade Law, the main law covering international trade, was revised in 2004. The Customs Law, which governs customs and related matters, was also amended in July 2000. For trade policy implementation, as a consequence of WTO accession, restructuring of ministries took place several times in China. In 2003, the State Development and Planning commission (SDPC) was reorganized into the National Development and Reform Commission (NDRC); the State Economic and Trade Commission (SETC) and the Ministry of Foreign Trade and Economic Cooperation (MOFTEC) were abolished, and the Ministry of Commerce (MOFCOM) was established.

DURING 2006-2009:

China's institutional and legal framework remained mostly unchanged since 2006. However, in 2008, an institutional change in the State Council took place involving reassigning of regulatory functions among ministries and agencies (and consequently establishment and abolition of ministries and agencies). The institutional change in 2008 included: the establishment of the National Bureau of Energy, the Ministry of Transport, the Ministry of Industry and Information Technology (MIIT), and the Ministry of Environmental Protection; and also the abolition of the Commission of Science, Technology, and Industry for National Defense (COSTIND), the Ministry of Information Industry (MII), and the Ministry of Construction. The Ministry of Commerce (MOFCOM), despite all changes, still posses the main responsibility for policy co-ordination and implementation in respect of all trade-related issues. China's current constitution states, *inter alia*, that 'sole proprietorship', 'domestic private', and other non-public sectors of the economy, within the limits prescribed by law, are major components of the 'socialist market economy'. More precisely, Article 11 of the Constitution of Peoples Republic of China (viewed on March 2009 at http://english.peopledaily.com.cn/constitution/constitution.html) states: 'Individual, private and other non-public economies that exist within the limits prescribed by law are major components of the socialist market economy. The State protects the lawful rights and interests of individual and private economies, and guides, supervises and administers individual and private economies.'

From early 2006 to end-2009, there had been no change in China's judicial review process or for appeal regarding administrative actions related to the implementation of laws, regulations, judicial decisions, etc. in trade of goods and services, investment, and intellectual property rights. Between 1st January 2006 and 11th September 2007, the National People's Congress adopted 22 laws including five amendments and eight decisions concerning legal issues; it also abolished two laws. During the same period, the State Council enacted 48 administrative regulations including eight amendments and abolished 24 regulations; local people's congresses and their standing committees with legislative power adjusted 287 local rules, 16 SAR rules, 72 separate regulations and abolished 85 rules; local governments with legislative power enacted 105 local rules and abolished 305 rules. By end-2008, local governments from 31 provinces, autonomous regions and municipalities, and 49 large cities use to have the rights to formulate local regulations (these are called local governments 'with legislative power'). As per the Supreme People's Court website as on 31st March 2008, there were also several trade-related judicial interpretations of the Supreme People's Court and the Supreme People's Procuratorate including judicial interpretations on IPR cases issued in April 2007 and February 2008. Under the 'Law on the Procedures of the Conclusion of Treaties', as mentioned in the Ministry of Foreign Affairs online information dated 31st March 2008, the WTO Agreement falls within the category of 'important international agreements', subject to ratification by the Standing Committee of the NPC. As also mentioned earlier, the WTO Agreement and China's Protocol of Accession are implemented domestically through enabling legislation; individuals and enterprises can bring to the attention of the national authorities cases of non-uniform application of the trade regime.

With regard to legal structure and the legislative process, legislation in China includes the Constitution, laws, administrative regulations, departmental rules, local regulations, and rules. Obviously, the Constitution is the highest law, followed by laws and regulations; and national administrative regulations take precedence over local regulations and rules. The NPC has the power to alter or annul laws formulated by its Standing Committee. Similarly, the Standing Committee of the NPC has the power to annul administrative regulations that are deemed inconsistent with the Constitution and laws or local regulations that contradict the Constitution, laws, and administrative regulations. Accordingly, the State Council has the power to annul departmental and local government rules that contradict the Constitution and laws. As per Legislation Law, the 'basic' economic system, finance, taxation, customs, banking, and foreign trade must be governed only by law. However, if laws have not been enacted on any issue of these matters, the NPC or its Standing Committee may authorize the State Council to formulate administrative regulations. With regard to legislative bills on the agenda of a session of the NPC, the legal committee, relevant special committees, and the Standing Committee of the NPC must solicit opinions from related authorities and citizens through hearings, meetings, and seminars etc. The respective related authorities and citizens can make comments or suggestions concerning the draft bills. In 2006 alone, 101 legislative hearings and 1579 panel discussions were held among 29 local governments with legislative power and 45 agencies led by the State Council. Moreover, 490 proposed regulations were also subject to public comment procedures.

During the period under discussion, China has continued to adopt measures to increase the level of transparency of its trade and trade-related policies, practices, and measures. China's emphasis on cracking down on corruption was reiterated in a speech by the President at the 17th National Congress of the CPC, held in October 2007, where he categorically called upon CPC members to carry out a comprehensive anti-corruption campaign addressing both its apparent symptoms as well as root cause. The President, at the same time, also called for both prevention and punishment. According to a 2007 Corruption Perceptions index, published in Transparency international on 11th February 2008, which measured perceptions of corruption among public officials and politicians in 180 countries, China ranked 72nd, with a score of 3.5 out of 10. China also ranked 38th among 48 countries in the 2009 Opacity Index, which measures the degree to which countries lack clear, accurate, easily discernible, and widely accepted practices governing the relationships among governments, businesses, and investors. The complexity and opacity can leave scope for administrative discretion and thus corruption.

In order to reduce corruption by keeping the government open and transparent in exercising its power, the State Council promulgated the Regulations on Open Government Information on 5th April 2007, which came into force on 1st May 2008. Also, as a further step toward reducing the corruption, the Supreme People's Court and the Supreme People's Procuratorate jointly promulgated a circular on 8th July 2007 on the Opinions to address the Issues in Handling Criminal Cases Involving the Taking of Bribes. This circular explicitly classified certain acts by government officials, such as securing benefits for someone and, in return, accepting corporate shares from the person without due payment, as bribery.

Another landmark development during this period was the establishment of the National Corruption Prevention Bureau on 13th September 2007. This Bureau is required to monitor the flow of suspicious assets and corruption activities through an information-sharing process among the judiciary, police and banks. The Bureau, which reports directly to the State Council, is thereby responsible for assuring the transparency of government information at various levels in order to prevent corruption and also to study measures in preventing and reducing corruption. According to the Chinese authorities, laws and regulations that have been adopted or modified during 2006-2009 with a view to further increasing transparency include the Law on Response to Emergency, the Anti-Monopoly Law, The Regulation on Report and Investigation of Cases concerning Product safety, and the Rule on Administrative Punishment of Price-related Violations. Since February 2008, most of the administrative regulations promulgated at the legislative level of the State Council have been published on the China Legislative Information Network System, a single platform maintained by the Legislative Office of the State Council, for general public comments before promulgation. Departmental rules by the central government agencies have also been published through this system since July 2008. The Provisions on the Disclosure of Government Information, which came into force on 1st May 2008 specify: which agencies are required to disclose information; the process of disclosure; the scope of information for disclosure and the way to do it; and the supervision of the system. Since 2008, there has been no change to the Administrative Permission Law which stipulates that provisions on administrative permission must be promulgated before their entry into force and all administrative permission outcomes, except for those related to state or business secrets or individual privacy, must be published. By the end of 2008, more than 280 of China's laws and administrative regulations provided measures to promote transparency; and about 80 involved the publication of government information.

In terms of formulation, administration, and implementation of trade policy, China's main laws covering international trade include the Foreign Trade Law, the Customs Law, the Regulations on Import and Export Tariffs, and also laws and regulations relating to standards, SPS, anti-dumping, countervailing and safeguard measures, and intellectual property rights. During 2006-2007, various trade-related laws have been adopted or amended. They include: Company Law, the Agricultural Product Quality Safety Law, the Property Law, the Law on Enterprise Bankruptcy, the Law on Partnership Enterprises, Regulations on the Administration of Company Registration, Regulations on Customs Statistics, Regulations on the Administration of the Import and Export of Endangered Wild Fauna and Flora, Regulations on Export Products Responding to Anti-dumping Cases, and the Regulation on the Administration of Commercial Franchises. The Property Law, which entered into force on 1st October 2007, defined, for the first time in China's current regime, the ownership of property and also stipulated the protection of property rights of rights holders i.e. private or public entities. During 2008-2009, also various trade-related laws and regulations have been adopted or amended. Laws and regulations that entered into force during this period included: the Provisions on the Disclosure of Government Information (1st May 2008), which stipulated disclosure requirements of government agencies; the Enterprise Income Tax Law (1st January 2008), which unified income tax rates for all companies including domestic and foreign invested; the Interim Regulations on Value-added Tax (Amended) (1st January 2009), which transformed VAT from production-based to consumption-based tax; the Anti-Monopoly law (1st August 2008), the first comprehensive competition law in China; the Patent Law(1st October 2009), which increased penalties against infringement; the Administrative Regulations on Foreign Investment in Telecommunications Enterprises (Amended) (10th September 2008), which lowered the minimum registered capital requirement for foreign-invested basic telecommunication providers; and the Regulations on the Administration and Supervision of Securities Firms(1st June 2008), which strengthened supervision of securities firms and protection of consumer rights. Other trade-related laws, regulations and rules (as well as their amendments) that have entered into force during this period include: the Implementing Regulations for the Enterprise Income Tax Law (1st January 2008); the Regulations on the Risk Disposal of Securities Firms (23rd April 2008); the Provisions on Thresholds for Prior Notification of Concentration of Undertakings (3rd August 2008); the Regulations on Foreign Exchange Control (Amended) (5th August 2008); the Administrative Regulations on Contracting Foreign Engineering Projects (1st September 2008); the Measures for the Examination and Approval of the Entry-Exit and foreign-related Joint Research and Utilization of Livestock and Poultry Genetic Resources (1st October 2008); the Interim Regulations on Business Tax (Amended) (1st January 2009); and the Interim Regulations on Consumption Tax (Amended) (1st January 2009).

In conclusion, it is evident that as a consequence of its accession to the WTO, China has, so far, sincerely sought to incorporate WTO rules into its legal, administrative, and regulatory systems. Similarly, the multilateral trading system, to which China has already been a member for more than nine years, has also contributed to china's socio-economic growth and legal reform.

CHAPTER – SIX

China's WTO accession – development and trade-policy reforms in agriculture

Economic liberalization and structural changes, introduced in 1978, have, so far, produced substantial growth in China's economy. The average annual growth rate of gross domestic product (GDP) was 8.5 percent from 1979 to 1984 and 9.7 percent from 1985 to 1995. The average GDP growth continued at 8.2 percent annually from 1996 to 2000 despite the Asian financial crisis. During 2001 to 2009, the average annual GDP growth was almost 9.0 percent. In other words, from 1978 to 2009, China's GDP grew by an average of 9.6 percent a year. For 2010, World Bank predicted the GDP growth of 9.9 percent.

During the eve of China's accession to WTO, it had been following the ninth Five-Year Plan (1996-2000) for the development of its national economy and society. China's ninth Five-Year Plan required it to accomplish two major goals in its economic and social front: to establish a socialist market economy as well as to attain a higher standard of living. While achievements in agriculture and in rural economy had been remarkable during the ninth Five-Year Plan, significant problems had also cropped up during this period that could not be ignored. In agricultural production, the share of forestry, animal husbandry, and fishery continued to increase compared to crop farming. The average standard of living of farmers continued to improve. The percentage of farmers' incomes derived from secondary and tertiary industries had been increasing – from 32.65 percent of the net productive incomes in 1995 to 46.65 percent in 2000. Even though the growth of farmers' income slowed down year by year during 1996-2000, the per capita net income increased from Y1,577.70 in 1995 to Y2,253.40 in 2000 – 4.7 percent average annual increase after adjustment for price changes. In 1995, farmers' spending on food was 58.62 percent of per capita living expenses, which was reduced to 49.13 percent in 2000. Compared to 1995, electric fans owned by every 100 farmers' households increased by 34 percent, black-and white televisions by 38 percent, color televisions by 32 percent, refrigerators by 7 percent, washing machines by 12 percent, and motor cycles by 17 percent at the end of 2000. Even the per capita housing space increased from 21 to 24.82 square meters. The most significant achievements were - the remarkable expansion of the production capacity of grain and other farm produce; the historical transition from the long-standing short supply of major agricultural products to balance in aggregate and even surplus in the years of good harvests. The achievements in grain production made during 1996-2000 were of historical significance to the development process of the Chinese economy and society. Since the foundation of People's Republic of China in 1949, 'taking grain as the key link' was emphasized for years to alter the situation of food shortage. Still the problem continued. In 1992, grain rationing system was terminated which improved the food supply situation. However, in the first four years of the ninth Five-Year Plan period, China's annual grain production surpassed 500 million tons, leading to a continuing situation of supply exceeding the demand. Continuous improvement of the basic rural policies was one of the causes that contributed to the significant growth in grain production during this period. Increase in the contract purchase price for grain had also provided an incentive for farmers to increase production. To make up for the effect of consumer prices rise on farmers, the Chinese government raised the contract purchase price for grain by 40 percent in 1994, and again by another 2 percent in 1996. Scientific and technological progress had also been responsible for nearly 40 percent of the agricultural growth in China. The 'seed project' introduced a large number of improved varieties replacing the poor varieties. The 'white revolution' extended technology in the cold and dry areas in the northern part of

China in order to advance sowing time while improving soil moisture conservation and repressing weed growth. Water-saving technologies had also been developed during the period. The flood irrigation practice had been replaced by micro-irrigation methods to comply with the needs of crop growth with less water. In general, stable and explicit agricultural policies as well as many scientific achievements facilitated growth in grain production during this period.

However, the decreasing growth in farmers' income was the biggest problem in China's rural economy during ninth Five-Year Plan period. While farmers' net income increased by 9 percent in 1996, such rate of growth declined to 4.6 percent in 1997, 4.3 percent in 1998, 3.8 percent in 1999 and 2.1 percent in 2000. Not only that, the severity of the problem lied primarily in the sustained decrease of income from agricultural production. The productive net income of farmers in 2000 increased by Y142 over 1997compared to the decrease in the net income from agricultural production by Y132 - a reduction of 10.4 percent. The average farmer's income from agricultural production declined progressively between 1998 and 2000 - decreasing by Y30 in 1998, Y57 in 1999 and Y44 in 2000.

Since China adopted reform and open economic policies, Chinese agriculture has experienced restructuring. In October1998, the Third Plenary Session of the 15th Central Committee of the Communist Party of China adopted the decisions on major issues of agriculture and rural work. The basis for the new thinking was the major change in the pattern of agricultural supply and demand. The Chinese Central government stated at the National Conference on Rural Work at the end of 1998 that the development of Chinese agriculture and rural economy had entered a new stage.

In early 2001 the Central government emphasized that the fundamental objective of the strategic restructuring was to ensure increases in farmers' income. This initiated a new stage of strategic restructuring. Securing income growth for farmers became a priority of the Chinese Central government after basically solving the quantitative contradiction in agricultural supply and demand. At the National Economic Conference in November 2000, then

Secretary General Jiang Zemin and Premier Zhu Rongji specified that increasing farmers' income should be a key goal in the entire economic program. In February 2001, the State Council held a working conference on the reform experiment in rural taxes and fees to explore fundamental solutions to the burdens on farmers. During this period, the central government also held a series of major conferences on rural restructuring, increasing farmers' income, and alleviating burdens on farmers. The central task of the new stage of agricultural development was to implement strategic restructuring of agricultural production. It was strategic for two reasons. The first was to put the long-standing practice of pursuing quantitative growth in agricultural products on the track of stressing optimized variety and improved quality and efficiency. The second was the continued need to consider the constraints on the resource side and to pay more attention to the constraints from the demand side for the development of Chinese agriculture. Such agricultural restructuring consistent with the above goals obviously required changes in the relevant policies. Although those policy changes and/or adjustments primarily resulted from major changes in the patterns of agricultural supply and demand in China, they were, however, fundamentally consistent with the direction of China's WTO commitments.

Agriculture had always been at the center of China's negotiations over its entry into the WTO. It was partly because of the vulnerability of China's rural economy and also partly because of the importance of agriculture in the political economy of a number of developed nations with whom China negotiated its accession to the WTO. During the immediate pre-accession period, there had also been debates in different quarters on the future of China's agriculture. Some argued that the impact of WTO accession on China's agriculture would be substantial, adversely affecting hundreds of millions of farmers. On the contrary, others believed that although some impacts would be negative and even severe in specific areas, the overall effect of China's WTO accession on its agriculture would be modest. However, the confusion about the ultimate impact of WTO accession on China's agriculture would be traced to a general lack of understanding of the policy changes that might result from China's WTO accession. Moreover, the lack of clarity of the debate could also be traced to a lack of understanding of the fundamental facts about the nature of the distortions to China's economy on the eve of its WTO entry. One should remember that during the immediate past twenty years of economic liberalization until China's accession to the WTO, distortions had already been declined significantly. Therefore, post-WTO episode of agricultural policy reforms that accompanied China's accession to the WTO should be considered an extension of past efforts.

FEATURES, DEVELOPMENTS AND POLICY FRAMEWORK IN CHINA'S AGRICULTURE:

A. DURING 2001 – 2004:

Features and Developments:

Agriculture's contribution to China's GDP has declined since 2000. However, it is still an important sector. Agriculture accounted for some 13.1 percent of GDP in 2004, while it was 14.8 percent in 2000. Agriculture also accounted for over 45 percent of employment in 2004, and it was 46.3 percent in 2000. In 2004, farming accounted for 50.1 percent of total agricultural production, while fisheries contributed 10 percent and livestock 33.6 percent. There has been a decline in importance of agriculture as a source of employment. As of today, agriculture in China is mainly characterized by small-scale farming and by scarce land and capital in relation to labor. This is because of stronger growth elsewhere in the economy, the creation of township and village enterprises (TVEs) which have absorbed some of the agricultural labor surplus, and also relaxation in the *hukou* system. Despite the decline in employment, it has been evident that a large part of the current agricultural workforce is not productively engaged. Therefore, the excess labor has resulted in a high ratio of labor per unit of land and accordingly low labor productivity and agricultural incomes. The income gap between rural and urban households in China is increasing. The Chinese government strongly feels that one of main challenges of Chinais to guide migration of rural surplus labor in an orderly and stable fashion. That will require the development of an integrated urban-rural labor market.

Land tenure in China is based on a household contract system. Farmlands are owned by the village collectives. They extend contracts to individual households – currently 30 years for tillable lands, 30 to 70 years for forest lands, and 30 to 50 years for grass lands. The households cannot sell the land. They have the right to use the land, reap the yields, and transfer the rights granted by the contracts. Limited land-use rights have an apparently adverse impact on investment and also the development of a rural credit system. If farmers have full and absolute ownership of the land, they supposedly care more about preserving land fertility and higher productivity, controlling soil and water erosion, and also reducing pollution.

Grain is still the key crop in China's agriculture. However, its share in total crop production and in area sown has declined since 1990. The reason is partly because of changing structure of production favoring crops other than grains. In addition, progressive relaxation of the grain quota system and subsequently removal of the special agricultural tax on all goods except tobacco leaf are also responsible for the decline in grain production. Farmers have switched production to other more profitable crops, such as fruit and vegetables. Such adjustments are also in response to changes in China's domestic demand and to emerging export opportunities. The re-allocation of resources is also in line with China's comparative advantage, since fruit and vegetables are labor intensive products, while grain is land intensive – China's relatively scarce resource. In effect, both the level of grain production as well as the area sown to grains fell during 2001 to 2003. There was also some additional restructuring during 2001-2004 as land sown to corn increased, while land sown to rice and wheat declined. Such changes reflect a shift in focus from food to feed in conformity with changes in food consumption patterns, with demand shifting from the main staple grains, i.e., rice and wheat to meat, and in turn increasing demand for feed grains, particularly maize.

During 2001-2004, although the real values of agricultural imports and exports increased, their shares fell from around 8.7 percent to 7.4 percent for imports and around 6.6 percent to 4.1 percent for exports, reflecting an expansion of trade in other products. In 2004, China became a net food importer, after remaining a net food exporter up to 2003. Although imports of agricultural goods have been increasing since 2001, the growth was especially high in 2003 and 2004 – at around 39.5 percent and 39.7 percent respectively. The highest rates of growth were registered for imports of cereals (i.e. maize, rice, and wheat in 2003; and mainly wheat in 2004), oil bearing crops (mainly soybeans), and cotton. Such growth in imports was in conformity with the expectation that WTO entry would reduce protectionism in agriculture, which in turn would lead to an increase in imports of land-intensive farm products that would decrease national self-sufficiency to a certain extent, while exports of labor-intensive farm products, in which China continued to have a comparative advantage, could increase. For example, exports of fruits increased from USD227.1 million in 2000 to USD589.8 million in 2004, accounting for 2.4 percent of agriculture exports in 2004, up from 1.4 percent in 2003.

China's livestock production is the highest in the world. Since 2000, China's livestock sector has shown a remarkable growth mainly because of strong domestic demand, and is also expected to continue growing because of the increases in incomes of the Chinese people and urbanization – the two major forces driving the rising demand for meat and also shifting the dietary pattern. Moreover, as sanitary conditions improve, exports of meat and related products are also expected to increase. Accordingly, the net demand for feed grain to support the livestock sector is also likely to grow. Fisheries, which is another labor intensive activity, has also developed and grown very rapidly since 2000. Trade in fish products showed impressive growth; exports grew by 16.9 percent and imports by 19.4 percent in 2003. China's fish products export accounted for 27.5 percent of total agricultural exports in 2004.

Policy Framework:

In terms of policy formulation, and institutional and legal framework, there is a complex network of agencies that formulate and implement agricultural policies. At least 16 institutions, including ministries, banks, and commissions are involved in governing and guiding agriculture and its upstream and downstream sub-sectors. These governing bodies are divided into four tiers according to level of responsibility. Obviously, the co-ordination of policy-making and the implementation of the policies appear to be difficult because the functions of the different agencies involved are often fragmented and overlap. Co-ordination is particularly difficult because of the divergent priorities and interests of the different ministries. The problems also arise because of the gradual decentralization of the Chinese government over the past 20 years. Provincial governments have become more influential in the policy-making process and have often been free to decide how to implement Central Government policies, in many cases causing some variation in the implementation process.

China's agricultural sector is regulated by a number of laws and regulations. Agricultural Law, the principal legislation, establishes overall policy. Other laws, such as the Grassland Law, the Seed Law, and the Law on Promoting Agricultural Mechanization, deal with specific aspects of the sector. For policy implementation, more specific guidance is contained in regulations issued by the State Council and various administrative organs of the Central Government.

During 2001-2004, China had progressively reduced import tariffs, partially removed licensing requirements on imports and exports, abolished some quotas and converted others to tariff rate quotas (TRQs), removed some price controls, and somewhat liberalized the marketing system. Tariffs on agricultural products fell from 23.1 percent in 2001 to 18.2 percent in 2002, and then further to 15.3 percent in 2005, but were still higher than the overall average applied MFN rate of 9.7 percent in 2005. Tariff dispersion had also declined during the period. Tariffs on grain declined from 51.9 percent in 2001 to 33.9 percent in 2005. Tariffs on oilseeds also declined from 32 percent in 2001 to 11.1 percent in 2005. Tariffs on dairy products witnessed also a substantial reduction since 2001, from 35.9 percent in 2001 to 12.1 percent in 2005. Nevertheless, grain, and other traditionally highly protected agricultural commodities including sugar (29.9 percent in 2005) and tobacco (25.4 percent in 2005) were still enjoying benefit from higher than average protection. During the period under review, it seemed that lower tariffs applied to sub-sectors in which China apparently had comparative advantage i.e. labor-intensive farm products, such as horticultural and animal products. The varied levels of tariff protection across commodities used to be a potential source of distortion. The level of support to producer had increased since 1999 despite the decrease in tariffs. This could be attributed to the limited impact that tariffs might have had on trade flows and prices in China prior to 2000, when prices of basic crops, i.e., cereals, soybeans, and cotton were fixed by the state. State trading had been playing a key role in foreign trade. Domestic grain supplies were also secured through the grain quota system. Since 2000, tariffs, even if falling, seemed to be having more influence upon domestic prices as a result of a decline in domestic control.

During the period under review, tariff rates quotas (TRQs) were applied to 55 tariff lines. The 55 tariff lines included wheat and maslin, maize, rice, cereal flour, cereal groats, soybean oil, palm oil, rape colza, mustard oil, cane or beet sugar, mineral chemical fertilizers, wool and waste of wool. Although fertilizer is not an agricultural product under the WTO definition, it is included because of its importance as an input. TRQ was necessary to avoid large quantities of imports that would affect farmers' incomes and social stability. Upon WTO accession, China replaced quantitative import restrictions on sugar, cotton, and three types of fertilizers (DAP, NPK, and Urea) by TRQs. The size of the annual quota was based on China's commitments at the time of accession to the WTO. At the beginning of 2006, China's Ministry of Commerce (MOFCOM) promulgated an announcement to eliminate the TRQ on vegetable oils, implementing a tariff-only arrangement instead. With the exception of cotton, imports under TRQs had been low during 2001-2004. Imports of grain, with the exception of wheat, under TRQs had been especially low in 2003. Since 2003, quota levels for cotton have been increased to presumably supplement domestic supplies for the textiles and clothing industry. However, all cotton imports during 2002-2004, including those in excess of the quota, were charged the in-quota tariff rate.

In 2003, China notified the WTO that the agricultural products that are subject to state trading comprised of cotton, grain (i.e.

maize, rice, and soybean), silk, and tea. As of 1st November 2001, exports of soybeans were liberalized. The exports of tea were subject to designated trading prior to 2004. State trading was eliminated for silkworm cocoons and silk products from 1st January 2005. The continued use of state trading to export these commodities allowed the government to influence their domestic and export price.

Export restrictions remained in place to avoid domestic shortages and depletion of exhaustible natural resources, and to comply with China's obligations under international agreements. In 2004, global export quotas applied to exports were subject to state and 'designated' trading such as cotton, grains, silk, and tea. As of 1st January 2005, export quotas and licensing were eliminated for seven silkworm cocoons and silk products. In 2004 and 2005, destination-specific quotas applied to, *inter alia*, live cattle, live chicken and live swine exports to Macao and Hong Kong. During 2002-2004, China did not subsidize its exports of agricultural goods as Chinese authorities notified to the WTO.

The agriculture sector, on average, contributed around 4 percent to total tax revenue, and generated 15.5 percent of China's GDP during the period 2001-2003. This implied that the contribution of agricultural sector to total tax revenue was relatively low. However, such comparison did not take into account of the generally lower incomes in the rural sector and farmers' relatively lower ability to pay taxes. Nor did it take into account non-tax government revenue collected from the rural sector (i.e. fees and charges collected by townships and the villages), or the implicit taxation involved in the compulsory sale at below market prices, i.e., in state procurement system. Chinese authorities maintained that since China's accession to the WTO, such compulsory sale at below market price, or in other words mandatory purchases by the state had not occurred.

During 2001-2004, the main taxes levied on agriculture had been the agricultural tax, the animal slaughtering tax (prior to 2004), the special agricultural tax, and the VAT. The agricultural sector had been taxed differently from other sectors. In addition to agricultural taxes, farmers used to pay fees and charges levied at the sub-provincial level and provide 'labor accumulation' for the construction of communal facilities. Agricultural Tax reform was initiated on a trial basis in 2000 in order to increase farmers' incomes as well as to diminish the increasing urban-rural income disparity. In the same year the CPC Central Committee and the State Council proposed the tax-for-fee reform. The main objective of this reform was to reduce the farmers' burden by merging the township and village levies with the agricultural tax and eliminating all additional fees, levies, and compulsory investments and donations. Prior to this reform, villages and townships were financed mostly off-budget through these additional fees and levies operating mainly free of oversight from higher levels. Among other things, the Central Government aimed to control expenditures at the township and village level through this reform by bringing previously extra-budgetary revenues and expenditures under budget control and also to curb the excesses in 'taxing and spending' at the grassroots level.

Agricultural tax reform during 2001-2004 also included - (a) the elimination of funds collection from the rural population at the township level, including all administrative fees and charges, contributions to government funds, and farmers' contributions to farm related pooling funds; (b) removal of the animal slaughtering tax and other fees attached to this tax on 1st January, 2003; (c) removal of special agricultural tax on all products, except tobacco leaf, in 2004; (d) implementation of a new system in 2003, to calculate the agricultural tax, which stipulates that the tax may be levied at different rates in different regions, but should not exceed 7 percent; announcement by the government in 2004 for progressive elimination of this tax by 2009, with annual reductions commencing in 2004; (e) replacement of village levies by a surcharge of up to 20 percent on the agricultural tax (i.e. an additional 1.4 percent) to provide revenues for village activities; (f) abolition of accumulated labor service and voluntary labor service which refer to a certain number of labor days that rural workers had to work without any compensation in cash or in kind.

According to the government authorities, the farmers' burden was reduced by 20 percent in 2001 in areas where the tax reform had been implemented. However, the elimination of the agricultural tax and fees could mean a loss of up to 25 percent of tax revenue for local governments. Therefore, the success of the reform depended on the continued off-setting transfers from the Central Government to provinces and counties as compensation for lower sub-national tax revenues. Total national government expenditure on agriculture had increased to Y236 billion in 2004 from Y 123 billion in 2000. In 2003, expenditure to support 'rural production' accounted for 71.8 percent of total expenditure, while expenditure on 'capital construction' accounted for 24 percent. Expenditures on a 'subsidy for price increases' reached Y79.6 billion in 2004.

In order to increase grain production and rural incomes, a number of new price and income support policy measures were implemented in 2004 and extended in 2005. Direct subsidy was given to farmers growing grain, based on the area of land sown to maize, rice or wheat. This program was started in 2002 on a trial basis and was implemented nationally in 2004. The estimated cost of the program was Y11.6 billion in 2004, nearly 2 percent of the gross value of grain production. However, it had been widely suggested that these subsidies have had only a minor impact on production and rural incomes. The increase in grain production in 2004 was more likely due to high grain prices in the domestic and international markets in the first half of that year as well as favorable weather which also boosted grain yields. However, the subsidies were not high enough to make grain as profitable as alternative crops, such as cotton, fruit or vegetables. Therefore, they were not enough of an incentive to modify planting decisions.

China also sought to reduce the cost of agricultural inputs by providing tax relief to manufacturers as well as to service providers and also through price regulation of essential services. In order to lower the fertilizer price, its producers were given access to lower priced inputs, such as electricity and were also exempted from VAT. In another effort, improved quality soy seeds had been subsidized since 2002 in order to improve the oil yield of domestically produced soybeans. This scheme was extended in 2004, to encourage the use of improved seeds for rice, maize, and wheat. Also, from April 2002 to December 2003, rail shipments of maize, rice, wheat, cotton, and soybeans destined for export and the domestic market were being temporarily exempted from payment of the railway construction fee into the railway construction fund, which was 20 percent to 50 percent of total transportation costs.

During the period under review, China had progressively liberalized the price of agricultural products. Until mid-1997, farmers were required to deliver a fixed amount of grain at a quota price i.e. at an administrative price. In late 1997, in order to protect rice and wheat producers, the government introduced 'protective prices' for grain, at which the state guaranteed purchase of the total output of specific commodities, since the market prices of wheat and maize fell below the quota price. However, the scheme was under-funded due to budgetary constraints for many local governments in major grain producing regions. Some grain producing areas also faced storage difficulties. Given these problems, in 2000, the government decided to reduce protective prices and also the scheme's coverage. Hence, since 2000, different grains produced in different provinces were gradually removed from the scheme. In 2004, the scheme was completely eliminated. The protective price system was subsequently replaced by a minimum price system or 'lowest purchasing price' in major grain producing provinces. In 2004, it was applied only to paddy rice. Finally, as per decree by the State Council in May 2004, grain prices would be mainly determined by supply and demand. Government intervention in the pricing of grain had been minimized to the extent possible.

Since the latter part of the 1990s, Chinese farmers have had the option of selling most of their products, with the exception of cotton, grain, and tobacco, through diversified private channels. The State Council issued a new grain policy package in 1998. Accordingly, the State Trading Enterprises (STEs) were granted a monopoly to purchase all grain that producers wished to sell, at the state's 'protective price'. The STEs were also allowed to sell purchased grain at some profit. Implementation of the new policy ultimately encountered several problems. Hence, the government had to change its policy again. In 2001 policy decisions regarding grain marketing were decentralized to the provincial level. In the same year eight grain purchasing provinces were also allowed to liberalize their grain markets, signaling the abolition of compulsory state purchasing, with farmers no longer obliged to sell grains to the state at 'protective price'. In 2002, some other provincial governments also decided to liberalize their own markets either across the province or in major grain purchasing areas within the province. Chinese Central Government issued a new regulation on grain marketing in June 2004. In principle, the new regulation liberalized grain marketing by allowing 'qualified' non-state firms to buy and sell grains, effectively ending the monopoly position of the STEs.

B. DURING 2005 - 2007:

Features and Developments:

During the period under review, China had evolved into an industrialized economy, and the contribution of agriculture to GDP continued to decline. Agriculture's contribution to GDP in China fell from 13.4 percent in 2004 to 11.7 percent in 2006. Employment in the agricultural sector also dropped from 42.7 percent in 2004 to 39.9 in 2006. By the end-2007, labor productivity in agriculture was barely one fifth of the level in the rest of the economy. As a result, average rural incomes had fallen further behind the urban average and thereby widening the gap between rural and urban living standards. Another change concerning agriculture has been the shift from taxing the sector to supporting it. By 2006, most agricultural taxes were eliminated, and since 2004, farmers were provided with financial support. Low labor productivity in China's agriculture reflects its high labor intensity and also partially the lack of mechanization. Chinese authorities are very much aware of the need to raise productivity in its agricultural sector, improve farmers' overall welfare, and thereby further develop rural areas as a whole. China's rural reform process continued under the above scenario. Chinese Government also expressed its intention to continue the reform to improve farmers' welfare and to mitigate rural-urban disparities under the Eleventh Five-Year Plan (2006-2010), which has called for the creation of a 'new socialist countryside'. In order to facilitate the movement of rural workers, the State Council promulgated Certain Opinions in 2006, which called for the integration of the urban and rural labor markets. As per the Opinions, all regions and departments concerned would have to eliminate all discriminatory regulations and restrictions in regard to hiring rural workers in urban areas, and should remove the administrative approvals and administrative fees charged to enterprises employing rural workers.

The land tenure system, by which the state owns all land, remained unchanged. However, China's Property Law of 2007 formalized the right of the individual to use the land. Under this law, village collectives continue to be the owner of the farmland and they extend contracts to individual households. The Law also clarifies rural dwellers' rights and confirms firmer legal guarantee of their land tenure rights. As of 2010, Chinese authorities maintained that the majority of peasants have rural land tenure certificates which grant them long-term guaranteed rights to use the respective agricultural land.

While grain continues to be China's most important crop, there has been a shift in production from the traditional staples i.e. rice and wheat to corn and to other more profitable crops such as vegetables and fruits. This is very much in line with China's comparative advantage and the change in its economic policies, which allow farmers to choose what they plant, and is also a response to changes in food consumption patterns as incomes increase in China. Also, there has been a continued shift in focus from food to feed with the change in demand shifting from staple products to meat and other animal products. Output of meat reached 80.5 million tons in 2006 from 72.4 million in 2004. Milk production also increased to 33.0 million tons in 2006 from 11.2 million tons in 2000. These changes, in turn, increased the production of corn from 106 million tons in 2000 to 145.5 million tons in 2006.

China remains a net importer of agricultural products. In 2006, imports of agricultural raw materials grew by 21.5 percent. Imports of cotton continued to show impressive growth (more than 50 percent) in 2006. In general, China's exports of agricultural products grew by 13.3 percent and imports by 14.3 percent in 2006. However, the contribution of China's agriculture to its total trade continued to decline. In 2006, nearly 20 percent of China's agricultural imports originated in the United States. Also in 2006, China's major agricultural products i.e. fish and horticultural products accounted for 27.5 percent and 27.3 percent of its total agricultural exports respectively. Japan remains China's major market for agricultural exports.

Policy Framework:

There had been no changes to the institutions that formulated and implemented agricultural policies. As mentioned earlier, at least 16 institutions were in charge of agriculture-related issues, and thus coordination amongst these agencies remains difficult as their functions often overlap. The main laws regulating the agricultural sector also do not seem to have changed since 2004. A new law, namely, Agricultural Products Quality and Safety Law was enacted on 29th April 2006 to ensure the quality and safety of agricultural products, protect public health and promote the development of agriculture and the rural economy.

Chinese Government's key objective in the agriculture sector, as announced in the Eleventh Five-Year (2006-2010) Plan, is to build a 'new socialist countryside'. This involves a substantial increase in financial support for agriculture and rural development aimed at increasing farmers' incomes. The Plan also urges for the establishment of a mechanism for the industrial sector to support agriculture sector and for the cities to support the villages. The traditional objectives of maintaining a stable domestic production and of attaining food security to protect farmers' interests have, however, not been dropped. The policies outlined in the Plan are aimed at promoting agricultural development and farmers' incomes by: (a) increasing productivity in the agriculture sector through better land management, introduction of modern and advanced production technologies, improving extension services, reform of the rural circulation system and improving the quality of livestock, poultry and aquatic products; (b) increasing farmers' incomes through the development of agriculture-related industry, better managed agricultural enterprises, the creation of co-operatives, enhancement of subsidies for grain in order to cultivate improved crop strains as well as for purchasing agricultural machinery and tools, elimination of any remaining fees or charges imposed on farmers, and trade promotion; (c) improving services in rural areas through increased investment in basic infrastructure to ensure an adequate supply of water, electrification of rural China, telephone and internet access, availability of paved roads, and creation of a proper rural health care system; (d) improving farmers' education through enforcing the nine-year compulsory education in rural areas, elimination of tuition fees, and adequate training for farmers; (e) increasing public and private investment in rural areas through the development of an appropriate, stable and effective financial system to make sure that private funds can flow into agriculture; and (f) accelerating overall rural reform through improvement of fiscal management systems at the county and township levels, reform of public institutions at the town and townships levels and improvement of the household contract responsibility system.

As mentioned earlier, in 2004 China introduced direct subsidies to farmers, began to phase out agricultural taxes, increased spending on rural infrastructure and initiated subsidizing seed and machinery purchases. During 2005 and 2006, subsidies were made more widely available, while exemptions of the agricultural tax were extended towards whole of China and eventually eliminated.

In terms of policy instruments, the following measures continued affecting China's imports during the period under review:

(1) the average applied MFN tariffs for agricultural products (WTO definition) and non-agricultural products in 2007 were 15.2 percent and 8.8 percent respectively. Tariffs on grain (33.9 percent), sugar (29.9 percent), and tobacco (26.9 percent) benefited from higher than average protection.

(2) Imports of agricultural products remained subject to VAT. The rate levied on agricultural products was at 13 percent in 2007, 4 percentage points lower than the general VAT rate.

(3) In 2007, tariff-rate quotas applied to grains, sugar, wool, cotton and some fertilizers, covering 45 tariff lines (down from 55 lines in 2005). China eliminated the TRQs on vegetable oils in 2006, implementing a tariff only arrangement instead.

However, imports under TRQs remained low and quotas were generally unfilled, with the exception of sugar and cotton.

(4) Chinese government still has some influence on imports (as well as exports) through the state-trading system to ensure the stable supply and price of specific products (wheat, sugar, tobacco, and cotton). In 2006, trade of vegetable oils was liberalized and the TRQs were removed. Chemical fertilizers were still subject to state trading in 2008. China's TRQ system allows allocating part of the quota to a state-trading enterprise (STE) and part to a private enterprise. However, a substantial amount of the quota is still allocated to STEs and remains largely unchanged since 2005. Import of tobacco remains a state monopoly.

The measures that affected China's exports during 2005-2007, we observed the following:

1. At the end of 2007, the agricultural exports that were subject to state trading were cotton, rice, maize, and tobacco. These products were still subject to export quotas. With the exception of tobacco, part of these quotas could also be exported by private enterprises with approval from the appropriate authorities. State trading for exports was still in place to ensure a stable domestic supply of strategic commodities and in turn ensure price stability.

2. China continued to impose global (i.e. irrespective of destination) and destination-specific export quotas. The agricultural products that were subject to export quotas remained largely unchanged since 2005. In 2007, global export quotas were applicable to cotton, grains (maize, rice, and wheat) and tea. Destination-specific quotas still remained in place for exports of live cattle, live swine, and live chicken to Hong Kong and Macao. Non-automatic licenses were used to distribute these quotas.

3. Exporters of agricultural products were still entitled to VAT rebate at the time of exportation. Rebates varied according to commodity and were often lower than the statutory VAT rate.

4. In 2007, general export prohibitions applied to eight agricultural products. According to the authorities, those prohibitions were in place to reduce exports of products using large amounts of raw materials, low value added goods, or energy-intensive and polluting products.
5. During 2004-2007, China did not maintain or introduce any export subsidies as it notified to the WTO.

In terms of internal measures, China started to phase out agricultural taxes in 2004. Since then, four different taxes levied on agricultural products were eliminated. In January 2006, the Agriculture Tax was eliminated. On February 2006, the Special Agricultural Tax was replaced by a new tax, which was only levied on tobacco leaves. The Animal Husbandry Tax and the Animal Slaughtering Tax were eliminated in 2005 and 2006 respectively. Most of the fees and charges levied on farmers at the sub-provincial level had already been removed. Since 2006, farmers only had to pay fees for water and electricity. As of end-2007, village levies were still in place but were being reviewed. Total levy collection amounted to Y20 billion in 2006, down from Y43.5 billion in 2004.

Agricultural taxes were a major source of revenue for local governments in China. Therefore, during 2005-2007, transfers from the Central Government had increased as compensation for lower sub-national tax revenues in order to ensure that governments at county and township levels continue to have a stable source of revenue. Data published by the authorities shows that in 2006 alone, the Central Government transferred Y75.1 billion to local governments, of which Y41.9 billion was to compensate for the removal of the Agriculture Tax and the Special Agriculture Tax. There had also been transfers from the provincial and county levels to the townships. However, as reported by the authorities, local governments did not have to impose fees to compensate for their reduced fiscal revenues, because of the efforts by governments at the different levels in regards to local public finance. Despite removal of most taxes and fees related to agriculture, tax collection in the agriculture sector continued to rise during the period, reaching Y108.4 billion in 2006, up from Y90.2 billion in 2004.

In terms of price control, China had progressively liberalized the prices of many of the agricultural goods. However, the prices of some commodities remained controlled and some were still considered 'important reserve materials' and thereby subject to some sort of price control. Similarly, by end-2007, China had also liberalized most agricultural markets. However, the Government still used to intervene to stabilize the market, when deemed necessary – resulting some controls in the selling of agricultural products. China also announced regulations designed to liberalize grain markets by reducing the state's dominant role. However, such regulations stipulated that the Government could intervene in grain markets if prices would rise rapidly, and that government departments were responsible for ensuring that the supply and demand situation for grain remained balanced.

C. DURING 2008-2009:

The global financial crisis in late 2008 adversely affected incomes of China's farming population, resulting in an additional increased gap between rural and urban living standards since then. However, the Government remained eager to achieve coordinated and balanced development between regions by, inter alia, public spending on rural education, health, pensions, and a minimum livelihood guarantee, as well as concessions in the existing taxes and transfer payments to the less developed regions.

China is the world's top producer of agricultural products by value with a total production of about Y4,078 billion (USD536 billion). However, the contribution of agriculture to GDP continued to decline despite rising value of production, falling from 11.1 percent in 2006 to 10.7 percent in 2008 and to 10.6 percent in 2009 mainly because of even more rapid growth in other sectors of the economy. By the end of 2008 the average rural incomes fell further behind the urban average and the trend continued in early 2009, thus contributing to a widening gap between rural and urban living standards. In 2007, per capita rural household income was Y4,140, while per capita urban household income was Y9,997. In 2008, per capita rural household income was Y4,761, while per capita urban household income was Y15,781. Agriculture's share of employment had also decreased to 39.6 percent in 2008 from 40.8 percent in 2007. Lack of mechanization, low average size of farms, and obviously high labor intensity were to be mainly blamed for low labor productivity in agriculture. In this backdrop, the Government continued implementing agricultural reform in order to improve farmers' welfare and mitigate rural-urban disparities, and more recently to stimulate domestic demand in the face of the severe global economic slowdown since late 2008. China's exports and imports of agricultural products increased by 8.7 percent and 32.8 percent respectively in 2008, while agricultural products accounted for only 2.5 percent of total exports and 4.4 percent of total imports. Japan remained the top market for China's agricultural exports in 2008, with 18.8 percent of total agricultural exports. On the other-hand, in 2008, the main imports were soybeans from United States and palm oil from Malaysia.

POLICY OBJECTIVES:

Chinese Government's key objectives in the agriculture sector remained same as what was announced in the Eleventh Five-Year Plan (2006-2010), such as developing agriculture through improving overall agricultural production, promoting restructuring, improving infrastructure and services, attaining food security, and maintaining stable domestic production to protect farmers' interests. The main laws and regulations related to agriculture remained unchanged since 2008.

While the average Producer Subsidy Estimate (PSE) for OECD countries for 2008 was 22 percent and ranged from 1 percent in New Zealand to 65 percent in Korea (OECD, 2009b), the Producer Subsidy Estimate in China was 9 percent of the value of gross farm receipts in 2008, down from 11 percent in 2006, but considerably higher than in 1995-1997 when it averaged 3 percent. Support to specific commodities i.e. the Single Commodity transfer (SCT) during the period made up about 32 percent of the total PSE and also varied widely from one commodity to another. All such product specific support was provided through market price support.

At the end of 2009, structural adjustment remained a major issue in China's agriculture. Improving productivity would require bigger farms; but increasing farm size, which is happening slowly in China, can be a delicate social and economic issue because it will result in fewer firms.

POLICY INSTRUMENTS:

In terms of the measures that affected imports, the average applied MFN tariff on agricultural products in 2009 was at 15.2 percent, mostly unchanged since 2007. It would be relevant to mention that since China's accession to WTO, tariff on agricultural products (WTO definition) have been reduced reasonably. Protection obviously varies from one product to another, with higher than average tariffs on some cereals (40% - 65%), sugar (50%), tobacco (57%), and some beverages (42.3%-65%). Agricultural products imports are subject to lower VAT(13%) compared to other products (general VAT rate – 17%). Moreover, agricultural products produced and sold directly by small-scale farmers are exempt from VAT. In 2009, tariff-rate quotas (TRQs) were applicable to 45 tariff lines at the HS eight-digit level on wheat, maize, rice, sugar, chemical fertilizer, wool and wool top, and cotton (down from 55 lines in 2005). Grains (corn, rice, and wheat), sugar, tobacco, cotton, and some chemical fertilizers were subject to state trading. These commodities, except tobacco, were also subject to TRQs. In 2008, STEs had the right to import 90 percent of the wheat quota, 60 percent of corn, 50 percent of rice, 70 percent of sugar, and 33 percent of cotton quotas, unchanged since 2007. However, imports of tobacco remained a state monopoly. Some agricultural imports also remained subject to automatic licensing which covers poultry, vegetable oil, and tobacco. In order to monitoring imports, China began to apply automatic import licensing on fresh milk, milk powder from 1st August 2009.

In terms of measures affecting exports, the Chinese Government, between 1st January 2008 to 31st December 2008, imposed interim export tariffs ranging from 5 percent to 24 percent on 57 tariff lines (HS 8-digit) covering wheat, corn, rice, and soybeans. The objective of such measures, as the authorities maintained, was to conserve natural resources or to protect the environment. Some of these export taxes were subsequently removed or lowered including on wheat and rice from 1st July 2009. Eight agricultural products were subject to export prohibitions. These products were ivory, bezoar, musk, liquorice roots of the kind used in perfumes, peat, some plants of medical use, and black moss (a seaweed). State trading enterprises are only allowed to export cotton, rice, maize, and tobacco. During this period, China continued to impose global (i.e. irrespective of destination) and destination-specific export quotas. In 2009, global export quotas applied to cotton, maize, rice, wheat, and tea. Destination specific quotas, in end-2009, remained in place for exports of live cattle, live swine, and live fowl to the SAR of Hong Kong and Macao. During 2007-2009, China's exporters of agricultural products continued to be entitled to VAT rebates at the time of exportation. Such rebates vary according to commodity and are often lower than the statutory VAT rate. At the end of 2009, the VAT on agricultural goods was 13 percent, but the usual export rebate rate for agricultural goods was 5 percent.

Since 2004, China began to gradually phase out agricultural taxes and the same was totally abolished on 1st January 2006. At the end of 2009, the taxes that remained on agricultural products were the tobacco leaf tax (20% of the purchase price for tobacco leaves), the VAT (13%), the deed tax (levied when a land contract or the right to a house is transferred), stamp tax, and farmland occupation tax (levied when arable land is used for non-agricultural purposes). The Central Government so far has been transferring Y41.9 billion annually to compensate the governments at the county and township levels the loss of revenue from agricultural tax and other taxes.

The Comprehensive Subsidy on Agricultural Inputs, introduced in 2006, continued to increase during the period, from Y12 billion in 2006 to Y63.8 billion in 2008. In addition, support for improved quality seeds had also increased considerably in recent years, from Y4.07 billion in 2006 to Y12.07 billion in 2008. Moreover, the Central Government also provided a further Y4 billion in 2008 as subsidies for agricultural machinery and tools (up from Y2 billion in 2007). In addition to direct subsidies for inputs, China had, during the period, price control programs intended to reduce the cost of fertilizers through preferential prices for electricity and natural gas used by fertilizer producers, preferential transport prices, and exemptions from VAT and levy for the rail construction fund. In 2008, about Y15.1 billion was provided as direct subsidies (including those accorded to grain producers), and Y71.6 billion as general direct subsidies for grain farmers in order to assist them in meeting actual and envisaged changes in economic environment, such as price changes for agricultural inputs e.g. diesel and chemical fertilizers.

In terms of price controls during this period, a minimum procurement price scheme continued to be in place for rice and wheat in major producing areas. The Central Government raised the minimum procurement prices for rice and wheat twice in 2008 and again in 2009. The Outline of Middle and Long Term Plan for Grain security (2008-2020) aims to increase grain output and to maintain China's 95% self-sufficiency ratio.

With regard to land reform and other reforms relevant to rural communities, under the Real Right Law (Property Law) of 2007, farmland continues to be owned by village collectives. As stated by the authorities, at the end of 2008 majority of the farmers in China had obtained long-term contracts for guaranteed right to land and operation. By end-2009, more than 90% of farmers received their operation certificates. In October 2008, Chinese Government decided to relax the restrictions on the transfer of land-use rights and allowed exchange markets for trading such rights. The Chinese Government regard transfer of the land-use rights an important element of land management and thereby encourages these transfers. During 2008-2009, they allowed farmers to transfer the operation right of the land contract through various forms, including sub-contracting and lease swapping. However, at the same time, the Government maintained that the transfer should not change the nature of collective ownership of land. A pilot pension program for farmers was implemented in August 2009 in order to provide 'personal account' pensions and basic pensions to farmers over 60 who were resident of the pilot program areas. The basic pension use to be fully subsidized by the Government. Moreover, rural co-operative health-care system covering 85% of the rural population and free compulsory education, introduced in rural areas in 2007, continued to be in place in full force during the period.

In this backdrop, it can be concluded that China's agricultural sector reform has, so far, been successful. The reform has been able to reduce 'farmers' burden', which in turn promotes the creation of a harmonious society, and also have translated into an increase in farmers' disposable incomes. The latter is, in turn, expected to stimulate investment in the agricultural sector, and consumption.

CHAPTER – SEVEN

China's state-owned enterprises and their reforms till date

China, in the process of integrating itself strongly with the World's multilateral trading system, has been remarkably successful in putting in place many of the conditions for a market-based system. The progress the Chinese leadership made so far, in reforming the nation's state-owned enterprises is a prism through which to view China's committed attitude to shoulder the obligations of membership in the World Trade Organization. Repositioning China's generally inefficient SOEs to WTO's rule-based trade system poses a major challenge to the Chinese authorities. After more than three decades of experiments, while the other old formerly socialist countries have technically privatized all their former SOEs, China is still relentlessly seeking to re-invent and re-engineer these economic establishments. Implementing the modern corporate form is the centerpiece of their state asset management reform initiative for SOEs. They have also accelerated the modernization of the country's SOEs so as to improve their efficiency under the rigors of the international marketplace.

Prior to China's open door policy and associated economic reforms beginning in 1978, state ownership of the means of production and of other property had been the norm. The SOEs accounted for almost all output and employment. Additionally, in the absence of a domestic capital market, insofar as SOEs had not been fully self-financing, they had relied on loans from state-owned banks or direct assistance from the government. SOEs' investments had been motivated more by the output generated than their profitability, to the detriment of productivity.

With China's opening, however, private enterprises were permitted to operate alongside SOEs in certain sectors, especially manufacturing, so that SOEs by 2009 account for 35 percent of GDP. In particular, foreign direct investment (FDI) involving foreign invested enterprises (FIEs) were encouraged as a vehicle for technological progress and export-led growth. FIEs tend to have much higher levels of productivity than domestic private enterprises and SOEs.

STRUCTURE OF CHINA'S STATE-OWNED ENTERPRISES:

In China, SOEs consist of those wholly owned by the state (SOEs), and those in which the state has controlling shares (state controlled enterprises). The latter refers to enterprises in which the state, or another SOE, holds more than 50 percent of the equity; or, if the share of the equity is less than 50 percent, the state or another SOE has controlling influence on its management and operation. Also SOEs can be grouped into central-level SOEs, and local level SOEs. The State-owned Asset Supervision and Administration Commission (SASAC) is responsible for managing government assets and reform of central-level non-financial SOEs; and SASACs at local levels are responsible for managing government assets and reform of local-level SOEs. The number of central-level non-financial SOEs has continued to fall, from 159 in 2006 to 129 in December 2009. SASAC intends to bring down the number of SOEs that are subject to its management to 80-100 by end-2010.

SOEs are registered either under the Law on Industrial Enterprises (effective 1 August 1988), or the Company Law (revised and effective 1 January 2006). The key difference between enterprises registered under the two laws is that those SOEs wholly-owned by the people of China (registered under the Law on Industrial Enterprises) do not have a corporate management structure. That is, unlike those registered under the Company Law, these SOEs do not have a board of directors; rather, they are managed by general managers appointed by the Government. Although these SOEs can make their own managerial, operational, and production decisions, the State retains some control over the companies through the appointment of factory managers as well as by punishing, rewarding, or removing factory managers or deputy managers. At the same time, party committees play an important role in the management of these SOEs. The number of SOEs registered under the Company Law has been increasing and as per the guidelines laid down by the authorities the trend is to register all SOEs under the Company Law before the end of 2010.

As part of the corporate restructuring of SOEs, the Government has been stripping off non-core businesses from SOEs, such as provision of schools and clinics to employees and their families. Before being listed in stock exchanges, SOEs are typically split into two parts: the parent company, which assumes responsibility for the firm's debts, its non-productive assets and any excess staff; and the subsidiary, which retains the productive assets and restructures as a joint stock company. At end 2008, 1,254 SOEs had separated their social functions from core businesses.

There are three different types of shares for listed SOEs: state shares, legal person shares, and public shares. Only public shares are traded on stock exchanges, while the other types are non-tradable. Non-tradable shares of listed companies accounted for nearly 60 percent of total capital stock in capital stock markets at end 2008; the State owned nearly 70 percent of these non-tradable shares.

The China Securities Regulatory Commission (CSRC) issued circular on the Pilot Program of Non-Tradable Shares Reform of Listed Companies on 29thApril 2005, with a view to converting non-tradable shares into tradable ones. Certain shares of SOEs, depending on the sectors they engage in, must be reserved for the state: for example, 60 percent of shares in SOEs in the national defense industry, 51 percent in resource-based and high-tech industries, and 35 percent in agriculture and manufacturing must be reserved for the state. CSRC, as well as other related agencies such as the SASAC and MOFCOM, has issued various rules to regulate the conversion. For example, the conversion plan of a listed SOE must be approved not only by two-thirds of shareholders of non-tradable shares (including the SASAC) attending the share-holders' meeting, but also by two-thirds of public shareholders (holders of tradable shares) attending the meeting. Additionally, there is a lock-up period (on average three years) for conversion, during which the non-tradable shares cannot be traded. Following the conversion, as per policy issued by the Chinese authorities in June 2009, listed SOEs require to transfer 10 percent of their shares to China's social security fund with another 'lock-up' period. The reforms through creating more floating shares could reduce the reliance of the enterprises on retained earnings and accordingly on SOEs' savings which, in turn, would lead to a lower saving-investment gap. From January 2006, foreign investors can purchase A-shares (shares listed in China only; can be purchased by Chinese citizen only and can only be settled in RMB) of companies in stock markets; they need approval from the SASAC to purchase shares in SOEs. Apart from the shares reserved or regulated by the state, conversion of non-tradable shares had been achieved in 96.6 percent of all listed enterprises by the end of June 2007. Partly as a result of the transformation of non-tradable shares into tradable ones, China's stock markets have been developing rapidly.

China's SOEs have been retreating from some of the competitive industries, but still remain concentrated in certain industries with a state monopoly. These are the industries related to national security and overall economic development, including petroleum and coal. Profits of the SOEs also continued to rise. In 2009, profits of SOEs increased by 9.8 percent. Against the background of SOEs' increasing profits, the State Council issued the opinions on the Pilot Program of Budget Management of State-owned Assets in September 2007, under which, as of 2008, unspecified SOEs are to start paying dividends to the Government. In 2007, the Ministry of Finance, together with the SASAC issued regulations that determine the specific methods of dividend payment. SOEs at the central level are classified into three categories: resource-oriented SOEs (including those engaging in tobacco, coal, oil, power generation, and information industries) pay 10 percent of their net profits; general industrial enterprises (including those engaging in steel, automobile, and electronics) pay 5 percent of net profits; military enterprises and SOEs transformed from research institutions are exempt from paying dividends for three years, because their profits are usually low. The obligation to pay dividends will undoubtedly reduce the amount of retained earnings available to SOEs for financing their investments, thereby forcing them to rely more on external financing, involving new shares or debt, which should help the development of the capital market. Moreover, given their important signaling function in stock markets, dividend payments together with greater tradability of SOEs' shares could help improve the governance of SOEs, especially as far as investment is concerned. It follows that greater tradability of SOEs' shares and their obligation to pay dividends could contribute to a more efficient allocation of capital in China.

HISTORICAL PERSPECTIVE OF CHINA'S SOEs:

Since the Peoples' Republic of China was founded on 1st October, 1949, it witnessed the establishment of the primacy of the State over the economy and centralization of economic control at the national level during 1950s. By the mid-1960s, the State industries had an unshakable grasp on the economy. Fairly high rate of industrial growth was achieved by PRC through heavy investment from the 1950s through to the 1970s. More precisely, SOEs accounted for 42 percent of total industrial output in 1952. At the end of the first five-year plan (1953-1957), the percentage of output produced by SOEs rose to 54 percent. By the mid 1980s, SOEs accounted for about 83 percent of industrial output and 78 percent of all urban employment. However, the effectiveness of those early investments had suffered rapid decline by 1978. Productivity had stagnated or in true sense even declined. In the countryside, 900 million farmers were living in extreme poverty and their living standards were far below the living standards of the 100 million urban dwellers.

Mr. Deng Xiaoping, the Chief designer of China's reform program who came into power when Chairman Mao passed away in 1976, announced a program to reshape China's economy in late 1978. Initially, many reform measures began on a small scale and on an experimental basis. However, since that time economic reforms in PRC involved the relaxation of direct planning controls, the decentralization of decision-making rights, the development of state-owned economic entities, increased reliance on market forces in setting prices and output and an opening of China's economy to the outside world. The government transformed some SOEs into non-state firms in the 1980s. The rapid growth of non-state sector, particularly township and village enterprises (TVEs) and subsequently privately owned enterprises (POEs) caused the percentage of total industrial output produced by SOEs to decline while SOE output was itself increasing. In the process of transforming a majority of small and medium sized SOEs into private sector, China's central government identified a number of strategic sectors in the mid-1990s and determined to maintain a dominant position of state ownership in these sectors. By the end of 2005, one-third of total industrial production came from the SOE sector.

THE REFORM PROCESS OF SOEs (REFORMS DURING PRE-WTO ACCESSION PERIOD):

The main reform initiatives had evolved from the profit retention and the profit contract systems (1979 to early1980s) to the tax-for-profit system (1983-1985) and the contract management responsibility system (from 1986). These reforms were launched throughout the 1980s to improve SOE performance as a result of greater management autonomy and operational incentives such as profit-sharing and commercially rather than politically motivated corporate decision-making based on the principle of 'separation of government from management'.

SOEs had recorded improved performance in the second half of the 1980s along with the increase of management autonomy and incentives. However, increasingly competitive pressure was faced by SOEs as the planning mechanism steadily declined and SOEs activities changed course towards markets. As a result, there was a significant deterioration early in the 1990s in terms of profitability, market share and share of GDP in the performance of SOEs in spite of greater autonomy granted to them. The widely held belief behind such deterioration in performance was that SOEs' behavior had remained fundamentally unchanged. In other words, until then reform measures did not in any way address the economic inefficiency and loss made by the SOEs.

Quantitative reform initiatives were brought in rather than qualitative reform measures such as ownership and control in the state administration-SOEs dynamic. Consequently, a large number of SOEs continued operating at a loss and had to rely heavily on government subsidies to be bailed out.

The subject of SOE ownership reform requirement and procedure had been hotly debated for a number of years before the corporate reform was officially adopted. Some were having major concern and belief that corporate reform would amount to passing state property into private hands and would inevitably lead to privatization. They also firmly believed that it was crucial to maintain social stability in the course of economic reforms and for that public ownership was superior to private ownership. However, by early1992, decision makers had become aware of the repeated failings of their past efforts at delegating operational autonomy to SOE management. That was why the central government took a cautious but firm stand in promoting corporate reform. There were un-productive over investments in fixed assets. The problem was compounded by state-assets depletion. Awareness of these problems and the growing pressure of property rights reform provided impetus and prompted the central government to change reform strategy in 1992. The central leadership abandoned the traditional planning system and embraced 'socialist market economy' to create a full-fledged market economic system.

Putting forward the goals of 'Market Economic System' at the Chinese Communist Party's (CCP) 14th Central Committee meeting in November1993 towards introducing a broad program of corporate reform among China's SOEs, could be considered as the second phase of SOE reform. The founding of market economic system as the objective of the reform of China's SOE sector, specially large and medium sized SOEs, was crucial in order to establish and perfect the market system.

The market economic system was also crucial to the overall reform agenda as it dealt with the issue of how to effectively separate the Chinese communist party and other state administrations from the management of SOEs. During five years period from 1993 until early 1998, the implementation of the market economic system was undertaken by making a number of extended experiments of corporate reform which included 100 trial companies at national level; city level reforms; SOE sector formation of key national enterprises and transformation of small SOEs.

The core of corporate reform was ownership restructuring. Corporate reform was one of the key measures in the larger policy of market economic system. The working definition of 'market economic system' in general and 'corporate reform' in particular is 'reform', 'reconstruction', and 'restructuring'. 'Reform' means the adoption of new enterprise management mechanisms; 'reconstruction' consists of technical transformation and improvement; and 'restructuring' encompasses a reorganization of property rights and assets. Reform would be realized by reconstruction i.e. by establishment of boards of directors and board of supervisors in order to improve corporate governance and by adopting three tiers of operating mechanisms: (1) decision-making and investment center, (2) profit center, and (3) cost center.

The main features of 'corporate reform' were as follows: (1) clarification of property rights; (2) clear definition and clarity about rights and responsibilities; (3) distinguishing between government and management functions; and (4) scientific enterprise management. The first three features demonstrate how China's centrally planned economy transitioned to a market economy. According to regulations, the entrusted state-owned companies would be able to exercise three rights: (1) management rights including decisions on methods of business operations, appointing state assets representatives into subsidiaries etc.; (2) supervision rights including the right of regular evaluation and supervision of business operations and assets management; and (3) residual claimant rights including the rights of gaining business profit, and use of this profit under the permission and guidance of the SASAC or other relevant supervisory agencies.

In reality, the purpose of corporate reform reflected the revised goal of SOEs. By imposing very strict budgets on SOEs by the state, it was highly expected that SOEs would be forced to produce marketable goods and provide better services to survive in a competitive market. To date, SOEs have been able to show encouraging results and they have begun to actively develop their production targets focused on profits. It is virtually a result of both the top-down needs of the state to reduce subsidies and to generate more revenues and bottom-up pressure from SOEs to remain economic entities in a competitive market environment.

Some supplementary measures were also implemented in the second phase of the SOE reform. These measures included establishment of a social security system in an attempt to alleviate the social burden of SOEs for healthcare, pension, education, housing and further government reform. In 1998, the number of ministries was reduced from 40 to 29. Many former ministries were replaced by various industry-related specific bureaus, state-owned holding companies and industrial associations. The CCP Central Committee Enterprises Works Commission (CCCEWC) was established in 2000 in order to control large SOEs. In 2002, after the 16th National Congress, the State Economics and Trade Commission (SETC) and the CCCEWC merged together to form a new institution, the SASAC. To date, SASAC is the supervisory authority of all large SOEs under the central government. Proper attention has been put in place towards internal management reform by introducing performance based labor management, cadre management and income distribution and the re-emergence of capital markets in order to facilitate the share-holding reform. Having determined the prime objectives of the corporate reform, with all the supplementary measures in place, the Chinese central government seems ready to transform SOEs into modern corporations.

The process of SOEs transformation progressed through a series of policy initiatives. Under the Modern Enterprise System (MES), the new SOE reform suggested that 10,000 large and medium-sized SOEs were to adopt new accounting standards, employ new asset valuation techniques, and also implement the fourteen autonomous rights set out in 1992. One thousand large SOEs were to adopt new state asset administration regulations issued in 1994 and then they had to go on to clarify their property rights. Full corporate reforms were to be adopted by 100 SOEs. Ten municipalities were to undergo comprehensive reforms (actually 18 at the outset, subsequently expanded to 110 in 1997). All cities are now covered by these enterprise reforms.

It is noteworthy that most SOEs by the year 2000, established a new relationship with the state as planned by the State Commission for Restructuring the Economic System (SCRES). The ownership structures of most of the SOEs became also more diversified. The scale and prescribed timetable had been one of the most ambitious economic transformations in history, more rapid than any comparable reform even in advanced economies. More than 700 large and medium SOEs had transformed themselves into corporations by the end of 1999.

Through the corporate reform, China's central government has planned to change the ownership structure for more than 99 percent of China's 300,000 small and medium-sized SOEs, which tend to have higher levels of financial and personnel liabilities. At the same time, the central government has also set out to transform the large-sized SOEs into joint stock companies and limited liability companies. Although the private companies and employee share-holding co-operatives are dominant in terms of numbers, by far the most important forms are the joint stock companies and limited liability companies as they represent the majority of the large state enterprises in China.

The shares of both limited liability companies and joint stock companies can be classified into five categories. Out of these five categories, state-owned, institution-owned and individual-owned shares are the three main categories. The state-owned and the institution-owned shares were not allowed to be traded on stock-exchanges until late 2006, and even now there are restrictions in place as the transfer of state-owned and institution-owned shares require special approval from the appropriate authority i.e. CSRC. Moreover, only the shares of the joint-stock companies can be traded on stock exchanges, where only those with equity capital of over RMB50 million are eligible for listing.

The joint stock company is subject to the highest threshold among all the organizational forms. Higher levels of capitalization are required for them. Every joint stock company also must undergo a much more extensive and time consuming regulatory approval process. They are also subject to greater market discipline pressures as they are the only organizational form through which an enterprise can seek a public listing on a stock exchange. Joint stock companies can be of two categories: (1) companies that have issued shares but have not traded shares on a stock exchange; and (2) companies that have made public offerings and have traded shares on a stock exchange.

In November1994, corporate reform of large SOEs began on a trial basis. One hundred SOEs were identified and designed to be restructured along three fronts. Firstly, they were to establish corporate governance system according to company law. This involved the setting up of Board of Directors (BOD), Board of Supervisors (BOS), and the installation of a system of clearly defined rights and responsibilities between the board members and the management so that their functions were separated. Secondly, they were required to define specific owners of state assets controlled by each SOE. Finally, they were also required to streamline their internal operations by reducing the number of internal departments and employees, and bring in new investors in order to lower the debt-to-asset ratio. Those large SOEs were required to conclude the process of corporate reform according to a pre-determined time table. At the end of the trial, out of one hundred, seventy three SOEs took the form of wholly state-owned corporations and the remaining had diversified ownership structures.

While corporate reform itself is one of the key measures in the larger policy of Modern Enterprise System, shareholding reform is one of the principal elements of the corporate reform. It is often suggested that shareholding reform has several key advantages. It helps the government to reduce its liabilities and thereby easing out the budget constraint. Share-holding reform is also considered as a means of relocating capital resources effectively through merger and acquisition. It serves to reduce SOEs' debt through revenue from sale of stakes. Finally, it can improve corporate governance and management incentives through the introduction of clearer management roles and reporting structures.

Changing structure of ownership and control in China's industries are being reflected in corporations and listing of in the stock exchanges. The listing of large SOEs in the stock markets is one of the central elements of the current strategy towards the creation of modern enterprise system. Efficiency in share-issuing companies is generally higher for the very reason that good performance is essential to become joint stock companies in the first place. It is also expected that SOEs will be under better mode of enterprise governance through share-holding reform. By the end of October 2009, 750 of the 1,650 listed enterprises were state-owned or state-controlled enterprises. Also, by end-September 2009, SOEs in China accounted for 58 percent of market capitalization, down from 83.1 percent in 2007. As of today, still a small percentage of China's enterprises are publicly listed. It is, so far, widely argued that the listing of a company was usually decided not on commercial merit but on sector and political considerations. It is a very standard pattern of floatation in China where a newly formed joint stock company, in which its parent company has a majority share having control over the core operating assets, is getting floated and the parent company remains in control of the rest of the non-operating assets. In a typical Chinese listed state company, one can easily notice a typical mixed ownership structure consisting the 'state', 'legal persons' (normally state institutions or other state enterprises) and 'individual investors'being the three predominant groups of shareholders having roughly equal shares.

After 1994, Chinese government started to adopt a flexible reform approach towards SOEs. The Central leadership, at the Fifth Plenum of CCP's 14th Central Committee in September 1995, officially promulgated a new policy initiative to sort out the seemingly intractable problems surrounding SOEs. The policy which was popularly characterized with the slogan of 'grasping the large and letting go the small'(zhuada fangxiao), was reaffirmed and reinforced at the Fifteenth Party Congress in October 1997 as well as at the Ninth National People's Party Congress in March 1998. Since then, Chinese government has undertaken a nation-wide corporate reform, especially targeting large SOEs. One interpretation of 'grasping the large' is to keep about 1000 large enterprises as state owned, but for them to be maintained through the introduction of the 'modern enterprise institution', dominated by the shareholding system, and effectively privatize the small and medium-sized SOEs through selling, auctioning, merging and bankrupting.

The transformation of ownership took two main forms: listing on domestic and international stock exchanges in the case of larger SOEs, and sales to insiders, management and employees, and other parties in the case of small and medium SOEs. A program was accordingly set in motion in the Ninth Five Year Plan (1996-2000) to 'grab and reinvigorate' the priority SOEs selected by the central authorities, and the 'letting go' of small SOEs through a special fund to encourage their 're-organization, bankruptcy, debt write-offs, merger into partnerships, leasing, contractual operation or sales, as their respective circumstances permit'. The shareholding system has been the dominant institution for restructuring of the SOEs during this third stage by widening the financing channels and imposing the governance mechanisms of a joint stock system. The State has sought to retain ownership of the largest SOEs and use preferential policies to develop them to the critical production levels where economies-of-scale can be reached. Such policies include further liberalizing and or adjusting prices for state-controlled products, for example, coal; reducing SOE's pension burden by creating a new pension system combining contributions from enterprises as well as individuals; reducing the number of redundant workers by granting enterprises autonomy in employing and dismissing workers; and introducing a new policy of 'state investment for bank loans' to reduce the pressure on SOEs of interest payments.

While 'Zhuada fangxiao' policy reflected both recognition of how severe the problem was for SOEs and also desperation to prevent extinction of the state sector, the rationale behind this policy was also simple. 'Fangxiao' was an admission that it was impossible to rejuvenate all existing SOEs. Small and medium-sized SOEs, specially the city-controlled SOEs were therefore expendable. By the end of 2002, 81.6 percent of small SOEs were transformed, and the number of industrial SOEs reduced from 64,737 in 1998 to 42,696 through shareholding co-operatives, selling, leasing, and contracting and so on. Similarly, the banner of 'Zhuada' captured the ongoing efforts of the central government to select a number of large SOEs and to concentrate efforts on restructuring their management patterns. According to data analyzed by the World Bank, mainly small and medium-sized SOEs were loss making. Most of these enterprises were below optimal scale and were responsible for the duplication of industrial activities among provinces and countries. Conversely, large SOEs were mostly profitable, although the profitability probably came from their monopolistic or oligopolistic position in their industries rather than from enhanced competitiveness.

The fact that 15,668 large and medium sized SOEs accounted for about 80 percent of all SOE industrial output advocates that if the burden of small SOEs could be released and efforts regarding the restructuring of the state sector concentrated on the largest and most profitable SOEs, the reform of the state sector enterprises would become much more feasible. 'Zhuada' became relevant to create world-class large-scale conglomerates, to accelerate their integration with the international economy, and to enhance their international competitiveness in order to win more strength for the continuing development of China in the new world-economic order.

In addition, mainly strategic industries, i.e., key sector industries with strategic importance, so far, initiated implementation of 'zhuada' policy, so that the state would remain in a controlling position. Such key industries included public utilities industries, namely communications and transportation, water and electricity supply; basic goods industries including exploration of natural resources, iron and steel, non-ferrous metals etc; pillar industries such as machinery, automotive, electronics, petrochemicals, construction and so on; high-tech industries such as space navigation and biological engineering; defense industries; and finally the financial industry which is designed as a lever for the government to carry out macro-economic control and at the same time industrial re-structuring.

Precisely, five pillar industries such as machinery, automotive, electronics, petrochemicals and construction together with other strategic industries would continue to act as the core of the state-owned economy. China is seen to possess a potential advantage in these sectors. Reaching international quality standards quickly, increasing their share in international markets, and becoming profitable remained the goals of these pillar industries. State industries, thus, increasingly became concentrated on large-scale upstream activities leaving the small-scale down-stream activities to other ownership forms. Two-track reform strategy, namely, corporation based on the share-holding system and outright privatization were officially adopted by authorities as 'zhuada fangxiao' for ownership restructuring in the strategic and non-strategic sectors.

Large Enterprises Groups:

China's State Council issued a discussion document in early 1980s to encourage horizontal mergers. By the middle of 1980s, many SOEs began to pursue close co-operation and horizontal mergers under the government's initiative. In the late 1980s, the Central government set out a policy of encouraging conglomerates through the re-organization of China's individual plants into large, multi-plant businesses that could leverage economies of scale and scope. Primarily, SOEs were transformed into four types. The first type, of which the majority were small SOEs, were turned into private enterprises. The second types, mainly medium and large enterprises, were transformed into limited liability companies. The third types, of which the majority were good performing enterprises, were listed on the stock exchanges with the government as the major shareholder. A further development was the emergence of 'enterprise groups'.

China's State Council approved a proposal on 14th December, 1991, that called for quickening the development of large conglomerates. Fifty-seven key state-conglomerates were specified. The State designated them to play a leading role in their respective industries. These enterprise groups were entitled to significant operational autonomy and decision-making power which were not normally available to other SOEs. A second group of nearly 100 national conglomerates were formed in 1996. Considering that these groups were the backbone of China's key industrial sectors, SOE reform marked a dramatic turning point in the reform of ownership in China. The State Council further issued the document on deepening the development of enterprise groups on 29th April, 1997. The main feature of the document was to clarify property rights of the previous conglomerates according to company law, and any newly established enterprise group would follow the guidelines of corporate reform. The change in policy between 1991 and 1997 signaled a new phase in the development of the enterprise group concept. Since 1997, enterprise groups have become limited liability group companies with mother-child company structure based on ownership linkages instead of contract-based co-operation as practiced earlier. During the same period (1991-1997), provincial and local governments also identified 2000 smaller potential conglomerates to be converted into limited liability group companies, which were contingent upon that they continue to be profit-making for at least three years prior to their application.

By 31st December, 2002, mother companies of 2019 enterprise groups had become corporations, of which the number of joint stock companies were 375, limited liability companies were 827 and wholly state-owned companies were 788. This accounted for 18.6 percent, 41 percent and 39 percent respectively of the total corporate enterprises. The remaining numbers of enterprise groups were privately owned. One of the major reasons of promoting state-sponsored enterprise groups by China's central government was to build-up international level conglomerates with economies of scale, resources and the economic strength necessary for competition in the international market. The idea perhaps developed from South Korean Chaebols model. Moreover, the policy was also designed to help the state to control the production output in key industrial sectors. Of course, above all the basic objective was to reduce the number of non-viable SOEs.

In order to revitalize SOEs, the State Council launched three important measures in September, 1997. Those measures were: (1) Written off bad debt, (2) Debt-into-equity reform, and (3) the availability of national bonds at subsidized interests to quicken technology upgrade and innovation. Debt-into-equity reform had direct impact on ownership and organizational structures of corporate SOEs. This involved converting the loans from government ministries and state-owned banks to investment so as to lower debts to assets ratios. Debts owed to other SOEs were also converted to investment. Since the vast majority of SOEs' debts were owed to the four major state-owned banks, four state assets management companies were established by those four banks. Industrial and Commercial Bank of China (ICBC) established the Huarong Assets Management Co. Limited (HRAMC), China Construction Bank (CCB) established the Xinda Assets Management Co. Ltd. (XDAMC), Bank of China (BOC) established the Dongfang Assets Management Co. Ltd. (DFAMC) and Agricultural Bank of China (ABC) established the Changcheng Assets Management Co. Ltd.(CCAMC). This preferential policy was restricted to large SOEs. The central government identified 580 large SOEs to implement debt-into-equity reform with total debts converted into equities of RMB 405 billion. The policy began on 1st April 2000. According to policy decision, shares held by the four major assets management companies should be gradually withdrawn within seven years. As argued that this plan was accepted because none of the corporations' creditors including ministries, banks or other enterprises had any possibility of recovering their money by any other method. The policy makers strongly felt that the chance of receiving dividends in future from a restructured profitable company was better than no return at all. Since 1997, the majority of small and medium-sized SOEs have been transformed into the private sector whereas the central government has focused its attention solely on the large SOEs. Large SOEs have explicitly been given a dual role. They have been expected to lead the large-scale sector into international markets but also to absorb large numbers of poorly performing small enterprises.

The transformation of ownership of small SOEs was very significant for China because, in contrast to the Soviet Union and Eastern Europe, most of China's industrial SOEs were small and medium-sized enterprises. Most of these enterprises were under the supervision of county and city governments which were given considerable latitude, leading to significant regional variations in the extent and depth of restructuring. In 1993, China's small and medium-sized enterprises accounted for 95 percent of total industrial SOEs, 57 percent in employment, and 43 percent in output of the State industrial sector. Over 80 percent of small and medium-sized SOEs have been transformed in the ways illustrated above. Between 1995 and 2001, China's SOEs halved their workforce to less than 40 million. Some of these jobs were not lost but reassigned the new entities as SOEs were reorganized into shareholding units or formed partnerships with other entities. It is also estimated that lay-offs from SOEs and collectives were 25.5 million during 1998-2001. Perhaps, 8.7 million of these workers did not find new jobs as reported by World Bank (2003). Never before, State employees had been laid off or state enterprises closed down. SOEs were required to establish 're-employment centers' for laid-off workers which provided retraining and job search assistance and paid unemployment benefits. If the laid-off worker remained unemployed for more than three years, the employer could sever the relationship. From 2002, newly laid-off workers received only unemployment benefits, and the re-employment centers were phased out by 2004.

In the new environment, two economic factors emerged that had considerable importance for alleviating the social cost of restructuring. One had been the development of the national social security system. The central budget expenditures on social security rose from 1 percent in 1997 to 6.3 percent in 2002. The other factor had been the promoting of the growth of new private enterprises including overseas funded enterprises to absorb laid-off workers from the state sector. Towards the end of 1990s, it had become apparent that the reform of SOEs had resulted in several major problems. The first was corruption of firm managers and state officials who had rights over the firms they were governing. The second was the drainage of state assets, as the state enterprises continued to under-perform. The contractual system also resulted in short-term behavior by the managers. For example, when the managers tried to make as much profit as possible during their contract term, they mostly neglected the maintenance of the assets. During 1994-2000, SOEs had lower interest coverage and were less profitable than other Chinese enterprises. Losses continued and while direct budgetary subsidies to SOEs were reduced, the SOEs tried to be supported by implicit subsidies through the banking system which, in the process, accumulated huge non-performing loans. Thus, the third problem became prominent that firms became more in debt to the banks. The State-owned banks usually maintained long-standing relationship with the SOEs, and in order to keep the firms running, government bodies encouraged the banks to give or renew loans to the firms, even though the firms were often unable to return even the interest on the loans.

Different case studies conducted during this period found that (a) lack of hard budget constraints i.e. a firm could keep running even though it was loosing money because the government couldn't afford to close them, as unemployment of the workforce might lead to social instability; (b) lack of legally clear and enforceable property rights i.e. while, in theory, the firm was owned by all the people and the state owned it on behalf of the people , in practice different government agencies could intervene in the activities of the firm claiming themselves as being the state; and (c) corporate governance problem arising out of lack of incentive as well as management accountability structures to induce firm managers to act in the interests of firm as the managers were politically appointed and thus their careers were less linked to the performance of the firm than to their political loyalty and competence.

In the process, policy makers came to understand that new and more radical efforts were necessary to make SOEs successful and profitable. The Communist Party also released its policy outline time to time for the continuing process of SOE reform in a number of documents. These documents were: (1) the decision on major issues concerning the reform and development of state-owned enterprises adopted by the Fourth Plenum of the Fifteenth Communist Party Central Committee in September 1999; (2) a policy statement issued by the State Development Planning Commission (SDPC) in January, 2000; and (3) the Tenth Five-year Plan (2001-2005) presented at the Fifth Plenary Session of the Fifteenth Congress of the Communist Party in October 2000.

Fifteenth Communist Party Central Committee decision in September 1999 specified that while state ownership would be reduced in many industrial sectors, SOEs would remain dominant in (a) pillar industries and backbone enterprises in high-technology sectors; (b) non-renewable natural resources sector; (C) public utility and infrastructure services sectors; and (d) sectors vital to the country's national security. This decision also urged greater corporate reforms of SOEs, and also re-iterated the importance of the Party retaining its leading role in SOEs. State

Development Planning Commission Policy Statement in January 2000 indicated that the government would actively guide and encourage private investment and would eliminate all restrictive and discriminatory regulations that are not friendly towards private investment, land-use, business start-ups, and import and export. This policy statement seemed to put the private sector on an equal footing with SOEs, and had been widely regarded as one of China's strongest endorsement in favor of free enterprises. The Tenth Five Year Plan (2001-2005) finally pinpointed SOE reform as the key link in China's structural adjustment and called for large and medium sized SOEs to deepen their reforms to establish a modern corporate system characterized by clear ownership, explicit rights and responsibilities, and disconnection between the government and enterprises.

In a very real sense, the reform of the SOEs was not about reducing the government's control over the key sectors of the economy, but it was about making that control more effective. If such effective control of SOEs could be achieved by stock-market listing, or introducing foreign investment, or leasing enterprises to private sector skills, then those things would have happened. It is evident that the short-term strategies that were introduced soon after Zhu Rongji took up his position as Prime Minister, turned out as efforts that would hopefully remedy some of the most immediate problems. The state intended to keep only those SOEs which were recognized as being most crucial to the national economy, while the others were sold, merged, turned into collectively owned firms, restructured to reduce overstaffing or just closed. Moreover, since then the SOE reform process had also been broadened out and acquired some new vision. For example, the scale of change had expanded to influence almost every kind of SOEs --- small, medium, large and very big under both central and local control; mass lay-offs became a wide spread phenomenon which was unheard of not so long ago; the role of the wholly state-owned non-financial company declined substantially in many areas; the range of restructuring mechanisms being used expanded dramatically to include bankruptcies, liquidations, listings and de-listings, debt-for-equity swaps, sales to both domestic and foreign private parties, auctioning of state firms and their assets and liabilities, standardize corporate governance techniques, and so on. Moreover, the whole reform process was propelled by the commitments made by China to the WTO to open up many of the sectors to foreign competition within a specific time frame.

REFORMS DURING POST-WTO ACCESSION PERIOD:

The current policy of the government in connection with SOEs is to concentrate on separating ownership and regulation of companies, and streamlining administration of state-ownership. At the central level, efforts were made earlier to transfer supervision to the National State Asset Administration Bureau and the Ministry of Finance, albeit with limited success due to opposition from other Ministries. In March 2003, the Government established the State-owned Asset Supervision and Administration Commission (SASAC). The SASAC is mainly responsible for reforming and managing government assets in the SOEs under its charge. The SASAC was originally charged with the management of 196 central-government-owned non-financial SOEs. As a result of consolidation, it appeared that as of December 2009, it managed 129 SOEs, down from 159 in 2006; these were involved mainly in defense, petroleum, electricity, telecommunications, metallurgy, coal, aviation, shipping, machinery, and civilian construction. According to the authorities, the government would maintain a controlling stake in companies having a bearing on national security, while gradually reducing state ownership of other SOEs. By December 2006, the SASAC enacted several departmental rules and a series of legal documents on performance evaluation, property management, and regulatory reform based on the 'Interim Regulations on Supervision and Management of State-owned Assets of Enterprises'. Another 260 regulations and legal documents that have implications for the work of the SASAC had also been revised by December 2006 to enable the SASAC to perform its work effectively. Some of the other activities of SASAC include to encourage, support and organize SOEs to recruit more management internationally, establishing competitive systems of remuneration for the SOEs, establishing equity exchanges to encourage equity trading for SOEs, increasing the involvement of international auditing firms in assessing the performance of

SOEs, continuing the restructuring of SOEs and continuing to advocate the divestment of social functions provided by the SOEs.

The reform of SOEs has been continued. This includes the reorganization of SOEs through mergers and acquisitions, as well as closing down and SOEs' corporatization and privatization. As a consequence, the number of SOEs fell from 929,152, i.e., 12.08 percent of all enterprises in China in 2004 to 730, 121, i.e., 8.46 percent in 2006. SOEs held total assets of RMB 29 trillion and provided employment to 39 million people in 2006 in comparison to total assets of RMB 18 trillion and employment of 42.3 million people in 2003. Moreover, mainly because of mergers and acquisitions, the number of SOEs managed by the SASAC fell from 196 in 2005, to 159 in 2006, and then to 129 in December 2009. The number of state-owned enterprises for which the State-owned Assets Supervision and Administration Commission of the State Council performed the responsibilities of an investor had decreased from 151 at the beginning of 2008 to 128 by the end of February 2010. Results of the Second National Economic Census, published early 2010, showed that at the end of 2008, China had altogether 4.959 million legal enterprises, among which 143,000 were state-owned enterprises, 36,000 or a 20 percent less than that at the end of 2004 that was published in the First national Economic Census. Meanwhile, at the end of 2008, the number of private enterprises was 3.596 million, up by 81.4 percent with an addition of 1.614 million. This clearly indicated that the non-public sector had been developing steadily and had already become an important component of the national economy by end-2009. Further restructuring of SOEs has always been undertaken in accordance with the Opinion on Guidelines for Promoting the Restructuring of State-owned Assets and SOEs, issued by the State Council. According to the Opinion, the Government intends to retain state ownership in industries involving national security, major infrastructure and important mineral resources, industries supplying important public goods and services, and important backbone enterprises in pillar industries and high and new technology industries. Seven strategically important sectors, namely power generation and distribution, oil and petrochemicals, telecommunication, coal, aviation, and shipping, would remain under state control.

The number of SOEs registered under the Company Law has been increasing. The authorities believe that there is a trend to register all SOEs under the Company Law by 2010. Corporate governance of SOEs registered under the Company Law has improved, as external directors have been introduced to Boards of Directors since 2004, and open procedures to recruit general managers commenced in 2006. Significantly 66 external directors had been introduced to 17 SOEs by 31st July, 2007. Corporate governance of SOEs has also been improved through their transformation into joint stock companies and their listing on stock exchanges. By end-October 2009, out of 1.650 listed enterprises, 750 were state-owned or state-controlled enterprises. On 29th April 2005, The China Securities Regulatory Commission (CSRC) issued circular on the Pilot Program of Non-tradable Shares Reform of listed companies with a view to converting non-tradable shares into tradable ones. Since January 2006, foreign investors can also purchase A-shares of companies in stock markets. However, to purchase shares in SOEs, they need approval from SASAC. Conversion of non-tradable shares, apart from the shares reserved or regulated by the state, had been completed up to nearly 97 percent of all listed enterprises by the middle of 2007. As on 31st December 2006, policy-led bankruptcies involved 4,251 SOEs which had been suffering losses for a long time and were gradually exiting the market. Since January 2009, all SOE bankruptcy cases are to be conducted according to the Law on Enterprise Bankruptcy. In this connection, it is to be noted that a significant change in China's corporate governance system is the promulgation of the Law on Enterprise Bankruptcy which is in effect since 1st June 2007.

The catalogue on encouraging, restricting, and prohibiting FIEs was revised, with a view to encouraging foreigners to invest in SOEs and some other key industries that are crucial to regional development, particularly in western and central China, as well as north-east China. The revised catalogue is in force since 1st December 2007.

The Ministry of Finance issued the Accounting Standards for Business Enterprises including SOEs on 15th February 2006, and the same came into force on 1st January 2007. The standards which apply to all enterprises in China including SOEs, are largely in line with international standards, with a few differences from the International Reporting Standards. The China Accounting Standards Committee has been in close co-operation with the International Accounting Standards Board (IASB) through regular meetings with a view to further aligning China's accounting system with international standards.

In October 2008, Law on State-owned Assets of Enterprises was adopted at the Fifth Session of the Standing Committee of the 11th National People's Congress, and established the legal framework for the supervision of state-owned assets. Introduction of corporate and share-holding systems for state-owned enterprises has further been advanced during 2008-2009 through participation of strategic investors, restructuring and going public. During the same period corporate governance structure has also been improved with measures such as establishment of standard board of directors and introduction of external directors, etc. The budget system for the use of state capital has also taken the shape during this period. Institutional improvement has also been advanced during 2008-2009 in areas such as financial supervision, ownership management and supervision by board of supervisors over the state-owned assets.

SUMMING-UP

We have mentioned earlier that four Chinese state owned banks (SOB) accumulated a huge amount of non-performing loans most of which were due to the SOEs. Four Asset Management Companies (AMCs), one for each SOB, used to receive money from the state through the Ministry of Finance, the Peoples' Bank of China and non-tradable bonds. In turn, the asset management companies provided money to the firms, and the firms pay their loan back to the banks. Using this system, the firms' debts were turned into shares held by the asset management companies on behalf of the state. Apparently, because of this debt-share swap system, banks appear to be in a healthier condition by getting rid of the bad loans in exchange for debt claims issued by the AMCs, while the SOE firms are less highly geared.

The negative aspects of the debt-equity swap policy, so far, appeared that it had deflected the AMCs from their principal role of disposing of those bad loans of the SOBs which were not part of the debt-equity swaps and which were the major component of the AMCs' portfolio. Disposal of the bad loans had been slow and also the recovery rate was low. The AMCs also remained notably unsuccessful in forcing governance changes in firms, the shares of which they held.

The causes of SOE inefficiency are generally well understood and mostly include the following: (a) in case of SOEs, the state owns SOE assets on behalf of the entire population of the country; there is no owner or group of owners with a personal interest in defending the value of the capital invested and actively demanding a good return on that investment, though SOE managers and supervising agencies have many de-facto rights to make wages, bonuses, investments and production decisions in their own interests. The government had been trying to overcome this problem since 1994. In 2003, the government established State-owned Assets Supervision and Administration Commission of the State Council (SASAC) at the central government level in conjunction with organizations and committees at the other levels of the government. Inventories of State-owned assets are made to ensure that state assets are not misappropriated. SOE performance is also appraised and rewarded. However, progress on this has been uneven so far due to number of factors, i.e., a lack of trained staff who should be independent of the old ministries, rearguard action by many of ministries concerned and finally unclear lines of responsibility at the ground level; (b) reward systems for both managers and workers were limited and linked to volume rather than quality variables. Performance indicators, at the same time, could be manipulated in order to meet the plan targets. Also, horizontal integration across firms and plans made it difficult to assess individual enterprise performance. It is well understood that once firm-level information becomes distorted, the incentive mechanism to encourage improved performance ceases to work. The government is also bound to become unable to distinguish good firms from bad; (c) while both direct budget grants and subsidized credit from the state banks to loss-making SOEs have declined in recent years, budget subsidies are still substantial. In addition, SOEs still obtain large transfers via inter-enterprise credits, the so-called 'triangular debt'. Triangular debt expands when SOE commodities become non-saleable, but basically it is caused by a failure to enforce payments for goods supplied. This situation has changed somewhat in recent years as many SOEs now face competition from non-state enterprises and a number of SOEs have been put into bankruptcy. However, the government has frequently re-iterated that bankruptcy will be used only as the last resort and even then priority will be given to protect the interests of managers and workers by exploring alternatives such as mergers, acquisitions and reconstructions. Such forbearance is obviously absent for collectives and private sector firms; (d) the positive as well as negative incentives for SOE managers are weak. The salaries and bonuses paid to successful SOE managers are low as compared with the salaries of comparable managers in private and joint-venture firms. The negative incentives for poor performers are also weak. Managers of loss-making SOEs earn nearly as much as those of profit-making ones and are unlikely to be sacked. Should managers fail to perform, the worst that they can expect is a transfer to another position. Loose control over operational costs such as business entertainment, trips and executive cars can result from SOE managers' dissatisfaction with their salary packages; (e) even with the issuance of improved accounting standards, there are some other impediments in implementing meaningful accounting practices. Tertiary businesses' assets, implicit liabilities and costs, especially social obligations, are unclear. Many SOEs are heavily indebted to other SOEs. Inconsistencies also exist within a single enterprise group. Costs are often determined arbitrarily. In many SOEs, different independent profit center workshops or production units still rely on an 'internal banking system'. Most units and the 'internal bank' lack sufficient information to plan or to deal with working capital shortages. The fact is that most of the accounts and the financial control mechanisms in China's industrial SOEs still do not create strong incentives for transparency and efficiency. Enhancing the system of checks and balances and strengthening the control system to manage inter-enterprise debts are still needed.

Nevertheless, the short-term policies for the grasped large and medium-sized SOEs had been able to lay the groundwork for the starting of the long-term strategies aimed at SOEs. The three-fold longer-term strategies for the SOEs remained: (a) to build a new environment for SOEs in a market economy based framework in which the firms will operate in an internationally approved financial system, stock market, taxation, personnel, social security and others; (b) to go for industrial restructuring at the macro level, eventually resulting in the concentration of SOEs in several key industries that are considered to be the 'commanding heights' of the national economy, such as steel, iron, energy and national defense. Overall, around 30-50 giant state corporations and conglomerates have been nurtured with the aim of building them into globally competitive multinationals by 2010. Already, some have proven to be competitive internationally. The largest and successful Chinese corporations are mostly transformed SOEs in oil, steel and chemicals. For example, Legend Group is 65 percent owned by the Chinese Academy of Sciences; Petro China is 90 percent owned by China National Petroleum Corporation which is 100 percent state-owned; in China mobile, China life, Sinopec and Baoshan Iron and Steel – state ownership is 75 percent, 73 percent, 84 percent and 61 percent respectively; (c) to achieve clarified property rights, clearly defined responsibility and authority, the separation of enterprises from the government, and scientific internal management, etc. of SOEs. While the board-system has been introduced to bring guided supervision of the managers, the selection of managers should also be open, rather than political.

After three decades, Chinese reformers seem to have reached a consensus of where the reform of SOEs should be going. It seems that they strongly believe that when the reform plans are fully materialized, SOEs will thrive even in the global competitive market. Towards working to build a socialist market economy or socialism with Chinese characters, the goal of the Chinese reformers is to have a market economy with a group of substantial state-owned players in many key industries, such as manufacturing, electricity, transportation, communication, petroleum, and finance and banking.

Finally, it can be mentioned that China's State-asset management initiatives, so far, for improving the performance of SOEs reflect a serious commitment to reform within the context of the 'socialist market economy' framework. However, if China's

SOEs, in the medium term, are to operate competitively under WTO's international trading system, it can be argued that more than marginal adjustments to some current policies are still necessary.

CHAPTER – EIGHT

China's accession to the WTO: A study of the developments in few selected sectors

A. THE BANKING SECTOR REFORMS

China had a mono-bank system before its reform process began in 1978. People's Bank of China (PBOC) was the main national bank and also the sole commercial bank. In addition, PBOC was the only repository of deposits and the only lending institution. Effectively, enterprise surpluses were remitted to the government and then those surplus funds were re-allocated to priority firms and projects as per credit plan administered by the central and local branches of the PBOC in accordance with State Council's decisions. In essence, the PBOC acted as a cashier to Government.

Transformation of this mono-banking system took place in a number of stages, a prologue to WTO accession. Beginning in the early1980s, commercial banking, policy banking and central banking functions were being separated. All those functions had previously been carried out only by PBOC. Five stages can be categorized:

(1) during stage one (1979 – 1985), the restructuring of the banking system and the creation of separate banking institutions took place;

(2) during stage two (1986 – 1992), the diversification of institutions and the establishment of stock market took place;

(3) during stage three (1993 – 1997), independence of PBOC and the initial commercialization of the state banks took place;

(4) during stage four (1998 – 2002), early moves to resolve the loan problems of the financial institutions took place; and

(5) during stage five (2003 onwards), reforms to strengthen the banking sector ahead of the impact of WTO accession commitments.

There were some consistent themes in all the stages of reform. During 1993-1994, there was a marked change when the government's previously strong commitment to employment growth and support for the state sector gave way to an overall tightening of policy towards the state-owned banks (SOBs) and the SOEs. The government was frequently using SOBs to support SOEs to resolve temporarily their soft budget constraints and that was largely viewed, considered and found to be the main reason for the deteriorating financial performance for both SOBs and SOEs. Mounting losses of the SOEs led to a rapid increase in non-performing loans in the SOBs, putting the whole financial system at risk.

In December 1993, the government of China laid out a roadmap towards restructuring of the financial system and also promulgated the rules for such financial reform. The salient features were as follows:

1. The People's Bank of China would be allowed to play its proper role in implementing monetary policy and in managing and supervising financial activities. Essentially, the PBOC would be transformed into a real central bank.

2. It was decided that policy related finance was to be separated from commercial finance by establishing a network of financial institutions. State-owned commercial banks were to be the main entities, while various other financial institutions would co-exist with them.

3. A market-based system featuring openness, orderly competition and strict management was to be introduced. Towards that direction, the financial market would be opened further and additional foreign financial institutions would be allowed. Moreover, the specialized state banks were to be transformed into real commercial banks.

4. The government of China also intended that the exchange rate was to be unified so that the renminbi should gradually become a convertible currency.

In institutional terms, much of the above agenda had already been realized. Nevertheless, success of the reforms would remain at risk so long as the banks' bad debt problem should remain unresolved. Moreover, there had been a close inter-relationship between financial sector reform and SOE reform. In other words, the financial reform agenda became intertwined with that for the SOEs in many respects.

BANKING SYSTEMS DURING 1948 – 1978:

On 1st December 1948, China's present financial system was originated with the formation of the PBOC through a consolidation of the former Hubei Bank, Beihai Bank and the Xibei Peasant Bank – the three regional banks previously controlled by the communists under the earlier Nationalist regime of Chiang Kai-shek (Jiang Jieshi). It was then termed or called as 'mono-bank' system. In 1949, Bank of China was created from the PBOC mono-bank as a specialist foreign-exchange bank, and was made responsible for foreign investment, currency exchanges and the administration of exchange rate policy. In 1952, the Bank of Communications was given responsibility under the Ministry of Finance to allocate capital investments, but in 1954 it was replaced by the People's Construction Bank of China (PCBC) to act as the cashier of the Capital Construction Finance Department of the Ministry of Finance. All investment projects took the form of budgetary grants disbursed through the PCBC. It was noticed that the Agricultural Bank of China had three incarnations, in 1951, 1955 and in 1963. However, its business was eventually transferred to the Bureau of Rural Financial Management within the PBOC.

Chinese government inherited a system of private commercial banks and other financial institutions from the Nationalist regime when the People's Republic of China was formed in 1949. Government shares were added to the private banks creating state-private corporate banks during 1952-1955. During first five-year national plan between 1955 and 1959, the private shares gradually decreased until the People's Bank of China had total control of the banks under state ownership. In the process of this transition, the state-private corporate banks gradually changed to become branches of the PBOC until all were consolidated into the mono-banking structure.

A similar transformation took place also on the industry side amongst the private and share-holding companies left behind by the Nationalist government. Private enterprises produced 63 percent of national industrial output in 1949. However, that share had declined to 39 percent by 1952 as People's Republic of China quickly built up its state economy with support and aid from the erstwhile Soviet Union. The private shares were gradually reduced and eventually disappeared during the First Five-Year Plan (1955-1959). Actually, the transformation of private to public was completed in 1956. Control of the state-private corporations was achieved either by a purchase policy to convert them into SOEs or by changing them into collectives owned by local government bodies. Between 1959 and 1978, the SOEs dominated Chinese industries producing more than 86 percent of industrial output. In essence, SOEs functioned as agents of the government, relying on the State Planning Commission in the State Council and its subordinates in local government to determine production plans, sell products and to set processes for inputs and outputs. All the major activities of the SOEs including research and development, product innovation, marketing and investment plans were directed and financed centrally. As a result, during 1954-1978, virtually all financial transactions were routed through the mono-bank network under a credit planning system managed by the MOF and the State Planning Commission. Except the special credit allocation for rural development, all deposits were maintained with the PBOC and all business transactions were settled through the bank. Credit could only be obtained through the PBOC which distributed industrial and commercial credits in the form of government-directed loans.

THE INITIAL STAGES OF BANKING REFORMS, 1979-1985:

In most financial systems, a major function of the financial intermediaries is to transform household savings into finance for productive investment. In 1978, national savings in China were fairly high but almost all of this was government savings (15 percent of GDP) and enterprise savings (17 percent of GDP). Household savings were only 1 percent of GDP. However, since the reforms began, household savings have increased rapidly. The ratio of household saving to household income increased from 5 percent in 1978 to 21 percent in 1985. Household bank deposits have increased from 8.8 percent of GDP in 1980 to over 60 percent today. It is evident that the necessary concomitant to this process was the break-up of the mono-bank system. Also, the introduction of western-style financial intermediaries was seen as important for this development. There were numbers of steps involved in breaking-up the mono-banking system:

a. The Agricultural Bank of China was a specialized state bank. It used to provide working capital to state agricultural supply and marketing bodies in rural areas, and also to grant loans to township and village enterprises (TVEs). After 1978, as a reform process, the Agricultural Bank of China was transformed to become the first commercial bank. It shows that the reforms began in agriculture with the 'household responsibility system' and then spread to industry.

b. The Bank of China (BOC) was separated from PBOC in March 1979. However, BOC started working independently as a state bank with the function of a commercial bank specializing in foreign exchange in September1983. BOC had branches in every province, municipality and county as well as in overseas. The main domestic business of BOC involved savings, deposits and settlements for industrial, commercial and foreign trade enterprises. Moreover, BOC remained the dominant foreign-exchange bank and continued its leading position in foreign-trade settlement and other foreign-exchange business in China although the exclusive rights of BOC to handle foreign exchange ended in 1985. In fact, none of the specialized banks are now restricted to their originally designated business activities.

c. In December 1981, the Investment Bank of China (IBC) was formed. The main purpose of forming IBC was to attract medium and long-term capital from overseas and to facilitate financing with the World Bank.

d. The People's Construction Bank of China (PCBC) was created in 1954 under the direct control of the Ministry of Finance (MOF). Later, it became the China Construction Bank (CCB). In 1983, it also became a separate entity. As PCBC, it used to provide long-term loans for fixed assets and was also using its deposits to finance the construction of enterprises and big engineering projects. However, in recent years, CCB has diversified its business and has emerged as a full-fledged commercial bank.

e. The State Council, China's ultimate decision-making body, approved the creation of a separate bank in September 1983. This move led to the establishment of the Industrial and Commercial Bank of China (ICBC), the fourth largest state-owned bank in 1984, which took over the urban commercial banking functions formerly undertaken by the PBOC. ICBC opened branches in every province, municipality and county.

These institutional changes enacted the break-up of the mono-bank system. In 1985, the responsibility for the provision of funds to SOEs became that of the state-owned banks rather than of the MOF. Such a move effectively established a distinctive role for each of the specialized state-owned banks. Under the initial reforms during 1979-1985, a strict credit ceiling was imposed on the annual increase in loans of the specialized state banks under the Chinese credit plan. In its original concept, the plan was a highly negotiated process whereby lending quotas were allocated to lenders based on a balancing of the lender's deposits against the borrowing requirement of the lender's assigned borrowers.

THE SECOND STAGE OF BANKING REFORMS, 1986-1992:

During this period, there were continued diversifications of the products and deposits of the four state-owned commercial banks, along with the introduction of a more broadly based financial system. Such introduction came from the formation of new commercial banks and the development of securities markets, namely the Shanghai and Shenzhen stock markets.

During the second stage of reforms period, a number of national commercial banks, namely the Bank of Communication

(1986), CITIC Industrial Bank (1987), Huaxia Bank (1992), and Everbright Bank of China (1992), were established. Moreover, several regional banks were also established in the booming coastal areas in response to local government demands. Those regional banks were: Xingue Bank of Fujian Province (1981), Huiteng Urban Co-operative Bank in Sichuan Province (1985), Zhao Shang Bank in Shenzhen Shekou district (1986), Development Bank of Shenzhen City (1987), and Development Bank of Guangdong Province (1988). These national commercial banks as well as the regional banks, unlike the four state-owned commercial banks, were owned by the share-holders, usually state-affiliated agencies or large enterprises, local government bodies or private companies, and used to be managed by a board of major share-holders. The Bank of Communications was a large bank with a long history in Shanghai. It was included, sometime, with the State banks for statistical purposes. However, it was re-established in 1986 as a comprehensive share-holding bank rather than a specialized state bank, and since then it has been operating along the lines of a modern commercial bank with branches throughout the country. The regional banks are comparatively smaller and can only set up branches in one or few provinces.

In addition, Urban Credit Co-operatives and Rural Credit Co-operatives also have vast networks. The urban co-operatives use to be independent legal institutions, and their functions are similar to those of a small commercial bank. Their businesses involve savings, deposits and settlements for small urban enterprises, industrialists and businessmen. The rural co-operatives used to service rural households and TVEs, creating employment opportunities and supporting developments at the local level. Before they became independent i.e. until 1996, they had been operating under the guidance of the Agricultural Bank of China and were undertaking policy-directed lending.

One of the major developments during the second stage of the financial reforms came from the establishment of the Shanghai and Shenzhen stock markets in 1990 and 1991 respectively. During 1986-1992 state Council continued to play a central role in the allocation of credit, despite the growth of the range of financial institutions and the development of a more diversified financial system.

THE THIRD STAGE OF BANKING REFORMS, 1993-1997:

During the third stage of financial reforms expansion of the ranks of the non-state banks were continued. In 1995 the Hainan Development Bank was established. However, it was later forced to close in 1998 along with two other housing savings banks due to bad investments in Hainan's real estate market.

In 1996, a new nationwide commercial bank, Minsheng Bank was established with majority capital from non-state firms who are members of the China Industrial and Commercial Association. However, government officials tried to confirm that despite such private sector participation, Minsheng Bank was not a private bank as its major shareholders were state-owned corporations.

During the third stage of financial reform, a number of urban credit co-operatives were merged and consolidated in 35 large and medium sized towns as city co-operative banks. Also, some rural credit co-operatives were amalgamated into rural co-operative banks. In 1982, China first allowed foreign bank's entry in China. However, since 1994 with the implementation of the national banking law regulating the scope and entry of foreign banks, the number of foreign banks in China has increased substantially.

The major developments in this phase revolved around central banking, policy banking, and the SOE debt situation. The People's Bank of China obtained permission in November1993 from the Central Committee of the Chinese Communist Party (CCP) to acquire greater independence in conducting monetary policy. Such independence was necessary as the PBOC was required to be re-organized to separate the apparatus of monetary policy from the fiscal side of government.

On January 1, 1994, a new exchange rate system was introduced as a continuation of financial reform process that began after December 1978. Between 1979 and 1986, a foreign exchange retention system had been in operation, permitting exporting enterprises to retain a portion of the foreign exchange they earned. Firms in the SEZs could hold back 100 percent of their earnings. Such percentage varied by location and sector for the firms outside SEZs. Between 1987 and 1993, a dual exchange rate system was in place. A 'swap' market was introduced, and swap centers for foreign currency were established across the country enabling the foreign-funded enterprises (FFEs) and certain domestic firms to trade directly in foreign exchange at below official rates. Until 1993, about 80 percent of foreign currency transactions occurred in the swap market at more market-determined rates. In 1994, the official and swap market rates were unified at the prevailing swap rate which represented a 33 percent devaluation of the official rate. As per 1994 reforms, the exchange rate of renminbi was subject to a unified and managed floating rate regime. Each bank designated to handle foreign exchange deals with clients on the basis of its own exchange rates, which were fixed within 0.5 percent of the floating range of the basic renminbi exchange rate. Current account restrictions were removed. Also domestic and foreign enterprises were free to use foreign currency for daily operations. The renminbi became fully convertible in December 1996 for international trade transactions. At that time, China also accepted obligations with respect to current account transactions. However, a range of controls were still in place to currency transactions associated with capital movements and full convertibility of the currency for the capital account.

In order to control the inflation, separating monetary policy from government fiscal outcomes was very important. Until 1993, credit was often extended in excess of the plan at the local level. The central bank PBOC was ultimately filling the gap and was contributing to money supply and thus increasing the inflationary pressures. Economic overheating during 1992 and 1993 convinced decision-makers that monetary policy and banking reforms were needed. In 1994, the policy lending functions of the PBOC and the four SOBs were withdrawn to separate monetary policy from government fiscal transfers. Instead, three new policy banks specializing in policy lending to three different areas were established. Formation of such policy banks removed the requirement for the PBOC to finance policy-lending by isolating the PBOC from the process of subsidizing the state-controlled sectors of the economy and also enabling PBOC to concentrate on central banking business. The specialized policy banks were Agricultural Development Bank (ADB), State Development Bank (SDB), and Import-Export Bank (IEB).

Agricultural Development Bank was formed to provide funds for government acquisition of output from the agricultural sector. State Development Bank (SDB) was primarily responsible for long term loans for infrastructure finance on selected key development projects. Import Export Bank provided support for the import of machinery and equipment associated with the modernization of industries duly assigned on priority basis by the government including income-earning export industries. In the case of SDB and the IEB, funding for the policy lending came almost entirely from the issuance of bonds, whereas for the ADB, central bank loans were a major source of short-term funds.

The People's Congress promulgated the Act of the People's Bank of China on 18th March 1995 and the Commercial Banks Act of the People's Republic of China on 10th May 1995 in order to provide a legal framework for central banking and commercial banking. The Act of the People's Bank of China legally confirmed the PBOC's status as central bank and defined its functions and organization. The commercial Banks Act insisted that commercial banks must assume responsibility for risk of loss, profitability, safety and liquidity, and to manage themselves separately from the People's Bank of China. Commercial Banks are also required to do business without any interference from any person or organization, and make loans in accordance with the credit worthiness of the borrower and do the best to ensure that loans can be repaid.

The Chinese central government maintained a strong commitment until 1994 to employment in the state sector that enabled state employment to grow on a par with that achieved in the non-state sector. However, maintaining this employment commitment required a steady flow of financial support to the state sector as the state sector's share of output was declining. The central government was providing such financial support to the state sector mainly with cheap credit from the state banking system using the credit plan as its principal instrument to control the banking system's credit allocation. Until 1994, more than 80 percent of the banking system's lending was directed to the SOEs. As many of these loans were not being repaid, a huge bad debt problem developed which put the entire financial system at risk.

The Chinese banking management committee in its meeting in 1995 first proposed that the bad debts of the four state-owned commercial banks be lowered. The government, as a first step, reduced its long-standing commitment to support employment growth in the state sector, which was the main reason for the soft budget constraints. Between 1995 and 1999, employment in the state sector was reduced by 26.9 million. On the other-hand, employment in the non-state sector increased by 50 million. The reduction of employment was most pronounced in SOE industries. During the four year period, the industrial SOEs released 19.9 million or 45 percent of their workers. The People's Bank of China (PBOC), as a second step, centralized and reduced its loans to SOBs, which had been an important source of funds in turn for their loans to the SOEs. Thirdly, the government began an effort to commercialize the SOBs by putting them in the position of assuming increased responsibility for their losses and bad debts.

Nevertheless, these actions at the onset of the crisis was something of a short-term fix leaving the long-term problems of the SOE debt to be addressed, and this was done more elaborately on the fourth stage of financial reforms.

THE FOURTH STAGE OF BANKING REFORMS, 1998–2000:

Financial sector reform accelerated from the very beginning of 1998. In November 1997, the top Chinese leadership participated in a major financial sector conference and they took a view that financial sector crisis posed a more serious threat to the Communist Party than unemployment.

During the fourth stage of banking reform, the following major changes took place:

a. In January 1998, the Chinese government abandoned the long-standing credit quota system for state-owned banks. Instead, banks' credit enhancement was henceforth managed using reference guidelines based on capital adequacy and deposit-to-loan ratios. The new system allowed the banks greater freedom to determine lending volumes and the distribution across sectors, provinces and business categories.

b. Although the government still continued to advise lending priorities, banks were expected and allowed to allocate lending predominantly by evaluating potential risks and returns, especially borrowers' capacity to repay. To ensure greater consistency with commercial lending criteria, bank managers and loan officers supposed to be responsible for new non-performing loans (NPLs). In March 1998, a new loan classification system was introduced in line with international standards, whereby loans were classified into five categories, i.e. normal, special mention, sub-standard, idle, and loss loans replacing the three categories classification for NPLs (overdue, doubtful, and bad loans) that operated before.

c. Introduction of the new loan classification system forced banks to upgrade their credit assessment and monitoring capabilities and in turn, to improve risk management capacities.

d. Capital adequacy targets were introduced in line with international standards. These targets necessitated a direct re-capitalization of the SOBs in 1998. RMB 270 billion were injected among all four banks. A second round of re-capitalization took place in 2004 and 2005 involving BOC, CCB and ICBC.

e. In November 1998, the People's Bank of China (PBOC) branch network was restructured along the lines of the US Federal Reserve system. Earlier, the PBOC had major branches in 27 provinces and 4 autonomous regions. Following the restructuring, it started operating from nine supra-regional offices, controlled from Beijing. The idea was to make the PBOC less vulnerable to provincial government pressure on provincial branches to expand bank-credit to fund local projects.

f. In 1998, the government undertook to introduce international accounting standards for banks and financial institutions along the line of reforms to the supervisory system.

g. In 1999 and 2000, a substantial component of NPLs was transferred from the balance sheets of the state-owned banks (SOBs) to asset management companies. The amount of debt transferred was around RMB1.4 trillion. Such transferred debt comprised mainly NPLs accumulated up-to 1995, much of which was associated with policy lending by the SOBs.

THE FIFTH STAGE OF BANKING REFORMS:

(a) DURING 2001-2007:

The banking reforms in this stage indicated a more determined effort to solve weaknesses in the banking sector at large, spurred on by the imminent implementation of China's WTO access commitments. Concluding 15 years of intense negotiations since 1986 when China applied to join the GATT, the predecessor of the WTO, China became a member of the WTO in November 2001. China entered into a bilateral market access agreement with United States as well as with European Union by May 2000. Most of the negotiations between China and its trade partners were about the opening up of China's service sector, and a wide-ranging agreement was reached covering various sectors including banking.

Against this backdrop and also keeping in view the evidences that earlier measures to resolve the bad debt problems of the banks were not having the desired results, the following additional financial reform measures were made on a number of fronts.

1. The State Council established the China Banking Regulatory Commission (CBRC) in April 2003 to take over supervisory and regulatory functions previously performed by PBOC. Having the objectives to protect consumers and depositors through prudential supervision of the banking sector, to maintain stability in the banking system, to enhance the competitiveness of banks, to encourage competition, to educate the public on the role of finance, and to eradicate financial crime -- the CBRC's main functions included: (a) formulating supervisory rules and regulations for the banking sector; (b) conducting on-site examinations and off-site surveillance; (c) penalizing non-compliance; (d) conducting fit-and-proper tests on senior bank management; (e) providing proposals to resolve problems in deposit taking institutions in consultation with the relevant regulators; and (f) administering supervisory boards of the major state-owned banking institutions.

2. The Law on Commercial Banks, the main legislation regulating the banking sector which was adopted by the NPC on 10th May 1995, was amended on 27th December 2003. Application procedures and requirements as well as prudential requirements for commercial banks were described in the Law on Commercial Banks. The Law on Regulation of and Supervision over the Banking Industry was effective from 1st February 2004. Moreover, under this Law, Commercial Banks may engage in some or all of the following business operations: taking deposits from the general public; granting short, medium and long term loans; handling domestic and foreign settlements; handling the acceptance and discounting of negotiable instruments; issuing financial bonds; acting as an agent for the issue, honoring, and underwriting of government bonds; buying and selling foreign exchange and acting as an agent for the purchase and sale of foreign exchange; engaging in the business of bank cards; providing letter of credit services and guarantee; acting as an agent for the receipt and payment of money, and acting as an insurance agent; providing safe deposit box services; and other business operations as approved by the banking regulatory authority under the State Council. According to this law, among other things, decisions regarding bank licenses must be made within six months from the date when the CBRC receives the application, within three months for any change or termination of a financial institution, and within 30 days for examining and approving the qualifications of senior officials of the financial institutions.

3. In 2003-2004, the Government used USD 45 billion of its foreign exchange reserves to partially bailout or in other words, to re-capitalize two SOCBs (Bank of China and China Construction Bank) as a prelude to a planned listing on the stock exchange over the following two years. The government created a state owned entity, Huijin Investment, to manage the Government's investment which was nearly one-tenth of its foreign exchange reserve holdings at that time. In March 2004, a special 'pilot scheme' was also announced for governance and supervision reforms for Bank of China (BOC) and China Construction Bank (CCB).

4. Efforts were also being made to gradually liberalize lending rates. Depending on the type of institution, lending in RMB was restricted to a maximum of 130 percent above the official benchmark interest rate until December 2003. In December 2003, the upper band on RMB lending was raised and consolidated at 170 percent of the benchmark rate, while the lower band was maintained at 90 percent. The upper band was raised from the previous ceiling of 150 percent to 200 percent of the benchmark rate for the Rural Credit Co-operatives (RCCs). In November-December 2004, the upper band was removed and the lower band was liberalized further.

5. In addition to the SOCBs, the government also put substantial efforts to address the problems of the Rural Credit Cooperatives (RCCs). In 2004, the government promulgated a number of measures including reforms of the ownership structure of the RCCs and efforts to improve corporate governance; changes in their management structure; and subsidies. A pilot program was also launched in 2003 in eight provinces to diversify ownership and to provide additional funding to RCCs. In 2004, the program was expanded to 21 provinces. In 2005, the authorities began efforts to restructure non-viable RCCs.

6. According to China's GATS schedule, foreign financial institutions with total assets of over USD 10 billion at the end of the year prior to application would be permitted to establish a subsidiary of a foreign bank or a foreign finance company or a Chinese-foreign joint bank or a Chinese-foreign joint finance company in China. In order to establish a branch in China, the foreign financial institution should have total assets of more than USD20 billion at the end of the year prior to applying. Furthermore, foreign financial institutions applying to engage in local currency business in China should have three years of business operation experience in China and required to be profitable for two consecutive years prior to applying. With regard to commercial presence, there are no geographic restrictions for conducting foreign currency business. For conducting local currency business, foreign investors were permitted in Shanghai, Shenzhen, Tianjin, and

Dalian upon China's accession to the WTO. The geographic coverage was gradually expanded to Guangzhou, Zhuhai, Qingdao, Nanjing, and Wuhan within a year following the accession i.e. by December 2002; to Jinan, Fuzhou, Chengdu, and Chongqing by December 2003; to Kunming, Beijing, and Xiamen by December 2004; and to Shantou, Ningbo, Shenyang, and Xi'an by December 2005.

7. On February 25, 2004, Hong Kong banks started accepting deposits in RMB – a further step towards making China's currency fully convertible.

8. Re-capitalization of SOCBs in China since 1998 amounted to over USD 93 billion. Big Four SOCBs were re-capitalized in August 1998 by the government through the issuance of over USD 33 billion in government bonds, which led to a more-than-doubling of their capital base. Between 2003 and 2005, another round of re-capitalization took place. During that period, the PBOC injected nearly USD 60 billion capital out of its foreign reserve into three of the Big Four SOCBs, namely, China Construction Bank, Bank of China, and Industrial and Commercial Bank of China. The Bank of Communications received a capital injection of nearly USD 4 billion in June 2004 through a transaction involving Huijin Investment Corporation Limited – a state owned Investment Company, the Ministry of Finance, the National Social Security Fund, and a foreign bank (HSBC) which acquired a 19.9 percent stake in the bank. Huijin subsequently also injected nearly USD 40 billion into the Agriculture Bank of China, and around USD 20 billion into the China Development Bank. Until end-2007, China's re-capitalization of banks represented the largest injection of fiscal or quasi-fiscal funds into any banking system in history.

9. Besides capital injection, restructuring has also been largely accomplished through the disposal of non-performing loans (NPLs), arguably one of the most important problems in the Chinese banking system. The Ministry of Finance established four asset management companies (AMCs), one for each of the Big Four SOCBs in order to deal with their NPLs. During 1999-2000, nearly USD 170 billion of NPLs were transferred

from the big four SOCBs to the AMCs. During 2004 and 2005, such transferred amount was nearly USD 146 billion. At the end of 2006, around USD 145 billion of the original transferred loans appeared to have been resolved, leaving large amount still on the banks. However, at end-July 2007, NPLs of all commercial banks amounted to nearly USD 153 billion (6.4percent of total loans) as per data provided by the authorities. According to independent estimates, NPL ratios might be higher if adjusted for the above-average loan growth in recent years.

10. These clean-up measures consisting of re-capitalization and NPL carve-outs were taken in preparation for the introduction of foreign strategic investors in Chinese banks and also for the subsequent listing of these banks in the stock markets. The strategy had also been adopted to diversify ownership, improve corporate governance and to facilitate transfers of know-how. Foreign strategic investors have not only acquired shares of the largest SOCBs, they have also been attracted to the smaller joint-stock and city commercial banks. By the end of 2006, 29 foreign financial institutions had invested a total amount of USD 19 billion in 21 Chinese commercial banks, of which USD 16 billion in the big four SOCBs. In all, at the end of 2006, the major SOCBs had raised nearly USD 47 billion.

11. In 2006, a key step was taken in the further opening-up of the banking sector in China. In November 2006, the Regulation on the Administration of Foreign-funded Banks was promulgated by the State council and it was followed by the CBRC's Rules for Implementing the Regulations on the Administration of Foreign-funded Banks. As a result, on and from December 11, 2006, geographic and customer restrictions on RMB business, as well as other non-prudential restrictions on foreign bank operations were lifted. By September 2007, six operational foreign-funded banks were allowed to conduct retail business, and nine foreign banks were in the process of converting branches into subsidiaries.

12. Improving corporate governance has also been a priority of reform in recent years. In May 2006, the CBRC issued

the Guideline on the Corporate Governance Reforms and Supervision of State-owned Commercial Banks and set up a quantitative benchmark based on seven parameters covering net return on total assets, net return on equity, and expense-revenue ratio (operational performance); asset quality (NPL ratios); and capital adequacy ratios, large exposure concentration, and coverage ratio of loan-loss provisions (prudential operations).

13. During 2005-2006, further reforms had also been introduced into rural credit co-operatives, including changes to the corporate structure and management. Accordingly, 27 provinces established integrated provincial credit co-operatives; Tianjin established a rural co-operative bank with separate legal entities at the municipal and county (district) level; and Beijing and Shanghai changed the Rural Credit Co-operatives into rural commercial banks.

14. The CBRC, as part of its effort to bolster the rural banking sector, launched a pilot program in 2006 creating three new type financial institutions – microloan companies, rural mutual credit cooperatives (RMCC), and village/township banks (VTB) – which are specifically aimed at expanding financial services in the rural areas. In 2007, the programme was rolled out nationwide as the success of this initiative exceeded expectations.

15. The reform of the postal system and the establishment of the China Postal Savings Bank (CPSB) marked a significant development in the banking sector. On 31st December 2006, the CPSB was established as a wholly owned subsidiary of the China Postal Group. At the beginning of 2007, it had a deposit base of nearly USD 207 billion with over 36,000 outlets throughout the country, and more than two thirds in rural areas. Although CPSB is supervised as a commercial bank by the CBRC, it used the national postal network for its operations and was also expected to provide basic financial services including retail and fee-based services to town and village communities and rural residents.

16. The CBRC, as part of its policy to support rural areas, relaxed the market entry policy for banking institutions in

rural areas as per the Guidelines on Adjusting the Market-entry Threshold for the Banking Institutions in Rural Area of December 2006. As a result, existing commercial banks and rural co-operative banks were being encouraged to set up branches in under-banked rural areas; while the investors (including foreign) were also being encouraged to invest in rural financial services by establishing village and township banks, lending rural companies, and funding rural co-operatives. The creation of CPSB and the reform of the Agricultural Bank were part of this policy. Other regulatory initiatives in 2006 included the Guidelines on Rural Co-operative Financial Institutions' Lending to small enterprises, the Guidelines on Corporate Group Loans by Rural co-operative Financial Institutions, and the Guidelines on Banking Institutions Carrying out Agency Business in Rural Areas towards promoting innovation in the rural banking sector.

17. The Rules Governing Capital Adequacy of Commercial Banks which were introduced in February 2004, were being revised in July 2007 by the CBRC. They were based on the 1988 Basel Capital Accord (Basel 1). Chinese authorities expressed its intention to implement the new Basel Capital Accord (Basel 11) gradually.

18. In an effort to enhance risk management and security standards in the banking sector, measures dealing with electronic banking were introduced in 2006. All banking Institutions applying to establish an e-banking business were required to have sound internal control and risk management system as outlined by the CBRC Administrative Measures on Electronic Banking Business and the Guidelines on Electronic Banking Security Evaluation of January 2006. These guidelines also stipulated that they should not have any major faults relating to their primary information management and operations processing systems in the year prior to application..

(b) DURING 2008 - 2010:

1. In terms of reform, re-capitalization of the Agricultural Bank took place in late 2008 and a process of its conversion

into a shareholding bank started in 2009. In July 2010, Agricultural Bank got listed in Shanghai and Hong Kong. This was followed by Everbright Bank's IPO on 18th August 2010. Twenty-two new locally incorporated banks, four new subsidiaries, and six new branches of foreign banks were approved in 2008; and 16 new locally incorporated banks, 4 new subsidiaries, and 3 new branches of foreign banks were approved in 2009.

2. The disposal of NPLs also improved during the period. The ratio of NPLs to total loans of major commercial banks was at 2.4 percent at the end of 2008, compared with 7.0 percent at the end of first quarter 2007. In end-2008, the NPL ratio of rural commercial banks was somewhat higher, at 3.9 percent. NPLs of the state-owned commercial banks (SOCBs) amounted to Y1,115 billion (about 8.1 percent of total loans outstanding) at the end of 2007; they had fallen to Y420.8 billion (about 2.8 percent of total loans outstanding) at the end of 2008. NPLs of the state-owned commercial banks amounted to Y364.2 billion (1.86 percent of total loans outstanding) at the end of third quarter of 2009. Chinese authorities maintained that the five largest SOCBs did not transfer any NPLs to asset management companies in 2008 or 2009.

3. The main legislations regulating the banking sector which include the Law of the People's Bank of China, the Law on Commercial Banks, and the Law on Regulation and Supervision of the Banking sector, have not been changed since 2008. The main regulatory and supervisory responsibilities of CBRC have remained largely unchanged. PBOC also retained its broad supervisory powers, beyond the macro-prudential control of the financial sector. .

4. As mentioned earlier, the establishment of a commercial bank requires CBRC approval and the issuance of an operating license. The licensing requirements and procedures, including the expansion of domestic branch-network, remained unchanged during the period. Also, there has been no change during 2008-2010 in the minimum registered capital requirement to establish banks or to maintain capital adequacy ratio (CAR). Commercial banks required specific

authorization to deal with some services, such as derivatives and wealth management, in accordance with prudential principles and depending on the capacity of individual bank. More specifically, separate licenses were required for all these services. However, authorized commercial banks having obtained the relevant business qualification from the CBRC could conduct investments on behalf of both domestic institutions and China's residents, in certain financial products outside China.

5. Since 2008, China has been gradually promoting the establishment of fund management companies owned by commercial banks on a trial basis. The pilot program in 2008 on 'comprehensive operations' by commercial banks included: a pilot program on equity investment by commercial banks in insurance companies; allowing some commercial banks to establish subsidiaries to engage in financial leasing; and a pilot program for commercial banks to establish fund management companies. The China Minsheng Bank Corp., Merchant Bank of China, Shanghai Pudong Development Bank, and five large state-owned banks obtained approval to establish fund management companies in 2008.

6. As part of China's ongoing reform of the regulatory environment for banking, CBRC issued rules aimed at strengthening supervision of bank-lending for fixed assets and project financing after the outbreak of the global financial crisis in 2008. The existing Rules Governing Capital Adequacy of Commercial Banks, based on the 1988 Basel Capital Accord (Basel 1), were issued in 2007. Large commercial banks that play an active role in other countries' or regions' financial markets, and whose overseas businesses constitute a substantial share of their total business activities were to start implementing Basel 11 at the end of 2010 and no later than end of 2013. Other commercial banks, including foreign bank subsidiaries, were free to apply Basel II on a voluntary basis.

7. From 1st January 2008, taxation of the banking system changed significantly upon entry into force of the Enterprise Income Tax Law. A unified tax rate of 25 percent has been applied

to domestic banks as well as operational foreign-funded banks. The business tax rate is 5 percent, and is assessed on gross income from interest and fees, minus income from financial institutions and agency fees on government bonds. Banks are also allowed to deduct 1 percent of the balance of loans from income before taxation. Additionally, all write-off loans can be deducted before taxation.

8. At the FX Week China Congress in Beijing on May 20, 2009, CBRC outlined reforms that need to occur before the Yuan can reach reserve currency status by 2020. Guanping Zhang, deputy director-general at the CBRC highlighted the development of the capital markets and banking industry, which have lagged behind the country's GDP growth in recent years. He said, despite the steady progress seen in the swaps, forward and spot markets, far more liquidity is needed, while the product range should extend to plain vanilla FX options.

9. Pursuant to the promulgation of the Guideline on Risk Management of Annexation Loan by Commercial Banks on 9th December 2008, commercial banks that met the standards in the Guideline were allowed to engage in annexation loan operations relating to financing merger and acquisition transactions. However, as stipulated in the guideline, a commercial bank must design its business process for annexation loans and internal control system before starting such operations. The bank could formally start the operation after reporting to the supervisory authority. Chinese-foreign joint venture banks and wholly foreign-funded banks could engage in the same business operations as domestic commercial banks, both in local and foreign currency. Operational wholly foreign-funded banks willing to engage in local currency business must have had their business in China for at least three years, and should have been profitable for two consecutive years, prior to application.

10. The PBOC and other administrative authorities encouraged commercial banks to adapt their lending to specific borrowers in light of relevant government policies. Interest rates were subject to benchmarks. Commercial banks were able to charge lending rates above the benchmark, but not lower than 90

percent of the benchmark; and also could offer deposit rates below, but not above, the benchmark. Market-based interest rates were allowed in the money and bond markets. In that case also, commercial banks could charge lending rates above the benchmark, but not below 90 percent of the benchmark; and could offer deposit rates below, but not above the benchmark. Mortgage loans were subject to a different policy.

11. There were no restrictions on interest rates for foreign-currency-denominated deposits over USD3 million, foreign-currency-dominated loans, and foreign-currency-denominated deposits of less than USD3 million with a maturity of more than one year.

12. The Circular of the State Administration of Foreign Exchange on Issues Concerning Foreign Exchange Administration of Overseas Lending Granted by Domestic Enterprises entered into force on 1st August 2009, and broadened the financing sources of overseas lending by domestic enterprises. The domestic enterprises could decide the timing and number of overseas lending transactions at their discretion within the total approved amount of lending.

13. In 2009, the CBRC rolled out a pilot program allowing listed banks to start trading of bonds on the stock exchanges. While bonds had become an important part of banks' treasury activities, banks were also turning to bond issuances to replenish capital. In 2009, as the CBRC reported, 32 percent of the capital raised by commercial banks was through the issuance of bonds compared to only 17 percent in 2008. Banks were no longer permitted to provide guarantees for corporate bonds issuances.

14. In July 2009, the CBRC launched a pilot program for establishing consumer finance companies following the issuance of Rules Governing Pilot Consumer Finance Companies. The program was initially limited to four cities, namely, Beijing, Tianjin, Shanghai, and Chengdu. Nationwide roll out of the program which is expected in the near future, would certainly help the existing consumer finance companies to expand on a national basis and also to reach the scales of economy necessary for sustained profitability.

15. Since China did not have a deposit insurance scheme, Chinese authorities were considering the possibility of designing such a scheme.
16. The China Postal Savings Bank, inaugurated in March 2007, was recognized as a community bank or rural bank with extensive outlets across the nation, especially in the countryside. It was also subject to the same laws, regulations, and rules, as well as enterprise income tax, as other banks. In November 2009, deposits at the China Postal Savings Bank amounted to Y2.5 trillion.

Before the reforms started, financing constituted a closed circuit. During that period, under the mono-banking system funds were collected from state bodies and transferred to other state bodies. All financing was controlled by the state and all financing took place through the banking system. Most of the funds were funneled to the SOEs and state projects and a small portion went to agriculture. At the time of writing this book, after more than thirty years of reform, the role of the PBOC, the structure of the banking sector and the pattern of financing have been changed in a big way. However, in spite of the significant improvements since 1979, the structure of China's financial sector is still unbalanced, with a significant predominance of banks over other types of financial institutions. In terms of market capitalization, the Chinese stock market was relatively small, although the situation seems to be improving. Commercial banks' dominance of the sector is evident from their share of total assets in the financial system. It is also evident that the banking sector plays a predominant role as a source of financing for the non-financial sector.

The high degree of state-ownership and control is yet another notable feature of China's banking sector. The Big Four State-owned commercial banks, the three policy banks, the Postal Savings Bank, credit co-operatives, and even non-bank financial companies are either state-owned or state-controlled. Only foreign banks can be said to be truly non-state-owned or controlled. In addition, assets of the banking sector are also highly concentrated. The Big Four Banks account for more than 54 percent of total banking assets.

In course of reform, the role of PBOC has greatly changed. SOBs have taken over the commercial banking activities of PBOC. Three policy banks have undertaken policy-lending job. PBOC does not have the responsibility of bank supervision also. That responsibility is vested with CBRC, which is also the body that now overseas the reform and regulation of the banking sector, allowing the PBOC to focus on monetary policy. Although the State Council is ultimately responsible for key monetary policy decisions, the People's Bank of China Act (of 1995) guaranteed the PBOC a high degree of independence. In other words, the PBOC has partial independence. The PBOC is one of the departments under the State Council. Interest rate and exchange rate policy requires to be approved by the State Council. The PBOC decides other monetary policy independently. The PBOC has used this independence to change gradually from direct to indirect controls. In the recent period, the PBOC utilizes a combination of central bank loans, rediscounting, open market operations, interest rates, exchange rates and lending policy to control the macro-economy. Stability of the exchange rate and GDP growth have become the target of the monetary policy. The method of determining the value of Yuan has also been altered in the recent past to a currency basket system. Such currency basket contains as revealed by Zhou Xiaochuan, ex-governor of the PBOC, eleven currencies: the US dollar, Yen, Euro, Korean Won, Singapore Dollar, Malaysian Ringgit, Pound sterling, Russian Rouble, Australian dollar, Thai Baht, and Canadian dollar. The new system works as follows: In response to a fall in the US dollar relative to the other basket currencies, the PBOC would let the Yuan rise against the dollar if the overall value of the basket is to be held steady. However, being a managed float currency, the value of Yuan could be altered against the basket at the discretion of the PBOC.

China's banking sector has grown rapidly in recent years. Total banking assets grew at an average of around 17 percent annually between 2003 and 2006. Total bank assets were Y43.95 trillion by the end of 2006. By the end of 2009, as the CBRC reported, the total foreign and domestic currency assets of Chinese financial institutions rose 26.3 percent year on year to Y 78.8 trillion (USD11.54 trillion). The CBRC also reported that combined liabilities rose 26.8 percent in end-2009 from the same period in 2008, and up 80 percent from three years ago. In fact, the Chinese banking system is now virtually the same size as the U.S. commercial banking system. By comparison, at year-end 2009, assets of U.S. commercial banks were USD11.7 trillion. Assets of state-owned commercial banks in China were Y40.1trillion by the end of 2009, up 25.9 percent year on year, while those of joint-stock commercial banks were Y11.8 trillion, up 33.7 percent year on year. At the end of 2009, liabilities of China's state-owned commercial banks were Y37.9 trillion, up 26.9 percent year on year, while those of joint-stock commercial banks were Y11.2 trillion, up 34.1 percent year on year. The bad loan ratio among major commercial banks (state-owned commercial banks and joint-stock commercial banks) fell to 1.59 percent, down 0.86 percentage points from the beginning of 2009.

At the end of December 2009, China's banking sector comprised of, among others, 3 policy banks, 5 state-owned commercial banks, 14 joint-stock commercial banks, 143 city commercial banks, 11 urban credit co-operatives, 3,056 rural credit co-operatives, 43 rural commercial banks, 196 rural co-operative banks, 148 village/township banks (VTBs), 16 rural mutual credit cooperatives (RMCC), and 8 microloan companies. Market share of China's total banking business by Chinese banking institutions were: (a) top five state-owned banks - 51percent, (b) joint stock banks - 14 percent, (c) policy banks - 9 percent, (d) city commercial banks - 7 percent, (e) credit cooperatives and rural banks - 11 percent, (f) postal savings bank - 4 percent, (g) foreign banks - 2 percent, (h) others which included village and township banks, lending companies, mutual credit cooperatives, trust companies, financial leasing companies, auto finance companies, and money brokerage firms - 2 percent.

Low profitability still remains one of the main weaknesses in China's banking sector. However, after the recent set of reforms, the income portfolios of banks have improved and become more diversified as banks have expanded their product offerings. At the end of 2009, fee-based income accounted for an increased percentage of banks' total income compared to previous years. In addition, capital adequacy levels have also improved, mainly because of reform, restructuring, domestic and overseas initial public offerings (IPOs), the presence of institutional investors, and an increase in the issuance of capital instruments.

According to the terms of China's WTO accession agreements, as of January 1, 2007, foreign commercial banks gained the right to carry out a full range of domestic and foreign currency financial services on an equal footing with their domestic counterparts, without restriction. This change had been billed as the greatest challenge yet to the Mainland banking system. However, given the attention paid to foreign banks' entry during this period, as of December 2010, so far there is no evidence whatsoever of a foreign onslaught. In fact, one can generally find a striking lack of enthusiasm of the foreign banks for a big push into China by setting up new flagship branches in every city and township across the nation. In fact, no foreign bank is planning this now and it is suspected that no one will be planning such in the coming minimum 3 to 4 years period as well. Competing on an equal footing with domestic institutions is an apparently appealing prospect. However, the Chinese government maintains fairly onerous restrictions on new expansion for most banks, foreign or not, in terms of high capital requirements, branch-by-branch licensing, and approvals, which make it difficult to expand rapidly in a short period of time. As of end-2009, 33 banks from 13 countries and regions were locally incorporated which maintained 199 branches; and 194 banks from 46 countries and regions set up 229 representative offices in China. In addition, there were 2 wholly foreign-owned finance companies, 2 Sino-foreign joint venture banks (having 6 branches and one subsidiary), and 95 foreign bank branches established by 71 banks from 24 countries and regions. Moreover, 49 foreign bank branches and 32 locally incorporated foreign banks were approved to engage in the RMB businesses and 54 foreign banking institutions were authorized to engage in derivatives trading activities. As of end-2009, the total assets of foreign banking institutions operating in China, increased by 0.33 percent year-on-year to RMB1.349 trillion, accounting for 1.71 percent of total banking assets in China. Also their total liabilities increased to RMB 1.182 trillion, accounting for 1.59 percent of the total. In 2009, their profits amounted to RMB 6.446 billion. The total capital of foreign banking institutions operating in China increased in 2009 by 16.33 percent year-on-year to RMB 143.51 billion, accounting for 5.86 percent of total paid-in capital of all banking institutions in China. At the end of 2009, their NPL balance was standing at RMB 6.18 billion and the NPL ratio was at 0.85 percent.)

Fundamentally, the mainland economy is already over-banked. M2 i.e. the sum of cash, and demand and time deposits in the banking system is nearly 200 percent of GDP in China, twice as high as the Asian average, three to four times the average level in the US and the EU, and even a higher ratio than other Latin American countries like Brazil and Mexico. It is understood that foreign banks' earnings would come mostly from non-traditional areas such as wealth management, non-interest income and payments systems – not from corporate lending or retail deposit taking. Because, most of these deposits are held in the provinces where state-owned banks or majority state-owned banks have a branch network numbering tens of thousands in place. Therefore, it is difficult as well as unwise for foreign banks to consider pursuing a national strategy. Even in the major urban areas where foreign banks are already making inroads into trade and international services, core banking markets are already very crowded. In fact, Big Four State-owned commercial banks, joint-stock commercial banks and a host of city-level credit institutions are very aggressive in the cities in competing for market share. In this backdrop, what we precisely observe that foreign banks, so far, have taken a strategy not to depend on aggressive new branch openings, but instead to buy into existing players in the financial market. Of course, foreign banks are still establishing flagship branches in a few major cities, but in dollar terms the amount of funds spent on mergers and acquisitions during the period was already much greater than capital inflows into new branches. Therefore, in fact, as of end-2010, one can observe that there is no real additional pressure on the Chinese banking system because of the foreign banks' entry in China. Additionally, foreign strategic stakes in domestic institutions don't add to competitive pressures in any meaningful way. Instead, they simply represent existing capacity changing hands. Therefore, the fact remains that WTO liberalization does not really imply any significant change in the structure of the financial system in China so far.

After more than 30 years of reform in the Chinese financial sector and considerable institutional changes, we can conclude the following:

a) China did a clean-up program of historic proportion in its banking sector. In the mid-1990s, it is estimated that non-performing loan (NPL) ratios in financial system were as high as 60 percent of outstanding loan assets. The first round of clean-up program came in 1998, when the Chinese government decided to carry out re-capitalization of China's Big Four State banks with roughly USD200 billion of financing. This funding was made through quasi-fiscal bond issuance by state-owned asset management companies (AMCs) and direct injections by the Ministry of finance with limited support by the central bank. This program was successful in reducing the NPL ratio of the financial system from 60 percent to supposedly under 40 percent. Analysts routinely put the ratio at 35 percent or higher even at the end of 2001. In 2002-2004, China erupted into another period of over-investment and excessive lending, with property developers and infrastructure projects pushing credit growth rates up into double-digit levels. Perhaps, 25 percent of loans given in these years should be counted as non-performing. This implied a cumulative figure for excessive NPLs of roughly USD850 billion or one-third of all net credit extended over the 1991-2004 period. This made China an absolute record-holder among major countries for bad debt creation. However, since 2003 the Chinese government embarked on a clean-up program of historic proportion and by the end of 2007, NPLs of state-owned commercial banks (SOCBs) amounted to Y1,115 billion i.e. about 8.1 percent of total loans outstanding; they had fallen to Y420.8 billion i.e. about 2.8 percent of total loans outstanding at the end of 2008. At the end of third quarter of 2009, these NPLs amounted to Y364.2 billion i.e. nearly 1.86 percent of total loans outstanding. The Chinese authorities maintained that the five largest SOCBs did not transfer any NPLs to asset management companies in 2008 and 2009. It is estimated that between end-2003 and end-2007, as much as USD400 billion was allocated in support for the state banking system. Compared to the previous bailout program in 1998, this round was far more unorthodox in terms of instruments and financing. The Ministry of Finance played a significant role by providing direct resources and tax relief, but most of the funding came from PBOC in the form of outright transfer of official foreign exchange reserves, domestic currency refinance credit and flow earnings of the banks themselves. Such a reduction on the size of China's NPL problem could be marked as one of the largest cumulative clean-up in banking history. It must be acknowledged that bank clean-up and re-capitalization were themselves the key to further progress in financial system restructuring. Since then, both the banking system and the Chinese economy witnessed very significant changes that make it very unlikely that financial institutions will ever see high double-digit NPL ratio again.

b) Bank performance has also been improved significantly. Strong improvements are evident in terms of macro-economic regulation, banking supervision, internal operational controls, and even in the quality of borrowers in the system.

c) Until 2005, the financial system was mainly bank-based. Most saving was collected through the banking system and most capital raised by Chinese enterprises were bank loans. Comparatively, very little finance was raised through the corporate bond market or the new equity issue market. These organized financial markets were having a very limited role in allocating pricing signals. The vast majority of listed companies were majority state-owned, while only a handful of corporate bonds were traded. Moreover, until 2005, the financial system in China was fundamentally static. All levels of the banking system were mainly state-dominated. As stated earlier, the three state-owned policy banks and the four large nation-wide majority state-owned commercial banks used to make nearly 62 percent of total loans. The smaller regional banks and main banks of the SOEs which were owned either by local government or SOEs themselves used to make nearly 20 percent of total loans. The credit co-operatives, postal savings banks and non-bank financial institutions – all used to have shareholding ties with central, state, or local government or were controlled by SOEs. In this respect, the landmark decision to begin privatizing financial institutions came at the right time. During 2005 – mid2010, foreign banks and other overseas investors had purchased equity stakes in nearly two dozen Chinese financial institutions. Also the 2005 – mid 2010 period had seen a number of public listings on domestic and overseas markets. All the big four state-owned commercial banks were listed during this period in China as well as in overseas. By early 2007, the Bank of China and the China Construction Bank were nearly 25 percent foreign-owned and Industrial and Commercial Bank of China was not far behind at 18 percent. This scenario would have been unthinkable only a few years before. In 2010, the remaining large state bank i.e. the Agricultural Bank of China also got listed. The Chinese government still imposes a 25 percent foreign ownership cap in any Chinese bank, with no more than 20 percent by a single outside investor. After the unprecedented global financial crisis of 2008, it is unlikely that these ceilings are going to be relaxed significantly over the coming few years. However, things have been changed considerably in terms of different other aspects. By the end of 2009, the state sector accounted for a much lower share of total bank borrowing than it did even in the end of 2003. In other words, there had been a continued decline of SOEs' share to total bank borrowings, supposedly as low as 25 percent to 30 percent in 2009. The rising share of non-state firms including privatized former SOEs, the introduction of mortgage lending and consumer finance and gaining of market share by smaller, more aggressive commercial banks less susceptible to government pressure, are mainly the reasons for the difference in scenarios between 1997-1998 and 2007-2010 bank-loan portfolio.

Both local governments and central government still put direct pressure on financial institutions to lend to favored projects and sectors. But now they do so in a very different way. Commercial banks are also no longer treated like treasury arms of the State Planning Commission or the Ministry of Finance. In reality, banks now face a more balanced set of state pressures. In one hand, local governments push for higher lending to their commercial projects, and on the other hand, key central government agencies push for better credit practices and transparency. The quality of state borrowers has also improved significantly. The Chinese government undertook the historically unprecedented task of downsizing the state sector by closing unprofitable SOEs. Such downsizing was not a cosmetic one. Tens of thousand of unprofitable and non-viable SOEs were dissolved. More than 25 million workers of those SOEs were out of job. Consequentially, the remaining viable state industrial sector started earning higher profit. In essence, today when a Chinese SOE comes to borrow from a bank, the borrower is generally profitable on a current cash-flow basis.

d) During the period, financial innovations for diversified products and services took place in China in a big way. The CBRC also continued to improve its regulation on financial innovations by taking into account the lessons learnt from the latest international economic and financial scenario. Financial innovations took place mostly through (i) fast growth of bankcard business; (ii) solid growth of wealth management business; (iii) and robust growth of other banking services. Financial market innovations also took place during the period through engagement in bond trading as well as through gold futures trading.

As of end-2009, a total of 2.03 billion bankcards were issued by the banking institutions in China, a year-on-year growth of 14 percent. The total transactions volume of these bankcards was RMB162.8 trillion, representing a year-on-year growth of 46 percent. In 2009, among all bankcards, the number of credit cards were 165 million, and the transaction volume was RMB3.5 trillion including RMB1.9 trillion in consumption volume, accounted for 15.2 percent of the total retail sales (as compared to 3.1 percent in 2006), and for 5.7 percent of the GDP (as compared to 1.1 percent in 2006). Therefore, it is evident that the bankcard business is playing an increasingly important role in boosting consumption in China. As of end-2009, a total of 5,728 wealth management products by 98 commercial banks were launched with a total book balance of RMB974.4 billion. While the diversified wealth management products enabled Chinese investors to enjoy more flexibility in managing their assets and liabilities, they also brought to banks another solid source of revenue. Presently, while Chinese banks are increasingly exploring various innovative products and services for their household and corporate customers, they have also started serving as agencies for investment funds, insurance companies, and fee-charging entities. In 2009, a total of 34.25 billion electronic transactions of various kinds took place, marking a year-on-year growth of 49.34 percent. The number of e-banking transactions reached 13.71 billion in 2009 with more than 197 million e-banking customers, and having a total volume of RMB 325.96 trillion. In order to promote commercial banks' cross-sector operations in a prudent manner, in 2009, the CBRC proceeded with the pilot program of permitting selected banks to invest in insurance companies and trust companies, and set up financial leasing companies and consumer finance companies.

Finally, it can be concluded that at the time of this writing, the outlook of the Chinese financial system is much more stable and optimistic. However, there are some strong challenges ahead. Going forward, Chinese banks will surely face lower balance-sheet growth, lower interest rate margins, and rising competition from other financing sources. In other words, in the coming years, government's decisions in connection with capital account liberalization, interest rate liberalization, weakening of implicit guarantees, and more opening-up of alternative financing channels will have their influence on the profitability and attractiveness of the financial sector in general.

B. CIVIL SERVICE REFORMS IN CHINA

During the post-WTO accession era in China, the country's steady march toward a more market-based economy has eliminated thousands of state-owned enterprises and reduced the government's role in economic decision-making. Nevertheless, government management is still in place in all important sectors of the economy and the government's role as regulator is as significant as ever.

During more than three decades of reform, China's leaders have sought to increase the capacity and legitimacy of the state partly through civil service reform. China's political leaders have always attempted to make the bureaucracy more merit-based with an ever-improving governance through increasing accountability, predictability, transparency, participation, and efficiency and effectiveness accompanied by civil service reform. There have been continuous attempts to improve governance focusing on reform of the bureaucracy as the civil service plays a central role in China's political system. Good governance requires a strong civil service that operates within the law, is open and transparent, encourages the community to participate and finally is accountable to the political executives. For a high capacity and legitimate government, an efficient and effective civil service is also crucial.

The Chinese government has taken significant steps to reform the country's civil service system since 1993. It is still evolving. Service in the public sector carries considerable prestige in China. Central ministries are staffed by many highly competent and committed employees and conform in many respects to the required level of performance. While in less developed parts of the country, where the civil service is viewed as an employer of last resort, the quality and capacity of the civil service is considerably lower; more developed parts of the country are able to support a more efficient and effective public service.

In 2002, the public sector employed an estimated 70 million people. About half of the public sector workforce worked in government. The remaining half i.e. around 35 million people worked in state-owned enterprises. The total number of public employees has declined in recent years mainly as a result of the contraction of the state-owned enterprise sector. However, employment in Public Service Units (PSUs, in sectors such as education, public health, research etc.) has been relatively steady over the past decade.

China's civil service regulations define the scope of civil servants in China. This definition is broader in some aspects and less so in others compared to the definitions of the civil service commonly used overseas. Unlike in many western countries, the civil service in China includes the most senior politicians such as the Premier, Vice Premier, State Councilors, Ministers and Provincial Governors, Vice ministers and Vice governors, etc. – the leadership positions (Article 9, Ministry of Personnel, 1996). White collar government employees at both central and local levels, including towns and townships, are also civil servants. However, the scope of the Chinese civil service is also less inclusive than the scope of civil services in many western countries. The Chinese civil service definition excludes (1) all manual workers employed by the government; and (2) the employees of all public service units. Public service units i.e. schools, universities, hospitals, research institutes, radio and TV stations, government publishers and cultural organizations etc. have their own personnel management arrangements. Public service units are also funded through a variety of mechanisms. PSUs like schools, universities and hospitals are mostly dependant on the State for funding while others use to turn to economic enterprises and are expected to pay their own way.

Chinese Communist Party plays an extensive role in the management of personnel in all public organizations, including the civil service. The predominant principle of personnel management in China is that the Party manages cadres and civil servants are a part of cadres. One member of the seven-member Standing Committee of the Politburo, the highest organ of political power in China, is responsible for overseeing 'organization and personnel work' which also includes the management of the civil service. The CPC Central Committee has entrusted policy making for the civil service to its Organization Department. The State Council's Ministry of Personnel implements the policy. The Party and the government are tightly linked. By all accounts, Party and government bodies in charge of the civil service work seamlessly together. Party's Central Inspection Discipline Commission, the government's Ministry of Supervision and the People's Procuratorate handle the anti-corruption work. Civil servants recruited into human resources departments of all government bodies including the most specialized and technical, must be members of the Communist Party. Also all civil servants recruited into positions in the Ministry of Personnel are Communist Party members. The Party exercises control over appointments of public personnel and also dismissals of civil servants to leading positions including the lowest level leadership positions such as deputy section head. Essentially, the CPC is having the final authority to approve these personnel movements.

Hierarchy of China's civil service is organized into 12 levels ranging from Premier at the top to clerical staff at the bottom. The civil service in China is also structured into 15 grades that are determined by level of responsibility and degree of difficulty of the task and the civil servant's capability, political integrity, practical success, work performance, and work record. In developed capitalist democracies, political positions are not usually part of the civil service. However, in China, political positions are considered to be civil service jobs. In terms of grade, China's civil service is divided into leadership and non-leadership positions.

Paramount leader Deng Xiaoping put reform of the leadership system as early as 1980 on the Party's agenda. Deng realized that the cadre system which was borrowed from the Soviet Union in the 1950s and under which the Party managed all cadres according to uniform rules and regulations, had outlived its usefulness. The positions of managers, administrators and professionals became more specialized during the course of economic development and liberalization. The CPC, accordingly, designed a management system of cadres working as civil servants, that took into account both the non-market nature of much of government work and the existence of newly emerging labor and wage markets. The CPC also sought to reform personnel management of public service units to make them more market friendly. These reforms were designed to improve the efficiency and effectiveness of the civil service in order to boost its quality and integrity as well as to improve its performance. The gradual professionalization of the PRC government reflects a dynamic interplay of social, economic and political factors. In order to respond to the massive social changes during last 30 years, the government has made major efforts to enhance its legitimacy and governing capability by promoting efficiency, meritocracy, transparency, and reducing secrecy and favoritism. Civil service reform efforts have accelerated in recent years as the government has become increasingly composed of and scrutinized by a well educated and vocal population with ever-growing as well as ever-diverging interests.

Open and competitive selection processes, mechanisms that appropriately utilize talent, ensuring that all employees are appropriately trained, setting and communicating performance standards, evaluating performance and feeding back the results of the evaluation to employees, and linking performance to rewards – characterize high capacity civil service systems. The extent to which the Chinese civil service approaches the above model could be viewed in its endeavors in terms of recruitment, promotion, performance assessment, staff development and training and institutionalization.

ISSUES OF CIVIL SERVICE REFORMS:

Recruitment: In recent years, China's recruitment procedure have become more merit-based. As an important milestone, in the movement toward a transparent and merit-based recruitment process under clearly defined criteria, China re-instated the civil service examination for all junior positions in 1993. Now-a-days, the civil service examination attracts huge numbers of applicants. About 775,000 people took the examination in 2008 competing for roughly 13,500 positions. The number of test-takers was 21 percent higher over 2007. The largest number of applicants were mostly interested for the positions in the Ministry of Commerce, Ministry of Foreign Affairs, and National Development and Reform Commission.

Promotion: Not only recruitment, promotion decisions too, are now getting less influenced by personal rapport. Civil service officials are now subject to more professional evaluation processes as they move upward. Chinese Communist Party Organization Department Document, 2006 entitled the Method of Comprehensive Cadre Evaluation that embodies requirements of the scientific development concept, emphasizes a more comprehensive assessment process by introducing a limited use of peer review and public-opinion polling. This can be considered a significant move from the requirements of the PRC's early years when class background and ideological leanings were the main criteria for promotion. However, membership of the Chinese Communist Party is still an important requisite. Most senior level officials whether of municipal, provincial, or central government, are members of the CCP. But there are few notable exceptions which include Health Minister Chen Zhu and Science and Technology Minister Wan Gang. The central committee of the Chinese Communist Party introduced in 2002 the Regulations on Selecting and Appointing Party and Government Leading Cadres. These regulations allow public consultation in the promotion process for leadership positions. Government agencies, under the regulation, should announce decisions on newly promoted leaders throughout the relevant government agency, offering peers an opportunity to object to the promotion. However, public rejection and rescinding of promotion decisions are rare as the opportunity for peer review occurs only after a decision has been announced. Introduction of 'public bidding' procedure for vacant leadership positions is another important change which was also introduced in 2002. It allows any interested candidate to apply for a new vacancy. This procedure is being used infrequently and also mainly for mid-level positions. For senior level appointments at the local level, more rigorous standards are being observed. For example, for leadership posts at the county-chief level or higher, candidates must have completed a bachelor degree, specified training program at the CCP Central Committee School, and experience in two posts at a level of leadership immediately lower than the one applied for.

Performance assessment: The Chinese Communist Party Organization Department Document,2006 modified the cadre evaluation system significantly. In the early days of economic reform, job performance was judged largely on economic performance as defined by gross domestic product (GDP) growth. Growth still counts today, but less than in the past. Since 2006, evaluation system is linked directly to President Hu Jintao's scientific development concept which advocates comprehensive, sustainable economic and social development towards more balanced and economic growth. The 2006 Organization Department Document outlined a six-step evaluation process that included democratic nomination and assessment, public opinion polling, analysis of achievements, interviews, and comprehensive evaluation. The 2006 Document also clearly stipulates that GDP growth is no longer the sole criteria for performance. On the contrary, the Document defines excellent performance by providing a long list of considerations which include not only GDP growth but fiscal revenue, per capita income, education, worker-safety, social welfare, family planning, employment, conservation of land and natural resources, environmental protection, and investment in scientific and technological development. More recently, a green GDP standard has been another manifestation of Hu Jintao's emphasis on smart growth.

Training and staff development: Before China's reform era began and even in the early days of reform, the government training was largely confined to political and ideological indoctrination. While training for government officials is not a new phenomenon, it has become more systematic as of today. The Chinese Communist Party Central Committee has made training guidelines more detailed, practical, and quantified by introducing cadre education and training in 2006 Trial Regulations. Though training for government officials still include political education, it is far more likely to focus on providing officials with the skills they need to perform their duties effectively. These days, the CCP schools which play a key role in educating future leaders, increasingly focus on economics, business, management, and not alone the ideology. The CCP schools also routinely invite foreign experts as guest lecturers. In 2008, the State Administration of Civil Service was created to narrow the quality-gap between officials from inland and coastal provinces. They issued guidelines encouraging deputy division directors and higher officials from inland provinces to attend training in China's more developed coastal regions.

Now-a-days, more civil servants also receive training overseas. Since 2007, China has sent around 40,000 officials each year for training overseas. Denmark, France, Germany, Great Britain, the United States, and Singapore are the most common destinations. About 90 percent of the cadres at the ministerial level have had some training abroad. Overseas training ranges from a one-week course to a year-long degree. These trainings are occasionally provided at prestigious schools such as John F. Kennedy School of Government of Harvard University and the University of London's London school of Economics and Political Science. Besides improving the quality of officials, overseas training is used as incentives to retain qualified officials who may otherwise be tempted to move into the private sector with higher salaries. At times, the brain drain had been acute. From 1999 to 2001, MOFCOM lost 72.8 percent of all new recruits within the first three years of employment. Not only MOFCOM, many ministries faced the similar scenario. The 2006 Civil Service Law also helped to address this problem by allowing more flexibility in salary levels.

In the reform process, the average educational level of government officials today is considerably higher than it was thirty years ago. About 9.3 percent of central-level officials had a junior college degree or higher in 1978, such number reached more than 90 percent in 2008. This is surely due to the vast expansion of China's tertiary education sector and to the conscious effort of the Chinese government to enhance the educational background and overall quality of officials. Since 2007, to participate in the national civil service examination, the government requires the candidates to hold at least junior college degrees. The government also recruits many of its officials straight out of college. In that case, they require to compete against Foreign Invested Enterprises and local companies that often offer far more attractive salaries.

Today's civil servants also have more varied academic and professional backgrounds. Previously, candidates often lacked expertise or experience on jobs or issues outside the direct scope of the relevant ministry that recruited them. But now, the government attracts candidates with a broader range of professional experience from a wider range of backgrounds, including those with work experience in state-owned enterprises, law firms, and multinational corporations.

Level of professional outlook: An effective public personnel system is based on the rule of law that defines the rights and obligations of both employers and employees. Such a system facilitates predictability which is necessary for managing expectations. Systems that value the rule of law, accelerate reform becoming institutionalized. During the last 30 years, China's political system as a whole has become increasingly institutionalized. During the past few years, institutional restraints on China's leaders have also increased. A new higher level of institutionalization especially at the top is evident in the CPC's management of the leadership succession in 2002-2003. Of-course, such an environment is conducive for further institutionalization of China's civil service reforms.

China's civil service reforms must become a norm and a matter of routine in order to be implemented successfully. While some reforms in China have become institutionalized, some reforms have failed to live up to their expectations. The existence of numerous loopholes in the competitive selection process had undermined the reforms to a certain extent. Moreover, China's civil service reform, despite its advances, has not spread evenly across the country. Especially, at the lower local-government levels, less developed provinces have lagged behind coastal provinces in terms of government professionalization. Local-government training budgets in less-developed regions are considerably smaller than budgets in most coastal areas. In order to create jobs for local residents, poorer provinces still tend to recruit most of their officials from outside the civil service examination system. However, in totality, civil service reform in China has been able to create a scenario as of today where government officials are better educated, better traveled, more efficient, and more accountable.

Conclusion:

China is adopting many features from western civil service. But its system still retains important Chinese characteristics. Notably,

China's civil service remains loyal to the Chinese Communist Party as the CCP's Organization Department plays the leading role in the assessment of officials. Additionally, traditional Chinese concepts like hierarchy, face, and the importance of personal relationship still apply even when new breed of Chinese civil servants are already taking many positions. Although capacity of the civil service and the performance of the government bodies have improved in the past 15 years, such improvement will possibly be more visible and accessible with the following: (a) making personnel policies and practices as transparent as possible to enhance legitimacy and accountability and also to attract the best possible candidates to work for the government civil service; (b) reducing and gradually eliminating the practice of permitting entry to the civil service outside the established mechanisms; (c) ensuring by the authorities that the rotation system for officials is implemented as widely as possible and that leading officials, their offices, and their families are being audited on a regular basis to reduce corruption; (d) maintaining the salaries for civil servants at a competitive level and also ensuring that the pay-level surveys are being carried out regularly, their results are published and the recommendations are implemented; and (e) improving human resources in the poor areas through training and transfers of experienced officials from more developed areas.

C. CHINA'S STOCK MARKET REFORMS – AN OVERVIEW

China's stock market can be traced back to 1869 when the Shanghai Stock exchange was first set up by foreign firms during late Qing Dynasty. The first Chinese-operated stock exchange, namely, the Beijing Securities Exchange was established in 1918. These stock exchanges never played an important role in the economy as the stock market was basically oriented towards agriculture and family operations. In 1949, the two stock exchanges were closed after the establishment of the People's Republic of China as the stock exchanges were considered as speculation place, a capitalist phenomenon inconsistent with the communist ideology. Since then for about 30 years, the stock market disappeared in China. Since 1978, as the reform and the opening up of the economy progressed, China's financial system witnessed concomitant changes including the spontaneous development of share-like securities in the 1980s, the share-fever of the late 1980s and the formal setting-up of the Chinese securities exchanges.

THE SHARE-HOLDING REFORM, 1983 – 1988:

Under the influence of the opening up of the economy and economic reform policies, villages began establishing township and village enterprises (TVEs). Since capital requirements for these newly established TVEs were of such amount which a single family or even a village could meet, experimentation began with a co-operative shareholding structure. Such shareholding co-operative system proved successful very soon and became quite common in raising capital. The Baoan County Joint Investment Company, a Shenzhen town and village enterprise, became the first Chinese enterprise to issue share certificates to the public after the establishment of the People's republic of China. In July 1984, the Beijing Tianqiao Department Store was the first state-owned enterprise restructured as a company limited by shares.

Also the Shanghai Feile Acoustics Company issued irredeemable shares to the public in November,1984. These early shareholding transactions were unregulated but were symbolic for the future development that was gathering momentum. In 1986, Shenzhen government was the first to standardize procedures relating to the restructuring of enterprises into shareholding companies. On the national level also, the shareholding reforms were strongly supported by officials within the State Commission for Restructuring the Economic Structure (SCORES). During 1984 to 1989 period, many shareholding companies were set up all over the country and issued nearly Y 3.8 billion worth of shares. However, relatively little new capital was raised by issuance of stocks, as 70-80 percent of the shares came from conversion of existing state assets. Additionally, less than 2 percent were public issues to general investors and most of the stocks were issued to related companies or employees of the related companies. Initially, individual investors were not interested. The fact that shares could appreciate (or depreciate) with the economic performance of the share issuing company or even simply as a result of supply and demand, was not understandable as well as believable to them. In the initial period of spontaneous fund raising through the issuance of a wide variety of non-standardized shares, the share issuing companies had to pay dividends at fixed rates in excess of the bank deposit rate to entice individual investors. Some share issuing companies even promised to refund shareholders on demand. Thus, at that time, the shares were having a strong resemblance to debt securities, and the investors tended to hold rather than trade.

From the mid-1980s, issuance of equity shares became increasingly frequent and also such shares began to change hands through non-market channels. Shengyang was the first city to initiate formal over the counter (OTC) trading in August 1986 and was followed by Shanghai in September of the same year. In October 1986, the Shenzhen government also approved formal establishment of OTC trading at various financial institutions. There were nine financial institutions conducting OTC trading by the end of 1988. In April 1988, some Trust and Investment companies were allowed to establish OTC trading operations in Shanghai with a primary focus on treasury bonds. Eight trading counters were established in Shanghai in the following twelve months with central government supervision. Thus, Shanghai became the central government sponsored market for debt securities, while others were mostly informal.

DEVELOPMENTS DURING 1989 - 1990:

In March 1989, Shenzhen Development Bank, China's first financial institution limited by shares, announced a dividend based on its 1988 results. That dividend announcement marked a significant turning point in China's share market. Investors who bought the bank's shares for about Y20 in 1988, enjoyed a profit several times their original investment in 1989. Just before the Tiananmen Square incident in June 1989, the price of the bank's share soared in OTC trading to Y120 and ended the year at Y90. Prices for the publicly traded Shenzhen companies continued to rise rapidly and funds were pouring in from all across China throughout the summer of 1990. This tendency gradually extended to Shanghai also. By the end of 1990, total securities were valued at over Y200 billion. During this period, some shares traded at 20 times, 50 times, and even 100 times their face value.

In the aftermath of such craziness of share market, many measures were taken to cool the markets, including daily price movement limits, increased transaction taxes, and ownership-transfer stamp duties. The State-council announced restrictions in May1990 on the share-market experiment including its limitation to the state sector. The State-council also designated Shenzhen and Shanghai as the only officially recognized OTC markets. These measures virtually led to a collapse of the market in late 1990.

DEVELOPMENTS DURING END-1990 to 1991:

Given the official backlash against share reforms, only few companies had been listed on the OTCs in Shanghai and Shenzhen. However, these OTCs were inconvenient to use and also were difficult for local authorities to regulate. In the aftermath of Tiananmen Square incident in June 1989, one would have expected proposals to establish stock-exchanges to have been put on hold or even totally stopped. However, the opposite happened. In Beijing, a group of reformists working at the SCORES, Ministry of Finance (MOF), People's Bank Of China (PBOC) had been preparing plans for a stock exchange for quite some time. In Shanghai, Zhu Rongji, then party secretary and mayor of Shanghai, viewed that the stock exchange would be useful in his attempts to develop Pudong, Shanghai's new investment zone in the east of the city. The paramount leader Deng Xiao Ping also offered his support for the establishment of stock exchanges in China. The stock-market was a useful symbol of Deng's own reform agenda. Finally, a formal decision was passed to proceed with the establishment of the Shanghai and Shenzhen security exchanges with an intention to provide a formal venue for security trading in two administrative areas well under the control of the central government. Eventually, the Shanghai Stock exchange (SSE) was opened in December 1990 and the Shenzhen Stock exchange (SZSE) in February 1991. At the beginning, SSE and SZSE were called the Shanghai securities exchange and the Shenzhen securities exchange. Later Shanghai securities exchange unilaterally change its English name as 'Shanghai Stock exchange' in its effort to establish itself as an independent identity. Later Shenzhen also followed the same practice. Obviously, both exchanges were heavily promoted by their local municipal governments and had the approval of PBOC, the nominal regulator. OTC trading continued in other cities of the country, particularly in Shengyang, Wuhan and Tianjin, each one sought to establish a formal and recognized stock exchange but was not successful.

The establishment and start of functioning of Shanghai and Shenzhen stock exchanges were extremely important events in China's reform history. Two main types of shares, namely 'A' shares and 'B' shares, have been traded from the very beginning of the establishment of China's two stock exchanges. 'A' shares are common stock issued by mainland Chinese companies, traded and priced in Chinese Renminbi (RMB), bought and sold by domestic investors only, and listed in either of the two stock-exchanges. 'A' share market was launched in 1990. On the other-hand, 'B' shares are issued by mainland Chinese companies, carry a face value in Renminbi (RMB) but are traded in foreign currencies, notably, US dollars in Shanghai and HK dollars in Shenzhen, bought and sold exclusively by foreigners, and listed in either of the two stock exchanges. 'B' share market was launched in 1992. However, trading of 'B' shares was always thin and the capitalization was also small. Ultimately, 'B' shares have been made available for trading by domestic investors since February 2001. There are also several other types of shares besides the 'A' and 'B' shares. Since 1993, 'H' shares have been floated by Chinese companies, traded on the Hong Kong Stock exchange and priced in HK dollars. 'N' shares are American depository receipts (ADRs), issued by Chinese companies, traded on the New York Stock exchange and priced in US dollars. 'S' shares have been issued by Chinese companies, traded on the Singapore Stock exchange and priced in Singapore dollars.

DEVELOPMENTS DURING 1992 – 1996:

The process of development during 1992-1996 can be divided into two episodes: (1) the establishment of the State Council Securities Committee (SCSC) and the Chinese Securities Regulatory Commission (CSRC) with the eventual domination of the latter towards developing a regulatory structure within which the stock market could operate efficiently and in a manner consistent with the overall economic policy of the Chinese government; and (2) the role of the banks in stock-trading.

Prior to 1992, the overall stock market was quite small and relatively unregulated. Though extensive regulations were drafted in 1989-1990, they were never implemented fully. However, in early 1992, Deng Xiaoping undertook a historical trip to the southern province of Guangdong where his support for the economic liberalization in general and for the share-holding system in particular triggered an explosion of share-trading activity both domestically and internationally. Meanwhile, Chinese economy also recorded a very high rate of growth, real GDP of 12.8 percent growth in 1992, 13.4 percent in 1993, and 11.8 percent in 1994. Of course, such a fast growth was also accompanied by high rates of inflation which even peaked at 21.7 percent at the end of 1994. Those positive developments dramatically and significantly boosted trading in both the Shanghai and Shenzhen stock exchanges. On 16th February,1993, the Shanghai Stock exchange composite index peaked at 1558.98 compared to its base value of 100 in December 1990. Similarly, the SZSE composite index was 359.44 on 22nd February 1993 compared to its base value of 100 in April 1991.

After Deng's positive comments on China's stock market in early 1992, all related regulations and provisional measures were brought forward including the standard opinion and the corporate law towards imposing a standard framework on shareholding companies and the shares offered to the investors. The Standard Opinion and the Corporate Law define a number of different types of shares , namely, state shares, legal person shares, individual shares and foreign capital shares, reflecting the ownership characteristics of the assets contributed by the promoters of or investors in the new company. The Standard Opinion and the Corporate Law define state shares as shares held by governmental agencies or authorized institutions on behalf of the state. State shares include: (a) the shares converted from the net assets of SOEs which have been transformed into joint share-holding companies; (b) the shares purchased by government departments, although initially issued by companies; and (c) the shares initially issued by companies and purchased by the investment companies, assets-management companies, and/or economic entity companies authorized to invest on behalf of the state. Trading of state shares are not allowed on an open market. Legal person shares are the shares of a joint stock company owned by another company or institution with a legal person status. The owners of legal person shares can be four types, such as state-owned, collective enterprises, private enterprises, foreign invested enterprises, and institutional legal person. Trading and transfer of legal person shares are also restricted. Individual shares refer to shares that may only be owned by Chinese citizens and it is officially recognized as 'A' shares. 'A' shares can be freely traded and transferred in domestic markets. Foreign capital shares refer to 'B' shares and overseas-listed shares i.e. 'H' shares, 'N' shares, 'S' shares and so on.

Following the emergence of the share-holding system, policy makers were concerned about the trading of state shares and legal person shares. They were afraid that such trading might erode the state's position of majority shareholding in state-owned enterprises. Policy makers were also concerned that the trading of state shares and legal-person shares would undermine the state's holding of its assets with the result of the loss of their dominant position in the national economy. Therefore, the Provisional Measures on the Regulation of State-owned Shares Issued by Companies Limited by shares was enacted in 1994. This law confirmed the predominance of the socialist public ownership system in the shareholding by maintaining the controlling position of the state-owned share rights. This policy, during the period of conversion of enterprises into shareholding companies, resulted in the expected dominant position of state-shares with state-owned legal-person shares occupying a second, and the third, non-controlling, minority position of individual shares. Obviously, a hierarchy had been created in the primary markets for shares of the state, legal-person, and individuals. The government also designed accordingly a peculiar secondary market aimed at maintaining the same hierarchy of classes of shares created in the primary market.

With the rapid growth of stock markets, restrictions on trading state and legal-person shares have had various adverse effects. The enormous amount of non-tradable shares restricted the function of stock markets as a mechanism to evaluate the management performance of listed companies and posed a serious threat to the secondary market.

The role of People's Bank of China (PBOC) in the securities market also became a serious concern to the Chinese government. Before October 1992, PBOC was not a real central bank and it was responsible for all aspects of the regulation and administration of China's financial system, broadly defined to include the traditional financial sector, insurance sector, and securities. The PBOC with other state-owned banks, the Ministry of Finance, and local finance departments were also permitted to establish their securities agencies to participate indirectly in the securities market. Thus, the PBOC was both the regulator of and an active participant in the securities market. However, the policy makers realized very soon that the PBOC as an institution was unsuitable as market regulator. So, in October1992, the Chinese Securities Regulatory

Commission (CSRC) and the State Council Securities Committee (SCSC) were set up. The SCSC was a ministry-level government organization and was authorized by the State Council to enforce security laws. During the period October1992 – mid1998, SCSC was the immediate superior of the CSRC. The CSRC was a quasi-government, vice-ministry entity and was designed to be the implementing apparatus for the SCSC. The CSRC eventually became the dominant regulatory body. In essence, we observed the establishment and consolidation of authority of Chinese Securities Regulatory Commission (CSRC) over the securities and future markets during 1992-1993. In 1996, the CSRC took the full regulatory control over the Shanghai Stock exchange and Shenzhen Stock exchange.

DEVELOPMENTS DURING 1997 – 1999:

The State Council Securities Committee (SCSC) was dissolved in mid-1998, and in 1999, the Chinese Securities Regulatory Commission (CSRC) finally became a full ministry-level organization empowered by the Securities Law of 1999.

During 1997-1999 period, with the regulatory framework in place, the Chinese stock market experienced fluctuations which are not uncommon to stock markets. Stocks listed on the Hong Kong Stock exchange for companies which are having significant interests in mainland China were called Red Chips. Chinese stock market also witnessed brief Red Chips craze associated with the handover of Hong Kong by Britain to China in mid-1997 and the subsequent deflation and again revival of stable market until the end of the century.

From the second quarter of 1996, Chinese stock market began to recover. By mid-December1996, the average stock price rose by 120 percent in Shanghai and by over 300 percent in Shenzhen. In real terms, on 11th December1996, the Shanghai index reached a high of 1258.69 and the Shenzhen index was up to 473.02 – the highest in three years with a daily turnover of Y37.4 billion. However, due to the disclosure of illicit speculation by the Shenzhen Development Bank, Chinese stock market witnessed a 'Black Monday' on 16th December, 1996. Essentially, Chinese government took strict measures to punish the offenders and also to ease the overheating of the market. As a result, stock prices fell dramatically both in Shanghai and Shenzhen stock exchanges. Within a week's time, both 'A' share indexes fell by approximately 40 percent. However, the lull was short-lived. Trading in the Red Chip stocks became increasingly frenzied as the Hong Kong handover of July 1997 approached. There were 16 initial public offerings (IPOs) of such companies in 1997 alone. Consequentially, both Shanghai and Shenzhen Stock exchanges experienced a sustained upturn in stock prices for about a year with some downward correction in the weeks leading up to the handover on July1, 1997.

China was not totally immune from the Asian financial crisis of 1997. Its export growth shrank drastically and growth in committed foreign direct investment turned negative in 1998 for the first time since the early 1990s. Number of new equity issues also decreased significantly. There were only 106 new issues domestically and two internationally in 1998, compared to nearly 200 in the previous two years. During the first six months of 1999, there were only 39 'A' share issues, no 'B' share issue, and one issue of 'H' share.

During the early second quarter of 1999, Chinese government announced some stimulatory measures which were initiated one after another. Such measures included allowing state-owned enterprises to enter the securities market, imposing a tax on interest earnings from savings accounts, expansion of brokerage capitalization, and also allowing up to 5 percent of the assets of 25 insurance companies to enter into the securities market. The Securities Law also took effect on July 1, 1999. All these measures boosted the market sentiment. People's Daily proclaimed in its editorial on 15th June, 1999 that the upturn reflected a fundamental improvement in the overall economy.

DEVELOPMENTS DURING 2000 - 2002:

As mentioned earlier, by second-half of 1999 Chinese economy was showing a concrete sign of recovery. Exports increased and deflationary pressures were reduced. Large and medium-sized state enterprises were mostly showing signs of recovery. Retail prices were starting to pick up. Above all, on 16th November,

1999, China and the United States reached their historic trade agreement on China's WTO entry. All these positive developments obviously created a strong basis for a medium-to-long term rally of China's stocks market, especially for the shares of textiles, clothing, and high-tech industries which were likely to benefit from China's WTO entry. As a result, in early 2000, China's stocks market rebounded strongly expecting more market-boosting policies and sound economic growth in 2000. Several stimulatory measures were also taken in late 2000 which caused further surges in China's stocks market. Such measures include the establishment of a venture capital market in both the stock exchanges and the entry of pension funds into the stock market. During 2000, market capitalization increased from Y2647.117 to Y4809.094 billion and also the index of both the stock exchanges rose strongly. While the international securities markets fell at the start of 2001, China's stock market continued rising due to investor confidence. In addition, on 19th February 2001, Chinese government made an announcement allowing domestic investors to take part into the 'B' share market. Consequentially, household savings in foreign currencies of around USD75 billion was made available for stock investment. Obviously, since then 'B' shares prices surged. As a total effect of increased investor sentiment and increased 'B' shares trading, China's stock market steadily went upward to reach its highest point of 2245.43 in Shanghai and 664.85 in Shenzhen by mid-June, 2001.

However, such strong share-price growth started to reverse from July 2001. Chinese government announced its intention to reduce the percentage and quantity of state-shares in order to solve the non-tradable share problem (refer to the section titled Developments during 1992-1996 and also for 2002-2009). The government also announced its plan to complete the sales of state-shares over a five-year period with a total of Y251.51 billion worth of shares releasing to the market. As soon as the reduction of state-shares started in July 2001, prices on the Shanghai stock market plummeted to about 1514.86 points on 22nd October 2001 from its peak of 2245.43 in June 2001. The Shenzhen composite index also sank to 439.36 points on 22nd October 2001 from a high of 664.85 on mid-June 2001. The 'B' share market influenced by the collapse of 'A' share market, also experienced a sharp downward adjustment during this period.

Not only state-share reduction was implemented, rigid supervision measures and tougher rules to de-list debt-ridden firms were also introduced in 2001 which added to the bearish performance of the stock market in the second half of 2001. On 16th November 2001, the Ministry of Finance announced a stamp duty cut from 0.4 percent to 0.2 percent which triggered some upward trend in the following few months. In order to replenish China's under-funded social welfare system, the CSRC announced on 12th May 2002, that the state-share reduction scheme would be resumed in a new form. However, obviously stock market reacted adversely as investor confidence collapsed. The controversial state-share reduction scheme was suspended again in June 2002 arguing that the complicated plan would require a lengthy study before regulators could devise a comprehensive plan widely accepted by the markets. The government also mentioned that it had other ways to raise money for the social welfare system. Such announcement naturally boosted the market and initiated record volume of trade and daily turnover throughout June and July 2002. But from the beginning of August 2002, both the stock exchanges index fell steeply because of poor corporate results, frequent initial public offerings and especially a lack of policy incentives.

DEVELOPMENTS DURING 2002 - 2009:

The reform of state-owned enterprises' (SOEs) ownership, corporate governance, and financing mechanisms has accompanied the recent development of China's stock markets. China's stock markets remained moribund in the early part of the new millennium, trending downward from 2001 to 2004 amid the fall-out from a 2001 government plan to sell-off a large portion of its shareholdings in China's state-owned enterprises.

Since May 2004, Shenzhen Stock Exchange has had a NASDAQ- type small and medium-sized enterprise (SME) board which is open to growing SMEs with outstanding businesses, and to innovative high-tech start-ups. It is run semi-independently with its own index, trade code, and supervisory system. One hundred and two companies were listed on the SME board, raising a total amount of Y18 billion as at 31st December 2006. Market capitalization of the SME board amounted to Y201.53 billion, accounting for 11.3 percent of total market capitalization of the Shenzhen Stock Exchange.

Both Shanghai and Shenzhen Stock Exchanges, since their inception, have been among the world's fastest growing equity markets. More than 1,400 companies are listed on the two exchanges (about 840 companies at Shanghai and nearly 560 companies at Shenzhen), with a combined market capitalization of USD 4,475 billion at end 2007. These two stock markets together are now Asia's second largest, after Japan, and roughly on par with the Hong Kong SAR. While the performances of both the markets were poor between 2000 and 2004, there were impressive gains between 2005 and 2006 when market capitalization increased by 220.6 percent in Shanghai, and by 97.1 percent in Shenzhen, and also between 2006 and 2007 when market capitalization increased by 302.7 percent in Shanghai and by 244.2 percent in Shenzhen. Growth also continued in the first half of 2008. Total market capitalization increased from 36 percent of GDP in 2003 (the lowest level in the decade) to around 43 percent of GDP in 2006. Tradable stock market capitalization was much lower, amounting to only 12 percent in 2005. At the time of writing, authorities claimed that upon completion of the reform all corporate stocks have already been transformed to tradable shares, subject to certain 'lock-up' period during which major shareholders cannot sell shares.

The fast expansion of the equity market was the result of an unprecedented stock boom, which gave rise to various malpractices. In 2007, the CSRC reportedly fined 16 listed companies and two brokerage firms, warned more than 150 individuals, and banned 46 people from entering the stock market.

The Chinese stock market used to be characterized by a split-share structure, with large volumes of non-tradable state-owned and legal person shares. At end 2004, as per official information, non-tradable shares of listed companies accounted for 64 percent of total capital stock, and state-owned shares accounted for 74 percent of non-tradable shares. In other words, only around one-third of shares listed in both Shanghai and Shenzhen stock exchanges were subject to trading. Therefore, public investors were being put in an inferior position relative to the holders of non-tradable shares in making corporate policies and disposing of firms' profits and assets. After an experimental reform on the basis of the Circular on Issues concerning the Pilot Reform of the split Share Structure Reform of Listed Companies, and the Circular on Issues concerning the Pilot Reform of the Split Share Structure Reform of the Second Batch of Listed Companies, the CSRC issued the Administrative Measures on the Split Shares Structure Reform of Listed Companies on 4th September 2005. According to the authorities, the reform transformed non-tradable shares held by major shareholders in a listed company to tradable shares. Now, major shareholders, after a lock-up period defined in the respective reform plans, could decide whether to sell their shares in the secondary market or to continue to hold them. As a result of this split-share structure reform, investors' confidence resumed in 2006. After a downturn of more than four years, the fund balance of client transaction settlements at the end of 2006 exceeded Y1 trillion, and the number of investors increased by 5.13 million. The market value of tradable shares also reached Y2.5 trillion by the end of 2006. In addition, as an effect of initiated reform, there were currently three types of shares: A shares, B shares, and overseas listed shares. China's stock market had only few institutional investors. As per KPMG report of 2006, there were about 50 active fund managers, fewer insurers, and almost no pension funds in a market dominated by retail investors. Out of the 76.5 million accounts opened with the China Securities Depository and Clearing Corporation (CSDCC), only 380,000 were of institutional investors. Nonetheless, according to the authorities, market capitalization by mutual funds, commercial insurance institutions, social security funds, enterprise annuity, and qualified foreign institutional investors has been expanding rapidly, and as at the end of 2008, it was accounting for more than 40 percent of all tradable shares.

During 2006-2007, China's local share prices soared with the Shanghai A-share index doubling in 2006 and rising by a further 96 percent in 2007. Chinese banks witnessed unprecedented slowing down of savings account growth in China during 2006-2007. The

People's Bank of China cited enthusiasm for the stock market as the major reason for the decline in deposits as People's Daily reported on January 5, 2007. Chinese savings deposits fell by RMB7.6 billion during October2006 alone. Such type of outright decline was registered for a number of months in 2006. This trend continued into 2007 also. In fact, China Securities journal, 2007 reported that over the first four months of 2007, more than RMB70 billion was transferred from savings accounts into the stock market. This represented a sharp change from past practice, when most Chinese citizens had ignored the stock market and simply deposited their money in savings accounts. In fact, one rationale for the PBOC's successive interest rate hikes during 2007 was to slow the flow of funds from households and corporations into the stock market.

The rise in investor sentiment also coincided with rising discounts attached by foreign investors to the share prices of Chinese companies. As mentioned earlier, in addition to the A-share market for domestic Chinese investors, B-shares for foreign investors had been trading in US dollars in Shanghai and in Hong Kong dollars in Shenzhen since 1992. Many Chinese firms have also obtained listings in offshore markets – in the form of H-shares listed in Hong Kong and as American Depository Receipts (ADRs) in the United States. Like the B-shares, H-shares were technically equivalent to A-shares. Again, like the B-shares and H-shares, the ADRs remained theoretically equivalent to A-shares and had the same ownership rights. While it was not unusual for B-shares, H-shares and ADRs to trade at a discount to the company's corresponding A-shares, these discounts became wider during 2006-2007. Such wider discounts suggested that the Chinese companies were either being increasingly undervalued by foreign investors or increasingly overvalued by the domestic investors.

In 2008, A-share index of both the Stock Exchanges declined dramatically, more so than most other world markets. In October 2008, after the outburst of the world economic and financial crisis, the markets registered a more than 75 percent drop relative to its peak above 6000 in October 2007. The losses continued even after direct Chinese government intervention began in September 2008, with shares purchases by China's Sovereign Wealth Fund in the big state-owned commercial banks. Investor sentiment generally trended downward as the market fell just as it had trended up with the market in 2006-2007. The sharp stock market falls after mid-January 2008 had caused significant losses to the investment returns on the part of the consumers, with a sharp month-on-month drop in cumulative 12 month investment returns only next to the drop seen in November 2007. In 2008, after the full-blown global economic and financial crisis hit the world, Chinese government introduced some strong stimulus package in order to ease the credit crunch initiated by the banks. China Securities Regulatory Commission also suspended all new IPO listings from end-September 2008 in order to combat the crisis situation and also to partially avoid the adverse reflection of people's sentiment towards stock market.

However, by August 2009, the fact that China's stock markets were up over 70 percent showed that the country had been prospering and was banking on itself into the years ahead. By mid-2009, there had been a lot of interest and excitement surrounding China's decision to allow companies to list after a lull of almost a year. In July2009, the Shenzhen stock market welcomed its first initial public offering (IPO) after nearly a one-year pause. There were several hundred companies in the process of receiving final approval from the China Securities Regulatory Commission. So, many more IPOs were likely in Shenzhen and the much larger Shanghai bourse, making China the world's most active market for new listings in 2009-2010.

Nevertheless, concerns were growing about possible asset bubbles forming since the explosion of lending in China. It was also feared that the IPOs may drain a lot of liquidity from the market. It was presumed that too many firms would not be allowed to come onto the market at the same time as capital stability has been the primary goal of Chinese regulators. Regulators would certainly suspend IPO activity again should they deem this sector overheated. The amount of new lending in the first half of 2009 was equal to approximately half of China's GDP in the same period. Continued upward momentum in Chinese stocks illustrated how money had been flying through the economy even as much of the world remained in the grip of recession. Essentially, inflationary pressures at home and those imported from abroad are likely to rise as the economy continues to grow. However, until end-January 2010, the People's Bank of China did not signal any reversal of its loose monetary policy aimed at stimulating growth, mentioning only that it may need to fine-tune the program. Even such a remark of fine-tuning the stimulus package on early August 2009 by the authority immediately created panic amongst the investors. We observed that panic-stricken investors chose to take profit as they rushed to dump shares fearing that monetary tightening was imminent as Beijing fine-tunes policies. A consensus opinion among analysts is that the A-share market had re-entered bubble territory when excessive liquidity sent stock prices soaring.

While Beijing's four trillion Yuan (HKD 4.54 trillion) stimulus package unveiled late 2008 has had an impact on the economy with the GDP of mainland growing 7.1 percent in the first half of 2009, a big part of that stimulus package went into the stock market. A researcher with the China's State Council's Research Development Center, mentioned earlier that nearly 1.2 trillion Yuan of bank loans were illegally invested in stocks. However, China's chief economic planner, on March 6,2010, dismissed allegations that part of the mainland's massive stimulus funds had been used to speculate in the country's red-hot property market. 'Not a cent' in the program had entered the property market or been used for land purchases , Zhang Ping , minister in charge of the powerful National Development and Reform Commission , said on the sidelines of the annual meeting of the National People's Congress on March 6, 2010. While investors were pinning their hopes on a constant inflow of capital, bank loans in July 2009 were valued atY356 billion, only 25 percent of the amount in June 2009, a sign that bank credit could dry up in near future.

In essence, the trend for an economic turnaround is becoming more obvious, but the recovery is not on a solid footing yet. The mainland's trade improvement has been very fragile considering the uncertainties faced by the world economy. In 2009, exports fell 16 percent from the previous year, dragging down gross domestic product growth by 3.9 percent and putting more than 10 million people out of work. However, exports had been improving since late 2009 and grew 17.7 percent in December 2009, 21 percent in January 2010 and 45.7 percent in February 2010 year-on-year basis. Still taking account of the high un-employment rate and low savings in some countries which were hit hard by the financial crisis, a solid recovery in world's consumption and China's exports to return to pre-financial crisis levels will take at least two to three years. Notably, China's trade surplus also dropped 50.2 percent in the first two months of 2010 from the same period a year ago – proving that China was contributing to balanced world trade instead of emphasizing only on exports. Under these circumstances, a further drop in the stock market could easily be expected. But it would not be severe. More rightly, fluctuations would continue to dominate the market.

D. CHINA'S HEALTHCARE REFORMS AND LONG-TERM CARE FINANCING

The People's Republic of China has achieved significant improvement in healthcare for its population since 1949. During the past two decades, there has been a spectacular increase in life expectancy in China. There has also been a significant as well as gradual fall in the infant mortality rate. In 1993, infant mortality came down to 22 deaths per 1000 live births compared to 250 deaths per 1000 live births in 1973. During this period, the average life expectancy increased from 35 to 69 years. In 1998, China's life expectancy reached 71 and is expected to be above 75 in 2010.

Despite the improvement in health for the general masses, China's health-care system is still having flaws. Even today - after 30 years of economic reform, Chinese citizens clamor for rapid improvement in the accessibility and affordability of healthcare. However, China reached a turning point when it released the new health-care reform plan in early April, 2009. This reform plan has important implications not for just China's healthcare sector but also for the country's economic development. Because, as soon as Chinese citizens stop worrying that sickness means impoverishment, there will be less precautionary saving and a greater readiness to spend. In this way, healthcare reform plan can become a milestone in terms of support of a sustained consumption boom in China.

In early April 2009, China released two health-care reform documents. The first, the State Council's Opinions on Deepening Healthcare System Reform (Framework Plan), is a broad document that sets the reform framework through 2020. The second, for immediate priorities in healthcare system reform, the Ministry of Health's Implementation Plan 2009-2011 provides a more detailed roadmap for the next three years. Four major programs are involved for the implementation of the plan: Expansion of the three main existing medical insurance schemes, establishment of an essential drug system, improvement of primary care infrastructure and the pilot reform of public hospitals.

The first major program is the universal coverage of basic medical insurance. China's government aims to extend each of the three main medical insurance schemes to provide coverage to 90 percent of the population by 2011. Particularly, the Urban Employed Basic Medical Insurance Scheme will be expanded to cover students, migrant rural workers, temporary contract workers, and also retirees from bankrupted and closed-down enterprises, in addition to the urban employed. The government is expected to raise subsidies in 2010 for health insurance premiums to Y120 (USD18.00) per participant in the Urban Resident Basic Medical Insurance as well as New Rural Co-operative Medical Insurance Schemes, which together cover 900 million people. Moreover, the service scope, reimbursement level, and maximum amounts payable of the schemes will gradually be raised in order to narrow the huge differences in benefits provided by the various schemes. Eventually, China will gradually integrate the three main medical insurance schemes to accommodate population mobility. In the process, medical insurance handling bodies will directly negotiate with healthcare providers to contain costs. Direct settlement system between the Medical Insurance handling bodies and healthcare providers will also be created.

The second major program for the implementation plan of China's healthcare reform is the establishment of an essential drug system. Chinese government will publish a national essential drug list (NEDL) containing 400-700 items with many low-cost generics and traditional Chinese medicines. Provincial governments will be responsible for procurement and distribution. The central government will guide prices. For drug procurement and drug distribution, provincial governments will run open tenders in their respective region. The tenders will be supposedly open to private and foreign participants in order to have fair competition. Respective provincial government may replace up-to 10 percent of the drugs on the NEDL to tackle diseases that are more prevalent in their locality. As mentioned earlier, purchasing prices of all drugs on the NEDL will be fixed within central government guided retail prices. Grassroots healthcare providers which include county hospitals, township health centers, village clinics in rural areas, community health centers and community health service stations in urban areas, may not levy a surcharge on drug sales and they may store and retail only drugs on the NEDL. All other healthcare providers will be encouraged to use drugs on the NEDL as their primary choice drug. The government will also require all healthcare providers and retail pharmacies to store and retail drugs on the NEDL. Basic medical insurance will cover prescriptions of drugs on the NEDL at a much higher reimbursement level than non-essential drugs. In course of time, the NEDL is expected to largely define the drug market in all but the urban hospitals.

The third major program for the implementation plan of China's healthcare reform is to improve primary care infrastructure. China will construct and renovate county hospitals and health centers. China will also train and rotate healthcare professionals. In order to improve the quality of China's grassroots healthcare professionals, a training program will be conducted covering 360,000 healthcare professionals for township health centers, 160,000 for community health centers, and 1.4 million for village clinics. Medical graduates who choose to work in township health centers will be given subsidy in their university fees and student loans. Doctors in urban hospitals will earn promotions only if they have practicing exposure at-least for one year in rural regions. In addition, urban hospitals must support county hospitals on a long-term basis to transfer expertise. In order to strengthen the primary care system, patients will be referred to hospitals only if they have secondary or tertiary care needs. Otherwise, patients will be encouraged to visit health centers as a first point of consultation, or to receive visits from mobile medical teams. The health centers will essentially ensure the affordability of their primary care services by using appropriate equipment, techniques and essential medicines towards improving accessibility.

The fourth and final major program of the implementation plan of China's healthcare reform is the pilot reform of public hospitals. Under this program, the government will attempt to improve the governance of public hospitals and gradually reform their revenue structure. The Chinese government will introduce various community-level programs and also will launch a new television station for health education to strengthen the prevention and control of diseases. In order to strengthen infant and elderly care, those younger than 3 and older than 65 years will be entitled to regular examinations. Pregnant women will receive prenatal and postnatal check-ups. The national immunization program and the prevention and control of HIV/AIDS program will be continued. New programs which include the provision of folic acid for pregnant women to help prevent birth defects and supplementary vaccination against hepatitis B for those under 15 years, will be launched. In essence, China will continue the existing as well as launch new major public health programs to prevent and/or control major diseases.

China's plans to make healthcare accessible and affordable to its vast population may offer significant potential for companies that can provide low-cost medical products and services. However, once the reforms get underway, opportunities for multinational healthcare companies will likely remain open around drugs, devices, and services offered in Grade 3 hospitals which provide comprehensive medical services, including clinical specializations integrated with teaching and research functions and whose catchment area covers multiple communities with more than 500 beds and generally includes provincial hospitals and municipal hospitals in bigger cities.

Associated with the implementation of China's healthcare reform, the issue of population ageing is also high on the policy agenda in China, as it is elsewhere. Population ageing is one of the most significant demographic trends with far-reaching ramifications for the economic development and social stability. In 1949, China's population was 541.67 million. By 1969, it became 806.71 million. China has been implementing family planning to control the population growth since the 1970s. The basic demands of China's family planning policy are to have late marriage and late child-birth – also having fewer but healthier babies, more specifically, one child for one couple in the urban areas. Consequentially, the distribution of population in China has increasingly shifted in both the number and proportion of the population aged 65 and over. For example, in 1985, 55.57 million people, which was 5.3 percent of the total population in China, were over the age of 65 years. In 1997, nearly 88 million people in China were above the age of 65 years – 7 percent of the total population (China Statistical Yearbook 1998). According to World Bank report and forecast, by 2030, nearly 22 percent of China's total population will be over the retirement age.

Associated with the fact of ageing population, the need for long-term care (LTC) has evolved as a major social and economic challenge to China in the twenty-first century. The Chinese government is analyzing and examining various options of financing long-term care in China. Long-term care social insurance with contributions from individuals through a tax on savings income, employers through a business tax and the state by re-allocating state social-welfare funds, has been specifically considered focusing on its advantages and applicability to China. There is likely to be a growing care-gap in China between the needs of elderly people and the supply of care-taking people from their families. Several reasons are responsible for this: (a) China's 'one couple with one child policy' means that the generation who are going to be in their 70s in recent coming years, will have fewer children than any previous generation resulting lesser availability of care-taking people within the family, apparently two young persons will be required to take care four old parents. There is also decline in fertility.

(b) Many Chinese people will not have families to support them in future as their children is far away from them because of work, migration or marriage. Also, recently comparatively more people are willing to remain single. (c) Change of marriage patterns, recent trends of getting marriage as well as having first child at comparatively much higher age, decreasing marriage rates, increasing divorce, and a big increase in cohabiting couples – all these factors are likely to have negative impact on the future availability of one's own care-taking people. (d) The increased involvement of married women in the labor market and self-employment will also reduce their commitment to home care. (e) The rising cost of living, the need to pay towards further and higher education for the only child, and need to contribute towards personal pensions – all these requirements put increasing demands on family budgets and affect adversely and significantly on the capacity of families to have the time, energy and resources to provide the care.

Financing long-term care has become an important social and economic issue facing every country in the world. However, the particular concern to long-term care financing is the relationship between the elderly and the working population. There has been a considerable debate about the economic and social advantages of the cradle-to-grave protection system and the user-pays mechanism. Essentially, frequent assessments of demographic trends and periodic adjustments in resource allocation and social welfare benefits are necessary to ensure sustained economic growth and satisfy the financing needs for the long term care for the elderly.

Four basic methods, namely, provident funds, employer liability, social assistance and insurance to finance long-term care for the elderly have their advantages and limitations in terms of specific features, scopes and uses. Although, China is already a member of WTO since 2001, Chinese insurers still require some time in building up the capability of developing long-term care insurance products and gaining marketing experience. Also many Chinese families cannot afford to purchase such private long-term care (LTC) coverage. Therefore, a public contribution must be at-least part of the solution if China wants to expand the availability of LTC private insurance services for low and moderate-income individuals. Long-term care insurance can possibly be linked with health-care insurance in order to make an integrated health insurance system providing protection for the health and long-term care of the population. Solutions in connection with providing long-term care are multi-dimensional. It is undoubtedly a growing problem. The socialist cradle-to-grave protection is no longer available to Chinese people. Therefore, an alternative protection system needs to be established to provide sufficient resources to cover the long-term care of the elderly as and when they need it.

CHAPTER – NINE

China's WTO accession and Governance in taxation

In 2001, China became the 143rd member of the World Trade Organization after the successful completion of bilateral and multilateral negotiations which had lasted more than 15 years. WTO membership has provided China with increased market access for Chinese exports. China's accession to the forces of international competition would certainly require an ongoing process of both structural adjustment and further reform. In fact, China has been progressively reforming its economic system since 1979, and it introduced a major legal reform package in 1994 covering banking, finance, taxation, investment, foreign exchange and foreign trade.

On the basis of China's Accession Protocol and Working Party Report, China is obliged to ensure WTO compatibility of domestic laws and regulations including taxation which constitutes an important part of the Chinese legal system that relates to private sector economic transactions. At the time of negotiation of China's WTO accession terms, certain members of the Working Party suggested the need for further tax reform because of WTO incompatible provisions contained in the Chinese tax system. Working Party report also expressed specific concerns on the following areas:

a) The different indirect tax treatment of products of non-Chinese origin and Chinese products was mentioned as an example (national treatment obligation of Act III), as were the taxes and fiscal provisions whose impact depended, directly or indirectly, on the Chinese or non-Chinese origin of the goods traded. More specifically, some members complained that the application of some internal taxes, including VAT and sub-central measures, to imports was not compatible with Art III of the GATT 94. The Chinese side confirmed that it would provide non-discriminating treatment in accordance with the provisions of its Accession Protocol, and that it would repeal all laws, regulations and other measures the effect of which was inconsistent with WTO rules on national treatment (points 15, 16, 19, 20, 21, 22 WP);

b) As regards trade related investment measures (TRIMS) China confirmed that it would, upon succession, comply fully with the TRIMs Agreement without having recourse to the transitional periods mentioned in Art 5 of that agreement. Any local content or export performance requirements contained in private contracts would no longer be enforced. The allocation of rights to import or invest would no longer be conditional on performance requirements or secondary conditions e.g. to conduct research, use local inputs or transfer technology, or to provide industrial compensation;

c) Some member countries expressed concerns in general terms over the application of the non-discrimination principle by China to foreign individuals and enterprises and over restrictions on participating in the Chinese economy on the basis of nationality;

d) Some members complained that China's notification had been incomplete regarding prohibited subsidies. China indicated its intention to eliminate all export subsidies as well as all subsidies contingent on the use of domestic products over imported, by accession (points 166, 167, 168 WP);

e) As regards incoming investments, some member countries voiced concerns over the newly adopted investment guidelines. However, China confirmed that it would only impose or apply laws that would be compatible with the Agreements on Trade related Intellectual Property Rights (TRIPs) and Trade related Investment Measures (points 42 to 49 WP). Regarding the Special Economic Zones (SEZs), some members reiterated that WTO obligations should be applied to the entire Chinese territory. China confirmed that WTO rules applied nation wide including SEZs or other special zones where special regimes for tariff, taxes and regulations were established (points 71 and 73 WP).

International trade law entered into a new phase with the WTO both in terms of the substance of the rules and commitments it encompasses as well as in terms of the way in which existing substantive rules are enforced and the way new rules are created.

There were at least three major changes in the substance of international trade law. Firstly, the rules applicable to the cross-border supply of goods greatly expanded with the entry into force of the WTO agreements. Although the provisions of the GATT itself were hardly changed, apart from the fact that the agreement was now called the GATT 94 instead of the GATT 47, new tariff-reduction commitments were undertaken and a large number of additional agreements were negotiated. As a consequence, the traditionally highly protected agricultural and textile sector, which had largely escaped the application of the GATT disciplines, were brought within the framework of international trade laws. The Agreement on Agriculture (AA) started an ongoing agricultural reform process by providing for a step-by-step increase in market opening for internationally traded agricultural goods, and for a gradual reduction of all trade distorting support whether in the form of price support to domestic farmers, or in the form of subsidies for agricultural export. The Agreement on Textiles and clothing (ATC) essentially provided for a total phase out of quantitative restrictions by January 2005, thus made an end to more than 40 years of managed trade in this sector lastly under the multi-fibre agreement. Moreover, existing GATT disciplines were strengthened on the use of certain trade measures which could have an effect similar to a quantitative restriction like the agreement on Pre-Shipment Inspection (PSI), the agreement on Rules Of Origin (ROO) and the agreement on Import License Procedures (IL), on the use of product standards for public interest reasons, such as the health of humans, animals and plants, or environmental protection, and on the use of so-called defensive trade measures or trade remedies that seek to prevent injury to domestic industry caused by sudden import surges or by unfair competition as a result of dumping or subsidies. The Agreement on Technical Barriers to Trade(TBT), the Agreement on Sanitary and Phytosanitary Measures(SPS), the Agreement on Safeguards (SG) and Anti Dumping Agreement are few more examples in this regard. The Agreement on Trade Related Investment Measures (TRIMs) clarified that the GATT 94 national treatment obligation and its prohibition of quantitative restrictions should be understood as prohibiting national measures which require from, or provide to, domestic enterprises to use local input and/or to limit the use of imported input.

The second major change in the substance of international trade law brought in by WTO was to cover international trade in services through the General Agreement on Trade in Services (the GATS). The GATS potentially has a very wide coverage in at least three respects. First it applies, in principle to all service sectors with only a limited exception for public services and with a carve-out for public procurement. Second, it applies not only to the cross border supply and consumption of services but also to the cross border establishments of branches or subsidiaries or in the form of the cross border movement of natural persons. Third, the GATS disciplines apply to all measures that may affect the cross border flow of services and it has also a very wide scope. There are only limited exceptions, for instance, for measures taken in the public interest such as public safety, security, health, fraudulent practices, privacy protection, etc. and for regional integration initiatives between groups of WTO members. There are also some limited derogations for developing countries and in particular for the least developed countries.

The third major aspect covered under GATS is the Agreement on Trade Related Intellectual Property Rights (TRIPS) through which the WTO brought to its member countries the protection of intellectual property rights. TRIPS covers copyright, trademarks, geographical indications, industrial designs, patents, and layout designs of integrated circuits. By obliging Members to protect and enforce the intellectual property rights, TRIPS constituted a significant departure from existing international law.

The WTO constituted a qualitative change as compared to the GATT 47, both in terms of the substance of its trade rules and commitments as well as in terms of the way in which new rules can be created. WTO became a modern international organization that has an in-built mechanism to continue to develop international trade law by exercising semi-legislative authority. Apart from facilitating the implementation of the multilateral trade agreements, WTO also provides a forum for further negotiations. Thus WTO agreement allows for a further deepening and widening of international trade law. Deepening of international trade law is realized by providing the possibility to organize further negotiations that aim at the formation of new commitments and new rules. Widening of the geographical scope is facilitated through the negotiations with more than 30 countries which since 1995 has sought accession to the WTO. The Doha Development Round of multilateral trade negotiations could be considered as first round in this dynamic process. In the Doha Ministerial Declaration of 14th November 2001, negotiations focused on the one hand for further market opening through fresh liberalization commitments in the areas of agriculture, industrial products and services and on the other hand the possible extension of WTO rules in the areas that are closely related to trade, such as trade facilities, transparency in government procurement, competition and investment. Most of these issues have impacts on the income tax rules of the WTO members.

WTO also constituted a qualitative change as compared to GATT 47 because of the way in which existing substantive rules are enforced. Under Article III of the WTO agreement, apart from facilitating the implementation of the multilateral trade agreements and providing for a forum for further negotiations, WTO is also required to administer the newly created Disputed Settlement Understanding (DSU). The DSU ensures that the enforcement of existing WTO rules is in the hands of a semi-judicial structure of panels and an Appellate Body (AB), which are set up to hear all disputes between Members concerning the implementation of the multilateral trade agreements. The dispute settlement procedure is predominantly judicial. The competencies of the panels and the AB are wide, and the independence of their members is guaranteed. Moreover, panel and AB reports are almost automatically adopted by the Dispute Settlement Body (DSB), since unanimity is required to withdraw its incompatible measures in line with the rulings or recommendations of the

DSB. Non-compliance is sanctioned by the possibility for the DSB to authorize the complainant to take retaliatory measures if the defendant fails to implement the DSB recommendations within a reasonable period. The dispute settlement procedures are also relatively fast compared with other court procedures, because the DSU applies strict deadlines for all stages of the process. More importantly, whereas DSB recommendations have an immediate impact on the state parties concerned, a secondary effect may impact on private sector economic operators. The authorization of retaliation measures may lead to trade losses as a result of the punitive custom duties imposed on trade between the parties concerned.

It is now evident that WTO provides for a rules-based, multilateral trading system in which members are free to negotiate new rules as well as amendments to existing rules. But rules, once agreed, are binding upon all and enforced by a semi-judicial mechanism. As a result of the extension of the international trade law and the strengthened enforcement of the implementation of the rules and commitments WTO became much more effective in enforcing the way its members impose taxes on cross-border transactions irrespective of whether these are indirect taxes or subsidies on the cross-border supply of goods or income taxes or subsidies in respect of the cross-border movement of persons and companies.

TAXATION VS WTO RULES:

Taxation is a compulsory transfer of monetary resources from the private sector to the public sector without individual counter performance. There is a conditional working distinction between indirect taxes and direct taxes. Direct taxes include all taxes on income and capital such as personal or individual income taxes, corporate income taxes, capital gains taxes, and wealth taxes. Indirect taxes include all taxes on the supply of goods and services such as turnover tax or sales taxes and excise duties. Taxation is the financial interface between the private and public sector. Therefore there is a clear correlation between taxes and the WTO objectives of trade and investment liberalization. However, there are very few WTO provisions that explicitly relate to taxation.

Firstly, Article I and III of the GATT which prescribe non-discrimination inter alia as regards indirect taxes, and prohibit members imposing higher taxes on products imported from one member compared to taxes imposed on similar imports from other members (MFN obligations) and taxes imposed on similar domestic products (national treatment obligation).

Secondly, as per Art XVI of the GATT and the Agreement on Subsidiaries and Countervailing Measures(SCM), subsidiaries means and covers any financial contribution by a government which confers a benefit. A financial contribution includes not only direct payment, but also any measures such as tax incentives by means of which the government foregoes revenue that it otherwise would have collected. That is why the SCM Agreement refers explicitly to both direct and indirect tax incentives.

Thirdly, Art III and Art XVI of the GATT clarify that the border tax adjustments in international trade that belong to destination type indirect taxes are not GATT incompatible, neither as a discriminating tax on imported products, nor as a prohibitory export subsidy in respect of the exported product.

Fourthly, the General Agreement on trade in Services (the GATS) also relates to indirect taxes in so far as these are imposed on the cross-border supply or consumption of services. However, there is no explicit reference to indirect taxation in the Agreement. In addition, the GATS relates to income taxes, in particular where services are supplied by means of cross-border establishments in the form of a branch or subsidiary, or by means of the cross-border movement of economically active professionals. There is an explicit reference to income tax measures in the GATS, which essentially seeks to carve out tax treaties from the most favored nation obligation and income taxes from the national treatment obligation.

Finally, taxation may come up, may be without explicit reference, under other WTO agreements such as the Agreement on Trade-Related Investment Measures (TRIMS), which prohibits any measures that stimulate the use of local rather than imported content. Taxation may also come up under the many transparency obligations that are imposed on WTO members by practically all WTO agreements.

The answer to the general question that how multilateral trade rules as contained in the WTO agreements, relate to both indirect and direct tax measures of the WTO Members, can be summed up as follows:

1. As mentioned earlier, unlike many other international governance structures, the WTO provides for a rules-based multilateral system in which Members are free to agree any new international trade rules or amendments to existing rules. But any rule, once agreed, is binding upon all and is enforced by a semi-judicial mechanism. The strengthened mechanism to ensure implementation and enforcement of the rules and commitments have increased the potential impact of WTO law on the way WTO Members impose taxes on cross-border movements of goods, services and service providers (professionals and companies).

2. WTO rules that may affect taxation include the following three sets of rules that apply to trade in goods:
    a. There are the most favored nation and national treatment principles which prohibit indirect tax discrimination between imported goods and domestic goods.
    b. There is the more specific prohibition of discrimination by means of trade-related investment measures.
    c. There is the prohibition of export and import substitution subsidies under Art XVI and the Agreement on subsidies and countervailing duties.

    In addition to the above rules in the goods area, other WTO rules that may affect taxes and those that relate to trade in services (GATS), and in particular its most favored nation and national treatment provisions. Moreover, the transparency obligations contained in many WTO agreements, and in particular in the GATT, TRIMs, SCM and the GATS, may affect taxation measures.

3. The non-discrimination rules in the WTO which relate to indirect taxes, contain a rather strong and well developed prohibition on Members to impose a higher or protective indirect tax burden on imported products from different countries with most favored nation obligation, or on imported products as compared to similar or competitive

domestic products i.e. national treatment obligation. Whereas indirect tax measures rarely seem to violate the most favored nation obligation, there are case laws on tax measures that discriminate against imports. Those case laws interpreted widely the aspects of the tax system, and the types of taxes that may cause the discrimination. In view of the strength of the prohibition of discrimination rules and the important potential effect of non-neutral indirect taxes on international trade, it is no surprise that conflict resolution of indirect tax measures continue to constitute an ongoing service for the WTO.

4. The TRIMs Agreement defines a trade-related investment measures (Art III) and very widely defines the quantitative restrictions (Art XI). Any tax advantages or incentives that are conditional on either a local content requirement or a foreign input limit fall within that definition. An overlap between the SCM and TRIMs may occur when tax incentives are granted for exports and conditioned on the use of domestic products.

5. As per the Art XVI of the GATT and the WTO SCM Agreement, both indirect and direct tax incentives may qualify as a subsidy because they constitute a financial contribution by the government and confer a benefit. If they are granted specifically to certain enterprises, they are either prohibited, if contingent on export performance or on using domestic goods instead of imported ones, or actionable if they cause adverse effects to the importing country or its industry. The illustrative list annexed to the SCM agreement explicitly prohibits that the category of prohibited export subsidies may include tax incentives in the form of a reduction or remission of indirect taxes in terms of preferential rates, reduced taxable amount or special credits or of income-tax related tax exemptions, tax deductions including accelerated depreciation, reduced tax rates or tax credits. However, it has also clarified that foreign tax exemptions or credit in regard to profits out of export transactions do not constitute subsidies in so far as they seek to avoid double taxation of foreign source income of domestic enterprises that was already taxed abroad.

6. The non-discrimination rules contained in the GATS have a very wide potential scope of tax implications. The GATS

MFN obligation applies unconditionally and irrespective of whether commitments were undertaken in respect of the services sectors concerned. It prohibits indirect and direct tax discrimination between services and service suppliers of different home countries. Nevertheless, the impact of the MFN obligation in the income tax area must be assumed to be limited due to the exception stipulated for tax treaties. However, the non-treaty based income tax differentiation by one host member between service suppliers from different "home" Members would be WTO incompatible. As per the case law under Art III Paragraph 1 and 2 of the GATT, a country can neither impose a higher tax burden on imported services as compared to similar domestic services, nor tax imported services in such a way as to protect domestic services. The national treatment obligation also covers the income tax treatment of service suppliers, and therefore of foreign-owned branches and subsidiaries providing services in the host Member. Not withstanding the above very widely defined exceptions for domestic income tax measures are likely to cover much of the traditional way in which those entities are taxed under international tax law.

7. The principle of transparency of the WTO has imposed some routine obligations on its Member countries. Members are required to publish trade related regulations and make them available to the private sector. Member countries of WTO have also sometimes agreed to an ex-ante consultation process before a trade related measure can enter into force. Tax measures can be covered by a variety of WTO agreements, but rare are the explicit references to transparency requirements in the tax area. Important WTO agreements under which tax measures may have to be ratified include the GATT, GATS, SCM and TRIMs.

CHINA'S OBLIGATIONS AS WTO MEMBER IN THE AREA OF TAXATION

The conditions of China's accession to the WTO as well as discussion within the Working Party between China and the members in the run-up to accession, were reflected respectively in the Protocol of Accession (WT/L/432, hereinafter referred to as PA), which included the schedules of specific commitments undertaken as regards trade in goods and services, and in the Report of the Working Party on the Accession of China (WT/MIN/(01)/3, hereinafter referred to as WP). While referring to some elements of the discussions in the Working Party as regards to taxation, it became clear that China undertook the commitment to continue to improve its tax system (points 24 and 26 WP) with a view to ensuring full WTO compatibility by the time of accession, taking into account the terms of the Accession Protocol.

The Accession Protocol provided the following relevant issues:

On non-discrimination, China agreed to provide foreigners national treatment as regards the procurement of inputs for the local production of goods and as regards the prices and availability of publicly supplied goods and services. Point 3 of Protocol of Accession reads: "except as otherwise provided for in this Protocol, foreign individuals and enterprises and foreign-funded enterprises shall be accorded treatment no less favorable than that accorded to other individuals and enterprises in respect of: (a) the procurement of inputs and goods and services necessary for production and the conditions under which their goods are produced, marketed or sold, in the domestic market and for export; and (b) the prices and availability of goods and services supplied by national and sub-national authorities and public or state enterprises, in areas including transportation, energy, basic telecommunications, other utilities and factors of production." On indirect taxes, China undertook to ensure full WTO compatibility of its tariffs and internal taxes, to eliminate most export taxes and to accord national treatment to foreign individuals and foreign-funded enterprises as regards border tax adjustments. In this regard, Point II of Protocol of Accession clearly clarifies: "China shall ensure that customs fees or charges applied or administered by national or sub-national authorities, shall be in conformity with the GATT 1994. China shall ensure that internal taxes and charges, including value-added taxes, applied or administered by national or sub-national authorities shall be in conformity with the GATT 1994. China shall eliminate all taxes and charges applied to exports unless specifically provided for in Annex 6 of this Protocol or applied in conformity with the provisions of Art VIII of the GATT 1994. Foreign individuals and enterprises and foreign funded enterprises shall, upon accession, be accorded treatment no less favorable than that accorded to other individuals and enterprises in respect of the provision of border tax adjustments."

On subsidies, China agreed to fully notify all subsidies granted in its territory, to accept "specificity" of subsidies to state-owned enterprises in certain circumstances, and to abolish all prohibited subsidies upon accession. In this connection, Point 10 of Protocol of Accession specifies: "China shall notify the WTO of any subsidy within the meaning of Art 1 of the Agreement of Subsidies and Countervailing Measures (SCM agreement), granted or maintained in its territory, organized by specific product, including those subsidies defined in Art 3 of the SCM agreement. The information provided should be as specific as possible, following the requirements of the questionnaire on subsidies as noted in Art. 25 of the SCM Agreement. This notification was annexed as ANNEX 5A to the Accession Protocol. As regards Special Economic Zones, China agreed to notify any relevant legislation to apply normal tariffs, taxes and rules in connection with the trade flows from the Special Economic Zones into other parts of China, and to grant incentives in these Special Economic Zones on a non-discriminatory basis. More specifically, Point 2B Sub 1 of Protocol of Accession explains: "China shall notify to the WTO all the relevant laws, regulations and other measures relating to its special economic areas, listing these areas by name and indicating the geographic boundaries that define them. China shall notify the WTO promptly, but in any case within 60 days, of any additions or modifications to its special economic areas, including notification of the laws, regulations and other measures relating thereto."

Point 2B sub 2 of Protocol of Accession also specifies: "China shall apply to imported products, including physically incorporated components, introduced into the other parts of China's customs territory from the special economic areas, all taxes, charges and measures affecting imports, including import restrictions and customs and tariff charges, that are normally applied to imports into the other parts of China's customs territory." Furthermore, Point 2B sub 3 of Protocol of Accession clarifies: "Except as otherwise provided for in this Protocol, in providing preferential arrangements for enterprises within such special economic areas, WTO provisions on non-discrimination and national treatment shall be fully observed."

In Annex 5 to the Protocol of Accession, the notification of subsidies included subsidies in the form of cash payments or credit facilities such as grants to loss-making state enterprises, export performance-related priority access to loans and foreign currency, local content-related tariff preferences for automotive production, availability of loans from state policy banks, poverty alleviation subsidies, funds for technology, renovation and R&D, funds for aqua-infrastructure, tariff and import duty reductions or exemptions and low-priced inputs for special industrial sectors. The notification of subsidies also included subsidies in the form of tax incentives including tax forgiveness for loss-making state-trading enterprises, income-tax preferences applicable in specially designed economic regions, tax and tariff refunds for export products, preferential income-tax treatment for certain enterprises, VAT refund to the forestry industry, tariff as well as VAT exemption for imported technology and equipment of investors investing in areas encouraged by the government. It is to be observed that China did not harbor some of its tax incentives which it used extensively as part of its open door policy to foreign investment, under the special derogations and transitional periods on the basis of its status as a developing country to become a member of the WTO.

China agreed to apply TRIMs Agreement upon its accession to WTO, without having recourse to the transitional periods provided therein, and thus by accession to eliminate all local content and export or other performance requirements. In this regard, Point 7 sub 3 of Protocol of Accession specifies: "China shall, upon accession, comply with the TRIMs Agreement, without recourse to the provisions of Art 5 of the TRIMSs Agreement. China shall eliminate and cease to enforce trade and foreign exchange balancing requirements, local content and export or performance requirements made effective through laws, regulations or other measures. China will also not enforce provisions of contracts imposing such requirements. Without prejudice to the relevant provisions of this Protocol, China shall ensure that the distribution of import licenses, quotas, tariff-rate quotas, or any other means of approval for importation, the right of importation or investment by national and sub-national authorities, is not conditioned on: whether competing domestic suppliers of such products exist; or performance requirements of any kind, such as local content, offsets, the transfer of technology, export performance or the conduct of research and development in China."

On transparency, China finally undertook not to apply or enforce legislation unless published in an official journal. China also undertook to establish inquiry points where information would be made available on request both to WTO Members and private parties. More specifically, as per Point 2C sub 1 of the Protocol of Accession: "China undertakes that only those laws, regulations, and other measures pertaining to or affecting trade in goods, services, TRIPs or the control of foreign exchange that are published and readily available to other WTO Members, individuals and enterprises, shall be enforced. In addition, China shall make available to WTO Members, upon request, all laws, regulations and other measures pertaining to or affecting trade in goods, services, TRIPs or the control of foreign exchange before such measures are implemented or enforced. In emergency situations, laws, regulations and other measures shall be made available at the latest when they are implemented or enforced."

Finally, it can be observed that China's WTO Accession Protocol largely documented China's obligations to fully comply with WTO rules by the time of accession, rather than providing for transitional periods, derogations or exceptions. Regarding taxation, there are, in practice, no exceptions or transition arrangements. Particularly, the general non-discrimination provisions, the rules of subsidies, the rules on TRIMs and the general transparency requirements applied to China from the moment of its accession to WTO. In so far as taxation is concerned, the Protocol of Accession provides explicitly that no exceptions are applicable to China as a developing country.

CHINA'S MEASURES IN THE TAX AREA AND ITS WTO COMPATABILITY:

Since its accession to WTO, China adopted various tax reforms, including the unification of income tax rates for domestic enterprises and FIEs through the Enterprise Income Tax Law, which entered into force on 1st January 2008. Some of the other major tax reforms include: the increase in the exemption threshold for personal income tax; reform of consumption (excise) tax; abolition of the agricultural tax with a view to relieving burdens on farmers; the increase in stamp tax on securities transactions; continuation of the pilot project in north-east China to transform the VAT from a production-based tax to a consumption-based tax; and the reduction of tax on interest from bank deposits. During the period, China also implemented a series of tax policies in order to promote rural development, technological innovation, energy conservation, and environmental protection.

China's tax revenue has been increasing rapidly, with total tax revenue as a percentage of GDP at around 17.7 percent in 2009 (up from 16.5 percent in 2006 and 17.3 percent in 2008). China's total tax revenue was up by 18.9 percent in 2008, almost double the GDP growth rate. However, the tax revenue growth rate slowed to 9.8 percent in 2009.

Indirect taxes including VAT, consumption tax, and business tax, account for most of China's tax revenues (74 percent in 2009, up from 72.7 percent in 2006). Since its accession to WTO, China has continued to reform its indirect taxes with a view to lowering tax burdens and thereby encouraging consumption (except for some energy products such as coal and refined oil, whose VAT and/or consumption tax rates were raised to help save energy and thereby to protect the environment). China's consumption tax, which is essentially an excise, is levied on certain domestic and imported goods. There is no consumption (excise) tax on exports. As per Notice on Adjustment and Improvement of Consumption Tax Policy, issued by the Ministry of Finance and the State Administration of Taxation (effective from 1st April 2006), tax rates for various products and coverage were adjusted. China has been revising its consumption tax from time to time mainly to encourage energy saving and environmental protection. As of 1st September 2008, the consumption tax was increased for high-emission passenger vehicles, and reduced for low-emission passenger vehicles. Also petrol tax reform began in 2009; the Government raised the consumption tax on gasoline, diesel and other refined oils, but cancelled charges on six items including road maintenance fees.

China's value added tax (VAT), as the main indirect tax, accounted for almost 31 percent of total tax revenue in 2009, down from 47 percent of total tax revenue in 2006. Revenue from the VAT is shared between the central government and provincial governments at the ratio of 75:25 . For goods subject to consumption tax, the VAT is calculated on the domestic price (c.i.f price plus tariff for imports) plus the consumption tax. China's VAT is production based, thus capital goods are included in the tax base. From 1st July 2004, a pilot project was launched in north-east China to transform the VAT from a production-based to a consumption-based tax, covering certain industries. China adjusted the pilot project in 2007 in terms of its coverage, tax rebate application procedure, and tax credit and reduction mode for nationwide VAT reform. From 1st July 2007, the pilot program was expanded to 26 cities in 6 provinces in central China. From 1st January 2009, China transformed its VAT totally from a production-based to a consumption-based tax at the national level. Following this reform, VAT paid on capital is to be credited against VAT on the final product. Therefore, the VAT exemption on imported capital equipment was discontinued. In 2009, China's tax revenue was reduced by Y140 billion because of the transformation. VAT use to be levied at a standard rate of 17 percent and a lower rate of 13 percent on certain items. In 2009, VAT rate was lowered to 3 percent for small-scale tax payers, but was raised from 13 percent to 17 percent on mineral products, such as coal, aluminum, copper etc. Exporters are entitled to VAT rebates.

China's business tax is levied on domestic taxable services, transfers of intangible assets, and sales of immovable property, all of which are excluded from the VAT. The tax is not levied on imports. However, the business tax on imported services must be collected if the organizations or individuals receiving the services are within mainland China. Business tax rates are set at 3 percent or 5percent on business turnover, except business tax rates for imported entertainment activities are determined by provincial governments within a range of 5 percent to 20 percent. Chinese Government is considering, without fixing any specific timetable, to consolidate the business tax and VAT into a general goods and services tax to simplify China's tax structure. From 1st January 2009, under the Provincial Regulations on Business Taxes, jurisdiction for declaration and collection of business taxes have been moved from the place where the services are supplied to the place where the tax payer is registered. Only for construction services, business tax is still collected at the place where services are provided.

Direct taxes (individual income tax and enterprise income tax) accounted for 26 percent of total tax revenue in 2009 as compared to 27.3 percent in 2006. Revenues from enterprise income tax and individual income tax are shared between the central and local government at 60: 40. FIEs in China were subject to lower rates of tax than domestic enterprises, and also were benefited from various tax holidays under China's enterprise income tax system. But from January 2008, the Enterprise Income Tax Law introduced the unified enterprise income taxes for FIEs and domestic enterprises, with a transition period for tax incentives already granted to FIEs. Accordingly, FIEs established before 16th March 2007 (when the new law was issued), and those subject to a 15 percent income tax rate before 2008, paid income tax at 18 percent in 2008 and 20 percent in 2009, 22 percent in 2010, and will pay 24 percent in 2011, and the statutory 25 percent in 2012. FIEs that were subject to an income tax at 24 percent before 2008 began to pay 25 percent from 2008. FIEs that were benefiting from the tax holidays of 'two year exemption followed by a three-year half deduction' or 'the five-year exemption followed by a five-year half deduction', retain the tax holidays until they expire. If an FIE was entitled to such a tax holiday, but the tax holiday had not commenced due to accumulated losses, it would start benefiting from the tax holiday from 2008.

China's individual income tax is payable on income earned in China by non-residents, and on world-wide income for Chinese residents. From 1st March 2008, the standard threshold for payment of individual income tax was raised from Y1600 to

Y2000 with a view to reducing the tax burden for middle and low income people. Foreign expatriates are entitled to an additional allowance of Y2800 per month, making their threshold of Y4800 per month. By end 2009, the progressive income tax rates on salaries and wages ranged from 5 percent to 45 percent. The income from the production or business operations of individual, industrial and commercial households is taxed at rates ranging from 5 percent to 35 percent with deductions for relevant costs and fees. For other income including royalties, interest, dividends, incidental income, income from property renting i.e. rentals, a flat rate of 20 percent applies. Dividends distributed by domestically listed Chinese companies, are subject to a reduced tax rate of 10 percent. Dividends received by foreigners residing in China are temporarily exempt from the tax.

Interest income from bank deposits was exempted from tax from 9th October 2008. Following the lowering of the tax rate from 20 percent to 5 percent in August 2007, the exemption of interest income from bank deposits was intended to increase interest income from saving deposits.

In terms of other tax reform, since 1st January 2007, the city and township land use tax, previously levied only on domestic enterprises and individuals, has been levied on all enterprises (including FIEs) and individuals using land in China. But at the same time, the land use charge on FIEs and foreign individuals using land in China was removed. In 2008, the vehicle and vessel usage tax, applied to domestic enterprises and individuals, and the vehicle and vessel license tax, applied to foreign enterprises and individuals were unified into the vehicle and vessel tax, levied on domestic and domestic and foreign enterprises, individuals, and organizations. Before 2008, only domestic enterprises, organizations, and individuals were subject to farmland occupation tax. From 2008, the farmland occupation tax also covers FIEs and foreign individuals. Until 31st December 2008, domestic enterprises were subject to the house property tax, while FIEs paid the urban real estate tax. On 1st January 2009, the urban real estate tax was removed. Now, both FIEs and domestic enterprises pay a house property tax.

Tax incentives have, so far, played a significant role in China's Open Policy and in promoting foreign investment and thereby in its economic growth. China has been providing various forms of tax incentives involving major taxes, such as the corporate income tax, the VAT and the business tax as described in the Protocol of Accession. The enterprise income tax i.e. the corporate income tax incentives have been in the form of preferential tax rates (mostly of 15% or 24% instead of the normal 33%) for investments in specific regions which include special economic zones, coastal open economic zones, economic and technological development zones (ETDZs), old urban districts of cities where SEZs and EDTZs are located, high and new-technology industry development zones, Pudong New area, Beijing New Technology Industry Development Experimental Zone, Suzhou Industrial Park, bonded zones, export-processing zones, border open cities, and national tourism and recreation areas. The enterprise income tax incentive have been also in the form of tax holidays, tax refunds for re-investment, special deductions and credits for research and development (R&D) and the acquisition of certain domestic equipment and withholding tax exemptions or reductions. Tax incentives are also given to SMEs to facilitate their development. Small scale, low profit enterprises meeting certain requirements pay enterprise income tax at a rate of 20 percent instead of the statutory 25 percent. Moreover, in 2010, the taxable income is reduced by half for small enterprises with taxable income below Y30000. SME tax payers who were subject to VAT at 6 percent or 4 percent, now require to pay VAT at 3 percent. In terms of the cost-benefit analysis of several tax incentives provided by the Chinese Government, the authorities maintain that they are enhancing the evaluation of the tax incentives in order to improve their cost effectiveness as well as transparency. It is understood that the Chinese government while taking a policy decision on tax incentives, requires to take full account of the general WTO rules that may apply to incentives as well as the more specific commitments made by China in the framework of its accession process to WTO.

WTO members have a very wide discretion in designing their tax system. They have unrestricted right to choose which taxes to impose and at which levels and with what mix between direct and indirect taxes. They have also the right to decide for each tax who should be the taxable persons, what should be the taxable event, what should be the tax base or taxable amount after making the allowable deductions, at what rates the tax should be applied, and whether tax-payers should be granted tax credits for certain expenses they made. The right also includes authority to decide, for each tax, how to treat cross-border as compared to domestic situations. For income taxes, this means that a WTO member may decide whether to tax only source income earned by residents/nationals or also source income earned by non-residents nationals and world-wide income of residents/nationals.

WTO Members' discretion in deciding how to tax cross-border as compared to domestic supplies, is limited by GATT and GATS. It specifies that imports of goods and services from all developing countries must be taxed in the same way and that the tax on imported goods and the services of the services sectors for which specific market access commitments were undertaken, may not be higher than the tax on similar domestic supplies. WTO Members are allowed to apply border tax adjustments provided those are not excessive, and exempt exports from that tax. However, WTO Members are not allowed to impose a higher tax on imports as compared to domestic supplies that are similar, substitutable or in competition, as an incentive to domestic production or a protection of domestic industry. WTO Members are on the other hand, free to decide whether to reduce the tax burden on imports of certain products or exempt then altogether from tax as an incentive for whatever reason as this would mean that the imports are treated in a better and positive manner. There is, however, a limit to this possibility to provide tax incentives in the form of a reduction, remission or exemption from indirect taxes.

WTO Members are allowed to provide income tax incentives to foreign investors in the industrial sector, provided other WTO rules are honored. More specifically, those incentives should not constitute prohibited subsidies or local content requirements contrary to the SCM and TRIM Agreements. In terms of direct taxes, WTO Members are not allowed to provide tax incentives in the form of a tax reduction, remission, exemption, deduction or credit that are contingent either on export performance or on the use of domestic over imported products, as such income tax incentives would be prohibited by WTO rules, as they would be considered export subsidies, import substitution subsidies or trade-related investment measures. WTO Members may not impose a higher tax burden on income of foreign investors from different home countries, unless the difference in treatment results from a tax treaty. WTO Members also may not impose a higher tax on the income of foreign investors that supply services within their jurisdiction, either in person or with a branch or a subsidiary, than the tax on income of similar domestic tax-payers, unless the different tax treatment is aimed at ensuring the equitable or effective imposition or collection of direct taxes in respect of service suppliers of other Members. WTO Members, on the other hand, are free to impose a lower tax burden on foreign service suppliers as compared to domestic one.

In the framework of the accession process, China undertook to abide by both the non-discrimination rules and the rules on subsidies and TRIMs from the time of accession. China didn't negotiate any specific derogation or any transitional period for instance, for the gradual phasing-out of prohibited subsidies as available for developing countries under the subsidies agreement.

The Chinese government, therefore, is not under a WTO obligation to abolish all tax incentives for foreign investment. However, in providing those incentives, it should make sure that there is no breach of the GATT and GATS non-discrimination rules and that there is no contingency on export performance or on the use of domestic products over imported ones against any incentive to the manufacturing industry. Tax incentives should also not be industry or enterprise specific, as this would increase the risk of imposing countervailing duties by other WTO Members on the products that are exported by the beneficiaries of the incentives.

The following comprehensive observations can be made on the tax incentives that the WTO was notified of by China:

a. The subsidies from Central and local government to loss-making state trading enterprises, partly in the form of tax forgiveness, are neither prohibited subsidies nor prohibited TRIMs, but they are enterprise specific and risky because they constitute actionable subsidies to the extent that the subsidized products exported by these enterprises cause injury to the domestic industry of other WTO Members.

b. The preferential income tax rates and tax exemptions available to manufacturing enterprises in the SEZs and to FIEs neither constitute a prohibited subsidy, nor a prohibited TRIM, but they are region or enterprise specific and risky because they constitute an actionable subsidy to the extent the subsidized production and export activities from the enterprises concerned have adverse effects on, in particular by causing injury to the domestic industries of other WTO Members.

c. The VAT exemptions or refunds on the export of products including forestry products, do not constitute a WTO incompatible border-tax adjustment so long as the VAT refund is not excessive. Similarly, the VAT exemption for imported high-tech equipment does not constitute a prohibited subsidy unless contingent on export performance.

d. The income tax reductions or exemptions or refunds to high-tech enterprises, waste processing enterprises and enterprises in disaster-stricken regions, neither constitute prohibited subsidies nor prohibited TRIMs. However, those are region or enterprise specific and risky because they constitute an actionable subsidy to the extent the subsidized production and export activities from the enterprises concerned have adverse effects on, in particular by causing injury to the domestic industry of other WTO Members. This observation, however, does not apply to the similar incentives for technology transferring enterprises as those are services providers for which no subsidy rules exist yet.

On transparency, WTO agreements require its Members to publish all relevant laws, regulations and other measures pertaining to and affecting trade in goods and services, and also to provide, at request, all relevant information to other Members and to private persons. China in its Protocol of Accession, undertook not only to publish all trade-related laws and regulations and to provide information on request, but also not to implement any rules unless previously published. More specifically, as per Point 2(c) of China's Protocol of Accession, China undertook "that only those laws, regulations and other measures pertaining to or affecting trade in goods, services, TRIPs or the control of foreign exchange that are published and readily available to other WTO Members, individuals and enterprises shall be enforced"

As of end-2010, most of China's tax laws and regulations are published, and reasonable structural transparency measures are being taken including the publication of a monthly taxation gazette, namely "China Tax laws and Regulations". MOFTEC (The Ministry of Commerce) has also established an enquiry center to provide information on laws, regulations, measures and the WTO provisions and commitments in respect of foreign investment legislation.

However, different interpretation and application of the tax laws by the Chinese tax authorities in different regions seem to be the rule rather than the exception. Local tax authorities appear to have a rather large discretion when applying the laws. Moreover, a proper and official interpretation of the provision of tax law can be difficult to obtain as there is no presence of tax courts or tax chambers in the Chinese judicial system. The International Bureau of Fiscal Documentation (IBFD) recommended a number of practical measures including the following to improve the transparency of the tax laws as well as the way they are implemented by the tax administration and are interpreted by the courts:

a. To improve compliance, through a better understanding and acceptability of tax rules, the tax administration could consult regularly with tax-payers. A formalized feedback process could be created with taxpayers to test the new rules or interpretations through a consultative exercise before rulings on administrative treatment are issued.

b. Tax authorities should aim at improving voluntary compliance, instead of relying on revenue targets. Better voluntary compliance would not only lead to more tax revenue but also to less tax-induced distortions.

c. Legislations and implementing measures of the SAT should be published before they are enforced and applied in practice.

d. A full review of published and unpublished administrative guidelines to identify inconsistencies and remove unnecessary confidentiality.

e. A streamlining of procedures to publish guidance through the official journal and the establishment of a central interpretative clearing house to issue guidance and standards that are binding upon all local offices in a consistent manner.
f. Tightening of control over local tax administrations and local tax offices that arbitrarily implement local policies beyond their authorities and often in conflict with national policies which are published in the official journal.
g. Administrative regulations in China should be simplified. Further simplification could lead to a substantial reduction of compliance costs for taxpayers as well as administrative costs for tax authorities. China has taken steps in this direction.
h. Improvement in the communication between the designers of the rules and those who apply the rules.
i. Administrative tribunals which should have the power to interpret substantive provisions of tax laws, could be set up to improve dispute settlement and judicial review. Tribunal's decision should be binding on both parties in case of any dispute. Arbitration also should be considered as an alternative dispute resolution mechanism in resolving tax disputes.
j. Appropriate training should be given to those who deal with increasing important and complex issues relating to foreign investors including multinationals and other large taxpayers.

In conclusion, it is observed that on tax policy, China is heading towards the right direction. China transformed the production type VAT to a consumption type VAT, fine tuned excise tax, unified the two corporate Income Tax codes of domestic enterprises and foreign invested enterprises and foreign enterprises, reformed individual income tax, restructured local taxes and streamlined agricultural taxes. However, more emphasis should be placed on the tax administration aspects. The organizational structure of the tax administration should be restructured in line with the procedures of taxation. The Chinese tax authorities, and above all the Chinese Government are aware of the challenges and have already aimed at improving compliance with the rules, ensuring a more uniform nationwide application of those rules, and creating independent judicial review so as to solve any dispute between tax payers and the tax administration.

CHAPTER - TEN

World financial and economic crisis, 2008 – learnings and remedies

The brutal financial and economic crisis of 2008, the worst in over 75 years, was a major eco-political setback for the United States and Europe in particular and the entire world in general. This financial crisis deeply frightened the consumers and businesses, and in response they sharply retrenched. In addition, the usual recovery tools used by governments – monetary and fiscal stimuli – have been relatively less effective under the circumstances. The financial system was seen as having collapsed; and the regulatory framework was seen as having tremendously failed to curb widespread abuses and corruption. Under the circumstances, it is widely suspected that over the medium-short term, American and European governments will have neither the resources nor the economic creditability to play the role in global affairs that they otherwise would have played.

In search of stability, the U.S. government and some European governments nationalized their financial sectors to a degree that contradicts the tenets of modern capitalism. Much of the world turned a historic corner and headed into a period in which the role of the state became larger and that of the private sector became smaller. Hence, naturally this damage has put the American model of free market capitalism under a cloud. However, the damage is getting gradually repaired, but in the process, they have accelerated trends that are shifting the world's center of gravity away from the United States of America.

It is apparently viewed that the crisis arose because of the collapse of housing prices and the sub-prime mortgage market in the United States. However, collapse of housing prices as well as collapse of the sub-prime mortgage market in the USA – both were themselves the consequences of another problem. Analyticaly, it is evident that the lethal underlying cause of the crisis was the combination of very low interest rates and unprecedented levels of liquidity. Overly accommodating monetary policy after 9/11 of US government was reflected through the low interest rates. The liquidity reflected the "global savings glut" as Federal Reserve Chair Ben Bernanke mentioned. Until the mid-1990s, most emerging economies ran balance of payments deficits as they imported capital to finance their growth. But the Asian financial crisis of 1997-'98, among other things, changed that in most of Asia. The result was that, surpluses grew throughout the region and then were consistently recycled back mostly to USA and some portion to the European countries in the form of portfolio investments. This mountain of liquidity was facing low yields and therefore naturally sought higher ones. As it is commonly understood that yields on loans are inversely proportional to credit quality, the stronger the borrower, the lower the yield, and vice versa. Accordingly, to earn higher yield, huge amounts of liquid capital flowed into the sub-prime mortgage sector and toward weak borrowers of all types in the USA, in Europe and to a smaller extent around the world. This flood of mortgage money caused residential and commercial real estate prices to rise at unprecedented rates. In case of USA, in particular, the annual volume of sub-prime and other scrutinized mortgages rose from a long-term average of approximately USD100 billion to USD600 billion in 2005 and 2006. In effect, whereas the average US home had appreciated at 1.4 percent annually over the 30 years before 2000, the appreciation rate soared to 7.6 percent annually from 2000 through mid-2006. Moreover, amid rampant speculation in the housing market from mid-2005 to mid-2006, such appreciation rate was 11 percent.

However, like most spikes in commodity prices, such appreciation eventually reversed itself – and with a vengeance. After mid-2006, housing prices started falling sharply, and there was no stable indication that they would bottom out. This collapse in housing prices undermined the value of the multi-trillion dollar pool of lower-value mortgages that had been created over the 2003-2006 period. Additionally, countless sub-prime mortgages began to convert to more expensive terms which were previously structured to be artificially cheap. As a consequence, innumerable borrowers could not afford the newly adjusted terms and therefore delinquencies became more frequent. As a result, losses on these loans began to emerge in mid-2007 and quickly grew to staggering levels. Total home equity in the United States, which was valued at USD13 trillion at its peak in 2006, had dropped to USD8.8 trillion by mid-2008 and was still falling in late 2008. Americans' retirement assets, the second largest household asset, dropped by 22 percent, from USD10.3 trillion in 2006 to USD 8 trillion in mid-2008. Savings and investment assets excluding retirement savings lost USD1.2 trillion and pension assets lost USD1.3 trillion during the same period. Taken together, these losses totaled a staggering USD8.3 trillion. Such large, abrupt and sudden hits shocked US families. These occurred amid headlines reporting failing financial institution and huge bailouts. Americans also reasonably started to fear over the safety and accessibility of their deposits. That was the reason why Americans withdrew USD150 billion from money-market funds over a two-day period in September 2008, whereas average weekly outflows used to be just USD5 billion. Federal Reserve had to establish a special USD540 billion facility to help these funds meet continuing redemptions.

PERSPECTIVE OF THE CRISIS:

A combination of many events led to the scenario in which Wall Street practically destroyed itself in an orgy of delusion and greed and transformed into something else entirely. Wall Street's ultimate woe had its origins in an area it considered its biggest strength - its skill in devising financial products that hedged risks, which derived higher fees and enriched the investment banks. Starting in the 1980s, the combination of the intelligence and technology on Wall Street helped to expand its complex array of risk-management products. These usually involved slicing, dicing and repackaging everything from pools of mortgages to the future earnings.

The creation of complex investment vehicles enriched Wall Street but also gave those on the street a false sense of security. As the real estate boom unfolded, firms concocted even more elaborate ways of extracting fees from the sector. Although apparently, those instruments were aimed at mitigating risk, in reality, they injected enormous debt into the system, which would ultimately magnify the difficulties of concomitant with a decline in real estate prices and overwhelm the system. In the early 2000s, Wall Street applied its skill in developing complex investment products in the roaring housing market. First, homeowners were borrowing enormous amounts of money, mostly in the risky sub-prime mortgage market. Second, long payback periods for mortgages (30 years in most cases) provided a steady stream of cash flow that made investors in secured debt and related financial derivatives more excited.

Wall Street also dipped more heavily into elaborate investment products, such as credit-default swaps (CDS), collateralized debt obligations (CDOs) and collateralized mortgage obligations (CMOs) all of which essentially involved trading unregulated contracts outside regular exchanges. Such contracts were structured with a specific motive, for example, protecting against a corporation's defaulting on its debt, which was primarily covered by a credit default swap (CDS). As the housing market took off in 2002, investors became increasingly hungry for yield. The Federal Reserve had lowered short-term interest rates to 1 percent in 2003 to fight an economic slow-down. These low-rates, however, helped propel the housing market to even stronger growth, because low interest rates made the cost of financing much lower. It was, in a sense, easy money. The boom in mortgages, especially sub-prime mortgages presented Wall Street with challenge as how to effectively monitor this risky, high-yielding debt in a way that would attract the most buyers. The solution to this dilemma was audacious. Financial wizards concocted instruments that magically transformed sub-prime mortgage debt into something far more attractive. In true sense, they took all kinds of mortgage debt --- sub-prime, top-rated, and so on and threw them into a huge pot --- then swirled the debt around, stirred it and repackaged it into various bundles that bore all kinds of fancy names, e.g. collateralized mortgage obligations (CMO), collateralized debt obligations and so on. Even though a huge amount of foul-smelling debt had been tossed into the cauldron, when it came out in these repackaged bundles, the ratings agencies declared the debt to be top-rated. Since, there was no shortage of fishy debt at the bottom of the repackaged CMO or CDO, the interest rate or yield on the repackaged investments was nice and high. The ratings agencies played along with this game by happily rating everything that came out of the Wall Street investment bank as good investments.

The ease with which all of the mortgages, especially lousy ones, were repackaged and sent out into the system helped drive rapid growth. The Fed's easy-money policy didn't hurt either. As with all manias, things were carried on for quite some time before everyone discovered that the emperor was wearing no clothes. However, knowing that something had gone crazy and knowing when everyone would notice were two different things.

In our experience, the real estate party ran along fairly nicely for some time. The financial firms felt increasingly confident in the complex debt-related contraptions they had built and took on more and more risks. Banks, eager to earn more money and keep the mortgage boom rolling, trimmed back lending standards to draw more business.

The real estate craziness spread to other areas of the debt-market also. Companies found themselves able to borrow with minimal collateral. Many performance covenants to protect the lenders gradually disappeared as debt discipline diminished. We observed a collapse in standards and an explosion in lending in a world of easy money --- easy for real estate, easy for companies and easy for every kind of deals. In other words, lenders found themselves fighting desperately to win business.

In the corporate acquisition market, the collapse of standards in lending played out prominently. Private-equity funds acquire companies or divisions of companies with an eye toward fixing these companies and then later re-selling them either to another company or to the public via an initial public offering. The word 'private' in their name stems from their frequent habit of taking over publicly traded companies and making them private. In the past, borrowings by private-equity firms had required them to meet certain performance measures in order to protect the lender. So, the functions of private-equity funds were under control. But during the post-internet bubble era, private equity funds boomed as the borrowings became exceedingly easy and also interest rates became very low. They raised hundreds of billions of dollars and acquired a large number of companies. They were no more satisfied to play the typical quieter role of buying and turning around smallish companies or divisions of companies. They bought huge, and big name companies and deal volume soared to nearly USD800 billion in 2006 from a merely USD34 billion ten years earlier. However, such deal boom quickly faded amid the financial turmoil and many of those highly leveraged companies started facing challenging debt payments

Throughout the 2000s, Wall Street firms had boasted about their ability of spreading risk rapidly around the world to small banks, college endowments, unions and other investors. The theory is that by distributing the risk far and wide, if things go bad everyone would lose just a little rather than a single entity losing everything. However, since the financial experts had done such a good job of masking the dangers of real estate debt and making it a valuable investment because of its unusually high yields, it became very tempting to hold some of the investments in-house rather than sell them. Such temptation or greed peaked around 2006 and 2007, just as things started to go awry in the real estate markets. Many Wall Street firms at this period became risk gatherers as opposed to risk spreaders. Accordingly, they had acquired these debt-laden assets with borrowing of their own.

By the end of 2005 and well into 2006, doubts and questions about the sustainability of the housing boom rose sharply. There were frequent proliferation of statements that the boom had become a bubble. However, among others, Merrill Lynch, Citigroup, and Lehman Brothers continued to add mortgage-related debts aggressively to their Balance Sheets in 2007, when it became clear to even casual observers that the real estate market had taken a dark turn.

The year 2006 ended in a simple enough way. Real estate prices had started to slip in some parts of USA, but the slippage remained contained to bad debt. In much of 2007, the stock market had a surprisingly healthy tone. Merger and acquisition activity continued its strong pace, and takeover firms were busy raising tens of billions of dollars of new funds to acquire companies. As 2007 also closed with booming bonuses and talk of great things to come, some of course, could see parts of what was to come even if the whole picture was not yet clear.

One difficulty to see the full extent of the looming problems was the unchecked use of leverage seeped into the system in many ways duly facilitated by the financial engineers. This leverage became excessive and would eventually nearly overwhelm the system itself. The sources of the leverage were manifold. One of such sources was the selling of US treasury debt or so-called agency debt such as that issued by Fannie Mae and Freddie Mac, the mortgage giants, with the government's implied backing to developing nations. Developing nations, especially in Asia, had an abundance of savings. Rather than spend or invest that money at home, much of those savings made their way to the U.S., where they became part of the debt-building machine.

The financial engineers also found additional ways to add leverage to the system. The hedge funds that bought the leveraged assets borrowed money to do so. Even sometimes investors in hedge funds were investing with borrowed cash. Debt upon debt upon debt – piled up. Much of such debt tied to real estate which itself had become an enormous source of borrowing and leverage.

One curious aspect of the current financial crisis was its slow-motion build-up and dramatic apogee over the course of a bit more than a year. But maybe because of the size of the problems facing banks and other financial firms, finding solutions to the crisis proved very difficult even though there was time to try to find it. Lehman Brothers knew it faced significant solvency issues for more than a year, but it couldn't raise enough capital to offset its enormous amount of bad debts. Similarly, those at Bear Stearns and mortgage lenders such as Washington Mutual, Country-wide Financial and Indy Mac knew that they were facing problems. However, most observers still believe that the crisis unfolded at a comparatively leisurely pace, giving those involved ample time to find solutions before the economic tsunami hit in September 2008.

The origin of the crisis was the sub-prime lending market troubles. Individual homeowners began to fail on their sub-prime loans toward the end of 2006 and well into early 2007. It would always remain a wonder how these homeowners were qualified for a loan in the first place. The mind-set was probably that real estate prices would never go down. Moreover, if the borrower failed to repay the loan, the bank would just take over the house and re-sell it at a profit. In reality, as the sub-prime borrowers defaulted, those defaults led to foreclosures, an unfamiliar sight during the housing boom. Foreclosures outnumbered actual home sales by early 2008 in once booming Orange County, California. As the sub-prime failures mounted, the illogic and fragile sustainability of the arrangement among banks, investment banks, hedge funds etc. became more clear. Sub-prime defaults rippled through the array of mortgage-related debt securities that Wall Street had concocted during the housing boom.

During the summer of 2007, hedge funds run by the large French Bank BNP Paribas and Wall Street investment bank Bear Stearns ran into trouble and ultimately failed. Even though investors largely ignored the fund failures, the slowly shifting environment led to modest changes in lending practices. Banks got just a mild tougher with one another, especially with banks heavily dependant on mortgage debt. Surprisingly, the first big casualty of the U.S. housing and associated financial engineering debacle fell in a foreign land. Northern Rock, a amazing success story during U.K. property boom of the late 1990s and 2000s, found itself in the midst of difficulties in meeting near-term debt payments. Whispers of Northern Rock's difficulties led nervous individuals to worry about the money they had deposited in Northern Rock. By September2007, an old fashioned bank-run had started and lines of depositors encircled Northern Rock branches, trying to withdraw their money. We noticed confusing policy responses at this initial phase of financial crisis. The British Government initially declined to intervene to save Northern Rock or to protect its depositors by either investing in Northern Rock or guaranteeing deposits at the bank. However, eventually Northern Rock was nationalized and the deposits were guaranteed, although such resolution took few months.

The failure of Northern Rock led many in the U.S. start worrying about whether such an event could happen in U.S. also. Companies and banks who were mainly real estate-centric or were having substantial mortgage-related exposure, such as Fannie Mae, Freddie Mac, Country wide, Indy Mac, Washington Mutual, Wachovia, Bear Stearns, Lehman Brothers, Citigroup and Merrill Lynch came under more scrutiny from the investors. In early 2008, the mortgage giant Countrywide, saddled with failing mortgage debts and seeing few avenues of exit, became the next to fall. Finally, Bank of America acquired Countrywide at a rock-bottom price.

Policy makers began to take more concerted action to add liquidity to the financial system in the wake of the Northern Rock run. European Central Bank as well as the Federal Reserve injected hundreds of billions of dollars and euros into the system in the last two quarters of 2007. During the bailing process which continued deep into 2008, banks grabbed for capital far and wide. In late 2007, Citigroup raised USD7.5 billion from Abu Dhabi. Merrill Lynch raised USD6 billion in December2007 from investors, among them Temasek Holdings, the investment arm of the Singaporean Government. In September2008, Goldman Sachs raised USD5 billion from Warren Buffett and others. Even General Electric tapped Warren Buffett for USD3 billion at the same time. However, for many of the firms, the level of bad debt was rising more quickly than the bailers could bail.

Bear Stearns faced a severe no confidence situation in March 2008. Bear Stearns, once famous for its risk-management acumen, found itself begging to convince that it was healthy and posed no counter-party risk. As little as two days before its failure, Bear Stearns publicly declared that it was in excellent shape, although nobody believed that. Hedge funds and other Wall Street banks began to refuse to do business with Bear Stearns and rapidly withdrew assets. Bear Stearns was forced to its knees. Bear Stearns became the first Wall Street casualty. J.P.Morgan Chase bought Bear Stearns for USD2.0 a share i.e. at USD236 million. Eventually that price rose to USD10 a share after a number of Bear Stearns shareholders squawked. The Federal Reserve guaranteed USD29 billion of Bear debt to help seal the deal. Questions were raised about the large and active role of the government in saving Bear Stearns. After the Bear Stearns rescue, the credit markets continued to tighten. Lenders grew more and more cautious of lending to one another. Lending for everything from car loans to mortgages slowed measurably. The vast credit markets act as a vital lubricant throughout the world's economy, helping businesses to operate and families to purchase a home or pay for college. When the credit markets falter, the economic effects can be swift and severe. Like the stock markets, the credit markets run on confidence. Buyers of debt are, in essence, lenders, and they expect to be paid back, with interest. Companies also raise the debt and pay back with interest. When companies fail and debts go unpaid, lenders get nervous. In usual circumstances, the lenders will simply charge higher rates and set tougher conditions for loans. But in the summer and fall of 2008, banks and others became wary about lending anything at all. Like an engine with no oil, the credit markets seized up. Many companies, large and small, had to face the situation where banks were either totally refusing or cutting down drastically the credit line during the credit crunch.

In the fall of 2008, the credit crunch led to large layoffs and other radical actions around the globe as companies grappled with the higher costs of doing business. In November 2008, in USA alone, the economy lost 533,000 non-farm payroll jobs. Citigroup cut 50,000 jobs. The credit crunch was most visibly illuminated when the most widely used bank-to-bank lending rate i.e. the LIBOR (the London Inter-bank Offered rate) rose sharply during the summer of 2008, negatively affecting credit card interest rates and adjustable-rate mortgages, harming further the economy. Such credit tightness persisted despite Central Governments and federal banks around the world, injecting hundreds of billions of dollars into the system. Lenders accordingly moved warily, fearing that anybody could face failure.

During September 2008, stock players were convinced that the mortgage giants Fannie Mae and Freddie Mac who were at the epicenter of the real estate and sub-prime crisis could not survive on their own. The share prices of the two firms plunged to near zero. A few weeks earlier, Congress had given US Treasury Secretary the power and authority to take over Freddie and Fannie if necessary. It came to that far more quickly than anybody expected. In essence, Fannie and Freddie became part of the US government, with tax payers taking on all the liabilities associated with the two firms.

The take-over of Fannie and Freddie sent a chill through the market place. In the two weeks after the Fannie and Freddie takeover, the credit spreads got worse. These spreads calculate the difference between interest rate paid by US Treasury's and other kinds of non-government debt. The wider the spread, the higher is the level of concern or fear in the marketplace. The rising credit spreads made borrowing exceedingly difficult and also incredibly expensive. This caused problems around the world for all sorts of companies dependant on credit, ranging from banks to electronics retailers and even the governments of some sovereign countries facing severe debt problems.

The credit market problems created severe situations for many financial institutions. Those included Morgan Stanley, a venerable firm descended from the House of Morgan; Lehman Brothers, once cotton merchants who had begun work in Alabama before the civil war; Merrill Lynch, the thundering herd with the largest brokerage network in the world; and AIG, a global insurance titan that had started by selling life insurance in Shanghai to the Chinese.

On September12, 2008, it became clear that Lehman could not survive. Lehman was continued to be known as vulnerable for more than a year. However, Richard Fuld, the company's tenacious CEO believed that Lehman, so often viewed as a potential takeover target, could weather the storm once more. His belief prevented Lehman from selling assets in a timely manner in order to raise badly needed capital to offset its large real estate related losses. On the week-end of September 13 and 14,2008, regulators rightly or wrongly felt some confidence that they could let Lehman Brothers fail without causing too much of a wider crisis. Thus, they were less willing to lend a hand, as they had in case of Bear Stearn, to help Lehman and potential bidders, notably Bank of America and Barclays Bank of the United Kingdom, to forge a possible deal over the weekend. As the various parties fenced, it became clear that Lehman Brothers would not be rescued. Bidders decided that Lehman's bits could be more easily and cheaply acquired through bankruptcy proceedings. Regulators including the Federal Reserve, the Securities and Exchange Commission and the Treasury, made it clear that they would move things quickly through such bankruptcy proceedings to mitigate the impact of Lehman's liquidation. Finally, Lehman Brothers faced bankruptcy filing on September 15, 2008.

Merrill Lynch was also looking to find a buyer. Though not nearly as unhealthy as Lehman, Merrill Lynch believed that a Lehman failure would leave it vulnerable to the negative views of short sellers and a fall in confidence that would make operating increasingly difficult. Merrill Lynch didn't want to test that scenario. So on Monday, September 15,2008, Merrill Lynch management agreed to an all-stock USD50 billion take-over by Bank of America which earlier had already edged away from the Lehman talks. Combining Bank of America and Merrill Lynch created, in the process, a banking and investment banking powerhouse. However, this created duplication of back-office and other support functions and that eventually led to reasonable number of job losses.

Contrary to the expectations of regulators, the news of Lehman's failure jolted the markets. Share prices plunged everywhere. By the end of the day, investors and policy makers had already started questioning the wisdom of letting Lehman go bust. But the bailout police at the Federal Reserve and the Treasury led by Ben Bernanke, New York Fed Chief Timothy Geithner and Treasury Secretary Henry Paulson, had little time to answer. Because by that time, AIG, the titanic insurance company with tentacles into every nook and corner of Wall Street and the broader global financial markets, was knocking at the government door for its rescue. Although AIG was known primarily as an insurance company it had gradually evolved into a complex financial services firm. It had been trading credit-default swaps (CDS), specially tailored investment vehicles and all manners of commodities. Its woes, similar to those of all the other companies in trouble, stemmed from bad real-estate bets and an excessive amount of borrowing that amplified its losses. As the financial crisis unfolded, AIG found itself holding enormous losses. US Government stepped in to rescue AIG, and within two months of the rescue, the company had already requiredUSD150 billion in aids to continue its operation.

On September16, 2008, the Asian markets opened after holiday and share markets plunged. Shares in Europe and the US followed suit. It became clear that the financial system faced a full-blown crisis. One of the US largest banks Wachovia based in Charlotte, North Carolina and investment bank Morgan Stanley started talks about a possible merger during chaotic, merry-go-round antics of those September days. Nothing came out of those talks. Soon, Wachovia started talking with Citigroup. Not long after, one more government-sweetened deal was announced that Citigroup taking over Wachovia backed by Federal Reserve loan guarantees for Wachovia's lousiest assets. However, finally Wells Fargo, a San Francisco bank emerged to make a non-government aided bid for Wachovia. After a bit of bickering, Wells Fargo won the deal.

Morgan Stanley, one of the top US investment bank, meantime negotiated over a three week period into mid-October before securing a USD9 billion investment from Mitsubishi UFJ Financial Group. The final terms of the deal was heavily in favor of the Japanese bank, but the capital lifeline gave Morgan Stanley the chance to survive, if barely. Within one week of failure of Lehman Brothers and also Bank of America's take-over of Merrill Lynch, Goldman Sachs and Morgan Stanley registered as bank holding companies, essentially ending the era of the big investment banks.

In September 2008, more large failures took place, including the collapse of Washington Mutual, better known as WaMu, largest savings and loan bank of USA. J.P.Morgan acquired WaMu for about USD2 billion. As a whole, it meant one less bank and thousands more jobs lost.

But the crisis was hardly over. Analysts believed that the large amounts of toxic real estate debt must be dealt with before the credit crunch could ease. Treasury Secretary Paulson prepared a USD700 billion bailout package aimed, initially, at removing this toxic debt from balance sheets by having the government purchase the bad debt. But the bailout plan ran into stiff opposition in Congress. On 29th September 2008, the initial bail-out vote failed and stocks dropped sharply with the Dow Jones Industrial Average plunging 777 points or just short of 7 percent, the Dow's biggest point drop on record. On 1st October 2008, the Senate passed a version of the bailout bill, and the House eventually followed suit. Since the Senate can't initiate legislation – the House used an old trick, digging up a dormant bill and using it as a shell. The House also eventually approved the new measure, giving the Treasury the cash to fight the crisis.

Failures, meantime, spread overseas and underscored the global nature of the crisis. Dexia, a Belgian lender, received a government bailout. In the United Kingdom, the Spanish Bank Banco Santander acquired Bradford & Bingley, a financial services firm with government help. Fortis, a Belgian financial services institution, found itself unable to raise badly needed capital and was eventually acquired by BNP Paribas, the French Bank.

By early October 2008, it had become clear that Lehman's failure, among other things, had set off a series of unexpected events and contributed to a systematic crisis in the financial system. Concerns were rising about the viability of the financial system. Governments in Europe, Asia, and the USA promised to do whatever it took to solve the financial crisis. But some governments had to rescue themselves first. Iceland was the starkest example which had been rocked by the crisis. This island nation of about 300,000 people, and as a member of the European Union, had an easy access to individuals across the continent and in the U.K. Iceland's banks grew dramatically and were dominating the Icelandic economy. The assets held on the bank's balance sheets dwarfed the country's GDP. However, many of those assets had links to lousy investments, notably real estate in booming property markets in the USA and Europe. As the financial crisis worsened, the Icelandic banks found themselves in a tough position. In true sense, the Icelandic banking system collapsed. The Government took over nearly all the private banks, and interest skyrocketed as Iceland sought to keep money from flowing out of the country. With its banking system frozen, Iceland watched retail supplies shrink and disappear.

As Iceland teetered, along with other countries such as Hungary, the credit crisis seemed bent on laying waste to the developed world's economic system. Essentially, nearly every country has been affected. Some places, such as Iceland and Hungary, faced severe issues, primarily because of bad bank borrowing and investing irrationally to overwhelm the local economy. Other countries, such as Ireland and Spain, faced problems from collapsing property markets. The U.K, with falling home values and carnage in its financial sector, had faced a deeper downturn than other major European countries. Russia also, like the U.K., faced a double blow. Its banks faced exposure to bad debt, and the plunge in oil prices, a main source of its revenue, had also stung. Russia's stock market had fallen dramatically and frequently had to be closed in order to restore order. Eastern Europe and most emerging economies also faced difficulties stemming from the financial crisis, either because of greater difficulty in borrowing money or because of economic downturn in key export markets. Eleven ex-Soviet Commonwealth of Independent States region as a whole faced the largest reversal of economic fortune over the near term largely due to financial turbulence and falling demand as mentioned by the International Monetary Fund in its six monthly World Economic Outlook in April 2009. Economic decline in 2009 in the region – comprising Russia and eleven ex-Soviet neighbors – was a dramatic setback after growth of 8.6 percent in 2007 and 5.5 percent in 2008. In recent years, most countries in the region relied heavily on foreign funding to finance debt and modernize their economies. But they found those funds dried up – as IMF reported. Countries like Russia that relied heavily on exports of oil, gas and other commodities hit hard by declining exports and falling commodities prices. However, another hazard for the region was high levels of borrowing denominated in foreign currencies, which appeared hard to service as local currencies in most states declined. As IMF reported, for Belarus and Russia, the proportion of credit in foreign currencies was about 30 percent, while it was about 50 percent for Kazakhstan and Ukraine and 70 percent for Georgia.

Governments in almost all countries kept trying to find a solution – lower interest rates, pumping money into the system by the Central banks, corporate rescues, government takeovers - but things only seemed to get worse until the end of 2008. Regulators across the world including the Federal Reserve, the International Monetary Fund and the European Central Bank dug deeper. Interest rates around the globe were cut, hundreds of billions in deposits were guaranteed, central banks pumped countless billions into the financial system and new policies were established to facilitate the purchase of scrutinized loans such as pools of auto loans and credit card debt. The coordinated effort to invest directly in banks, providing them with badly needed funds, seemed to lessen the fear of outright systematic collapse, though severe problems remained. By the end of 2008, the governments had pledged more than USD7 trillion in various loans and guarantees to try and solve the financial crisis. However, on the top of the financial problems, other economic crisis also grabbed the government's attention. The financial tsunami had spread deeply into the so-called real economy, with a prospect of deep recession and large job losses on the horizon.

At a time when the world was reeling under economic and financial crisis, China and India, despite being seriously affected by the same, emerged as drivers of global economic growth as World Bank said in its latest World Development Indicators (WDI) 2009. It is also to be noticed that while low and middle-income economies contributed 43 percent of global output as of end-2009, 7 percent up from 36 percent in 2000, the World Bank report said that China and India accounted for five percentage points of that increased share. We observed that the global crisis raged mostly in the financial sectors of developed nations, resulting in mounting losses, a string of bankruptcies, and a severe interruption in the flow of credit, particularly in the inter-bank money market. But Indian banks have not been seriously rocked by this global financial crisis because of their relatively small exposure to US asset backed securities and structural derivative products like collateralized debt obligations. Yet the global financial meltdown also casted its long shadow on Indian financial markets and thereby on the overall economy. The first major impact of the global financial tsunami was on India's capital inflows, particularly external commercial borrowings (ECB) and foreign institutional investment (FII) because of the close integration of the domestic economy with international financial markets as well as increasing relaxation of capital account transactions. ECBs and FII registered a steep fall as soon as the global financial meltdown surfaced. The huge financial crisis and the associated credit crunch, and a widening spread between the yield on private bonds and that on government securities were responsible behind the significant fall of ECBs. On the other-hand the need for repairing the balance sheets of developed country financial firms in the context of their mind-boggling losses, could be the most important reason behind drying up of FII flows to Emerging Market Economies (EMEs) including India even though the economic prospects of those FII seemed better than that of the USA. The reversal of capital flows led to a steady fall in the value of the rupee between October 2007 and November 2008 despite substantial running down of foreign currency assets by Reserve Bank of India. FII outflows also had a negative influence on domestic investment. A whopping USD3.2 billion FII equity outflows in January 2008 triggered a relentless bear run in the Bombay Stock Exchange, making it plunge by 52 percent between December 2007 and January 2009. Moreover, the global financial meltdown has had some negative consequences for India's credit financed economic activities despite the resilience of Indian banks. Indian banks became increasingly choosy in extending loans not only to traders but also to buyers of real estates and consumer durables who had so far played an important role in sustaining domestic demand. However, such caution was also warranted by the rise in non-performing assets (NPAs), the resulting erosion of banking capital and the far from rosy prospects of the domestic economy. The role and policy of Reserve Bank of India (RBI) during this phase was more or less similar to that of many central banks including the European Central bank. The RBI made a 250 basis points cut to 6.5 percent in cash-reserve ratio (CRR) on 11th.October and cut 100 basis points to 8 percent in repo rate on 20th October 2008. Also following the examples of China, the USA, the UK and other countries, the Government of India finally announced its first fiscal stimulus package on 7th December 2008.

During the period, the world also observed the resilience of China's economy to the global financial tsunami. However,

China's dependence on export-led growth left it vulnerable to the effects of the global economic crisis that started in late 2008. China's international trade was significantly affected by the global economic slowdown and the sharp contraction of demand in its traditional export markets. In 2009, China's exports and imports fell by 16 percent and 11 percent respectively. Also, China's trade surplus fell by 34 percent in 2009. Its exports and imports of goods and services accounted for 35 percent and 27 percent respectively of GDP in 2008, down from the 38 percent and 30 percent respectively in 2007. In the first half of 2009, both exports and imports under the 'processing trade' fell evidencing the difficulties of FIEs after the outbreak of the global economic crisis in 2008. Real GDP growth declined from 9.6 percent in 2008 to a year-on-year rate of 6.2 percent in the first quarter of 2009, the lowest rate in more than a decade. But growth rebounded in subsequent quarters to 7.9 percent, 9.1 percent, and 10.7 percent respectively in the second, third, and fourth quarters of the year resulting China's overall real GDP growth of 8.7 percent in 2009. Chinese economy grew by a better than expected 11.9 percent year-on-year in the first quarter of 2010. The blistering growth rate was the fastest since 2007 and the figure was 5.7 percentage points higher than the same period of 2009, and 1.2 points higher than the last quarter of 2009. China overtook Germany to become the world's largest exporter in January 2010, and remained the world's second largest importer, behind the United States. The Chinese Government responded to the effects of the global economic crisis by introducing expansionary fiscal and monetary policies to offset the sharp decline in external demand. During the period, China put more emphasis on domestic demand to drive GDP growth. In November 2008, China announced Y4 trillion (13 percent of GDP in 2008) economic stimulus package for investment in the economy in 2009 – 2010. In addition, in September 2008, the People's Bank of China (PBOC) announced a shift from a tight monetary policy to a moderately loose one to help stimulate domestic demand. Since last quarter of 2008, interest rates and reserve requirements have been cut several times and foreign exchange sterilization operations have been reduced. Also, while keeping benchmark lending costs unchanged during the period, the PBOC has been encouraging banks to provide loans through window guidance. In 2009, new bank lending increased rapidly, almost doubling from the previous year to Y9.6 trillion. However, in early-2010, the PBOC being conscious of the risks of excessively loose monetary policy contributing to inflationary pressures and compounding the misallocation of credit in the economy, began to reduce lending stimulus by increasing the reserve requirement ratio of the banks.

A fundamental difference between China and the rest of the world was that, when banks in other countries were being forced to deleverage, Chinese banks were actually pumping liquidity into the economy. In November 2008, China's central bank removed lending quotas. Consequentially, by the end of first-half of 2009, loan portfolio rose 34.4 percent on year-on-year basis – the strongest growth in 14 years. Chinese banks, in many aspects, appeared well positioned to face the global financial storm and the economic downturn. Firstly, they were having limited exposure to global financial markets because of strict foreign exchange controls and, therefore, suffered limited losses when the financial crisis began. Secondly, most of the China's banks already cleaned up their balance sheets through re-capitalization and restructuring during the last ten years, and were well prepared to absorb and deal with potential increase in non-performing loans (NPLs) during the period of economic downturn. The average NPL ratio of Chinese commercial banks was only 1.8 percent as of June 2009. Finally and very importantly, in terms of future potential activity, Chinese banks' leverage ratios were very low after years of monetary tightening and strict controls on lending. The loan-to-deposit ratio of US banks was nearly 100 percent in 2008, while only 66 percent among their Chinese counterparts.

Chinese households were also lowly leveraged and still in a strong position to spend. Nominal retail sales grew by 1.. percent year-on-year in the first half of 2009. This simply meant that Chinese were cushioned by their high savings. Chinese families saved nearly 33 percent of their total income, compared with a meager 0.5 percent by US families, pushing household deposits to over 70 percent of GDP in China in 2008. Similarly, household debt amounted to nearly less than 30 percent of disposable income in China in 2007, compared with over 120 percent in Japan, with even higher levels of debt in many other developed countries. In a deflationary situation, while highly indebted household sectors in many countries faced an increasing burden to service their debts, the real purchasing power of Chinese households actually improved. Therefore, household consumption growth in China will continue in the coming years even if economic downturn persists in the remaining parts of the world.

China's huge foreign exchange reserves and low short-term external debt demonstrate that China's external sector is also lowly leveraged. While global investors pulled money out of the emerging market since the beginning of the sub-prime crisis until early 2009 because of concern that the financial crisis would affect emerging market currencies, it caused a sharp depreciation in many emerging market currencies. But the RMB remained firm, appreciating 6.4 percent against US dollar between January 2008 and February 2009. China also had a solid external position with an enormous current account surplus of USD440 bn, or 9.7 percent of its GDP in 2008 and USD2.1 tn of foreign exchange reserves, more than seven times of China's short-term external debt obligations. Although limited currency depreciation might help to improve export competitiveness, a sharp depreciation could cause many economic damages, such as eroding the purchasing power of domestic entities, shaking business and consumer confidence, encouraging capital flight and discouraging FDI flows and finally provoking protectionism. All these damages could make economic recovery even more difficult. Although China's external environment is more challenging today than after the Asian crisis a decade ago, its domestic economic fundamentals have improved significantly over the last ten years and that should help China avert a protracted slowdown.

However, as mentioned earlier, Chinese exporters has been facing much tougher challenges since the crisis surfaced than they were after the Asian financial crisis. Firstly, the economic crisis of 2008 was more severe and global in true sense, forcing to a much sharper decline in final demand. Secondly, China's currency appreciated more sharply this time in terms of its real effective exchange rate. Between August 2007 and February 2009, real effective exchange rate of RMB appreciated by 25.1 percent. It made the Chinese exporters much less competitive. As a result,

China's exports could supposedly witness the sharpest decline since 1962 by nearly 15 percent in 2009. However, although exports were struggling, China's domestic sectors including banks, corporations, households and the government, were strong enough in order to be resilient to the current crisis and to outweigh the tougher external economic environment and to help the economy avoid a protracted slowdown.

Chinese Central Government also announced some additional measures in early March 2009 which were not part of the Y 4 trillion package. They included higher pensions for retired workers, pay rises for 12 million teachers, subsidies for farmers, Y600 billion in tax exemptions and reductions, and Y850 billion set aside for medical reform over the next three years.

It is evident that the commitments showed the Chinese Central government's seriousness about tackling economic crisis. It is also obvious that the stimulus package demonstrated the central government's determination to prod the economy.

China's fiscal deficit stood at 180 billion Yuan in 2008, or 0.8 percent of gross domestic product, down from 319.8 billion Yuan or 2.6 percent of GDP in 2003. The small proportion indicated China's sound fiscal health despite a series of tax cuts and mainland companies posting lower revenue. The Central Government re-iterated that the deficit was at a controllable level and the debt level was safe, thanks to efforts to cut the deficit in recent years. The budget deficit for 2009 was a record 950 billion Yuan, equivalent to 3 percent of GDP, a level still widely regarded as within safe limits.

A question may arise that how long can China's massive fiscal stimulus be sustained? In 2008, China's outstanding debt was less than 20 percent of GDP, one-fourth of the OECD average of 80 percent. The Chinese government planned a budget deficit of 3 percent to fulfill its pledge to stimulate the economy over 2009-2010. However, even if we assume such budget deficit of 5 percent of GDP during that period, the government has the wherewithal to pursue such a policy every year for at least a decade, before its debt-to-GDP ratio reaches the above-mentioned OECD average of 80 percent. It demonstrates the abundant room that the Chinese Government has to increase its fiscal spending.

Although China couldn't completely escape the most severe global economic downturn since the 1930s, it is now evident that its solid economic fundamentals would cushion it from a hard landing. Accordingly, China would also be able to offset a significant amount of the adverse impact of external shocks and putting the economy back on right track to achieve more than 10 percent growth in 2010. With such strong economic recovery, the Chinese government should presumably be able to phase out its fiscal stimulus policies in 2011 and the central bank might start increasing interest rates in second half of 2010.

In the wake of the severe economic crisis, many developed nations had hoped that China could lend IMF a larger part of its foreign exchange reserves – the world's biggest -- to bail out crisis-stricken economies and inject liquidity into the markets. Under the existing arrangements of the International Monetary Fund, the USA contributes 20 percent of the fund's capital, while China chips in 4 percent. If the quota stays the same, the US would have to come up with about USD100 billion to support additional loans while China would be responsible for contributing USD20 billion.

If China did agree to carry more of the IMF funding load, it could contribute an amount corresponding to its share of global gross domestic product – as several China based researchers maintained. China's GDP accounted for about 6.8 percent of the global total in 2009, so there should be about 3 percentage points of room to move over its existing 4 percent IMF contribution.

Like many member-nations, China also believes that IMF itself is a defective system because it has traditionally been tough on supervision of developing countries. This time, China is likely to ask first that better market monitoring for developed countries be introduced before any refinancing plan can go ahead.

The IMF usually matches its 185 members' rights with the money they put in. Only the USA with 16.77 percent of the voting rights, has veto power. Germany has 5.88 percent of the voting rights, while Britain and France each have 4.86 percent. China has 3.66 percent. Even if China increase it's voting rights by making a bigger contribution, there is no way the rights will match the collective clout of developed countries. More importantly, the voting rights will mean almost nothing if the IMF still functions as an emergency fund and has no enlarged power to supervise the world economy.

TWO YEARS ON, WHAT HAVE BEEN CHANGED:

Two years on from the collapse of Lehman Brothers, the world economy has certainly turned the corner. There seems to be definite light at the end of the tunnel.

DURING 2009:

Despite bailout measures, global consumer sentiment and the stock markets plummeted to an all-time low until mid-2009. However, from the third quarter of 2009, the world has been on a recovery mode. By August 2009, the silver lining became apparently visible. The plunge in output at the end of 2008 and in the early months of 2009 had been arrested. The economies of America, Britain, the euro area and the Asia started to be growing again. Still the policy makers and central banks are cautious and in no hurry to withdraw stimulus.

US Federal Reserve Chairman Ben Bernanke mentioned on September 15, 2009 that the worst recession since the 1930s probably over, although he cautioned that it would still going to feel like a very weak economy for some time because many people would still find that their job security and their employment status is not what they wish it was. During the twelve months period that ended on September 2009, he took many creative measures. He slashed interest rates; rolled out a dizzying array of new lending programs; backed the debt of Bear Stearns, a failing investment bank; agreed to lend to Fannie Mae and Freddie Mac, America's troubled, quasi-private mortgage agencies; argued for fiscal stimulus and mortgage write-downs; and proposed an expansion of the Fed's regulatory domain. By far Mr.Bernanke's most innovative response to the credit crisis had been the expansion of the Fed's tool kit from control to short-term interest rates to the deployment of its balance-sheet to restore liquidity to specific markets, such as that for inter-bank loans. In October 2008, 91 percent of the Fed's assets were invested in government bonds. In October 2009, the share was 52 percent. Finally, Mr.Bernhanke's declaration in September 2009 that the recession likely ended marked his most optimistic assessment yet of the economy. And his remarks came on the same day that the US Government report that retail sales jumped 2.7 percent in August 2009, the most in more than three years. Mr.Bernanke's speech at the Brookings Institution on September 15, 2009 was identical to the one he delivered at the Fed Conference in July 2009 in Wyoming that economic activity appeared to be leveling out after declining sharply at the end of 2008 and into the beginning of 2009. He also mentioned that the global economy was just beginning to emerge from recession.

By third week of August 2009, stock markets across the globe moved up, in most cases to their highest levels in 2009, a sure sign that people were willing to bet real money on the green shoots of economic recovery yielding a favorable harvest. A 3.7 percent rise in retail sales in August – the highest in three-and-a-half years – backed Bernanke's prognosis. So did the news that US industrial activity in August 2009 was at 0.8 percent, better than the expected 0.6 percent, and consumer prices rose a stronger than forecast 0.4 percent. Given that the US is by far the world's biggest economy and the one that triggered the year-old global economic and financial crisis, it was not surprising that good news from there was being treated as light at the end of the tunnel.

Things were also getting back gradually, although slowly, to normal in Britain as well as in Europe twelve months after the collapse of Lehman Brothers whose demise precipitated the worst crisis to hit the financial world in living memory. Second week of September 2009 offered some evidence of a return of such old spirits. Kraft Foods, the world's second biggest food maker launched a USD10.2 billion (Euro7 billion i.e.GBP6.2 billion) offer for Cadbury, the cherished British confectionary group. A day later, France Telecom and Deutsche Telecom said they were merging their UK mobile phone operations in a GBP7 billion deal, creating the largest operator in the U.K. The numbers might pale in comparison with those seen during the heady days of the last boom in mergers and acquisitions, but they had been eagerly welcomed by every quarters. Some were seeing them as the start of things to come as confidence was gradually recovering. UK equities i.e. FTSE100 ended July 2009 with a gain of 8.5 percent, its best monthly performance for more than six years, even though weak energy stocks dragged the FTSE100 index down from a seven-month high. Speculation about further blue-chip take-over activity following Kraft's hostile bid for Cadbury helped the FTSE100 index reclaim the 5000 level for the first time in a year. Miners were among the biggest gainers until the end of the second week of September 2009.

In Europe, the Euro-first 300 reached its highest level in end-July 2009 since November2008 as positive corporate earnings helped maintain buying momentum. The telecom and banking sectors led the way higher but energy stocks fell. By the end of the second week of September 2009, the Euro-first300 ended at an 11 month high after rising for six successive sessions on the back of optimism about a global recovery. Commerz bank rose sharply after pledging to start repaying state aid.

Optimism about the global economy was boosted by September '09 first week's pledges by G-20 Finance Ministers to maintain policies aimed at bolstering the recovery.

Asia's emerging economies were recovering much more quickly than economies in other parts of the world. They grew at an average annualized rate of around 10 percent in the second quarter, while America's GDP fell by 1 percent.

Asia's bounce had taken many forecasters by surprise. China, India and Indonesia were among the few economies in the world that continued to expand throughout the global downturn. However, the smaller, more open Asian economies were badly hit. Between September 2008 and March 2009, real GDP fell by an average annualized rate of 13 percent in Hong Kong SAR, Malaysia, South Korea, Singapore, Taiwan and Thailand. But the second-quarter GDP figures showed an impressive bounce. Comparing the second quarter with the first at an annualized rate, South Korea's GDP grew by almost 10 percent, Singapore's soared by 21 percent, China's by 15 percent and Indonesia managed a respectable 5 percent. Other countries in the region also showed a rebound. While output in Singapore and South Korea was still lower than a year earlier, but quarterly changes were more useful for indicating the turning points.

Industrial production in emerging Asia had also been revived in an impressive manner, jumping by an annualized rate of 36 percent in the second quarter, 2009. Emerging Asia was the only region in the world where output had regained its level before the crisis period. Although this was largely because of China, where industrial production rose by 11 percent in the twelve months to July 2009. However, it was evident that all the Asian economies witnessed a strong pick-up. By these measures, Asia's emerging economies were clearly leading the global recovery. Aggressive fiscal and monetary stimulus helped revive domestic demand across Asia. Asia has had the biggest fiscal stimulus of any region in the world. South Korea, Singapore, Malaysia, Taiwan , Hong Kong SAR and Thailand have all had a government boost of at least 4 percent of GDP, while China's package notably grabbed the headlines. At the time of this downturn most Asian countries except India, had sounder budget finances in comparison with their western counterparts. So they had more capacity to spend. In case of India, the government has had much less room to spur growth because of its dire fiscal situation (a budget deficit of 10 percent of GDP in 2008). Since exports announced for only 15 percent of India's GDP in 2008, compared with 33 percent in China, India has been much less affected by the global recession. At the end of 2009, public debt of the region as a whole rose around to a modest 45 percent of GDP, only half of the average in OECD countries.

Cheaper money had been more potent in lifting the spending in emerging Asian countries than its western counterparts. This was because, unlike in west, local financial systems were not crippled. Therefore, the banks were able to lend more. Moreover, Asian households and firms had not previously been on a borrowing binge and thus they could afford to borrow more. The easing of credit had been even more effective in China than its fiscal stimulus. In China, while lending slowed sharply in July 2008, new lending by banks in the first seven months of 2009 was almost three times its level a year earlier. In addition, pump-priming was also more effective in Asia than in America or Europe. Tax cuts or cash handouts in Asia were more likely to be spent than saved as Asian households were not burdened with huge debts. It was also true that in Asia, there were much room for spending by the government in worthwhile infrastructure projects – from railways to power grids.

Asian stock markets also finished July 2009 with gains in double digits. The Kospi index in South Korea hit a one-year high and the Nikkei average in Japan rose to a 10-month peak, as upbeat corporate earnings reports around the world were seen as more evidence that companies were coping well and poised to benefit from any recovery. Both Hong Kong and Shanghai stock markets recorded another month of hefty gains in July,2009, the seventh successive monthly gain for Shanghai and the fifth winning month for Hong Kong, fueled by positive earnings momentum and analysts' upgrades. The Shanghai composite index gained 15 percent in July,2009 – its biggest monthly rise in two years. The Hang Seng index gained nearly 12 percent in July 2009. South Korea offered more evidence of recovery in Asia, lifting the won to a nine-and-a-half month high. Industrial production rose 5.7 percent in June 2009 – more than twice as fast as was expected and the sixth straight monthly increase. Elections in India and Indonesia reflected as spurring investor-friendly changes and sparked big gains in those markets. The main Mumbai and Jakarta indexes closed at new highs for the year. Australian stocks also registered monthly gain of 7.3 percent in July 2009 taking the S&P/ASX200 index to its biggest monthly rise in nine years, led by banks and miners.

In early-October, 2009, International Monetary Fund further confirmed that in the second quarter 2009, real GDP moved mostly on the upside, with an expansion in France, Germany and Japan and at a slower pace of contraction elsewhere, including the United States. IMF also confirmed that emerging economies, led by China and India, turned around even more strongly. Region-wise, Asia appeared set to pull out of the global downturn faster and stronger than any other region. However, IMF insisted that fiscal and monetary policies in Asia should continue to provide stimulus till signs of sustained economic recovery are clear. IMF director (Asia and Pacific Department) emphasized at a press conference in Istanbul ahead of Fund Bank meeting in early October, 2009, that Asia's Central Banks generally possessed the room to maintain an accommodative monetary conditions until there would be clear signs of a sustained growth in private demand as pressures from inflation were muted. However, IMF director also pointed out in his speech in early-October 2009, that there was considerable heterogeneity within Asia as there were cases where inflation started to turn upwards.

In USA, former Federal Reserve Chairman Alan Greenspan said that the US government should not consider a new stimulus package, even if unemployment threatened to break the 10 percent barrier and stayed there for a period. US Labor Department reported early October 2009 an unemployment rate of 9.8 percent, the highest since 1983. Such report prompted President Barack Obama to say he would explore any and all additional measures to spur growth. Greenspan pointed out on ABC's 'This Week' program that only 40 percent of the USD787 billion economic stimulus package approved in February 2009 was in place. Therefore, it would be far better to wait and see how the momentum that already appeared to develop in the economy carried forward. Greenspan also added that the focus should be on trying to get the economy going, but also it needed a careful approach that in trying to do too much it could actually be counterproductive. In other words, it would be premature for President Obama and Congress to enact another stimulus package while the economy was recovering. In connection with the existing stimulus package, US Treasury Secretary Timothy Geithner vowed early October 2009 not to withdraw stimulus funds. Geithner said signs of economic recovery were stronger and appeared sooner than expected. But he reiterated that it was not yet time to roll back stimulus programs. Geithner's remarks followed a meeting of finance ministers and central bankers from the Group of Seven industrialized nations.

The sharp downturn in Asian economies in late 2008 painfully proved that the region was not immune to America's downfall. However, emerging Asia as a whole might probably enjoy annual growth of 7-8 percent over the next five years as analysts and researchers predicted. The speed and strength of the rebound in Asia, if sustained, proves not only that the sustained growth of this region is heavily chained with that of western countries, it also already posses its in-built economic power. It is to be noted that the gap between growth rates in emerging Asia and the G7 rose to a record nearly nine percentage points by end of 2009.

In terms of the future, pessimists may argue that Asia's growth over the coming years will be much slower than before the global economic and financial crisis because its main engine of growth viz. exporting to America, has broken down and it will probably take years to find a replacement. However, in answer, it is also to be noted that between 2001 and 2006 (when America's trade deficit peaked), Asia's trade surplus with America accounted for only 6 percent of the region's GDP growth. Growth will only be slower if the decrease in those exports cannot be replaced by domestic demand. In any case, it will never be massive.

DURING 2010:

In the first week of May 2010, Europe's sovereign-debt crisis looked dangerously close to contagion. The Greek debt was ballooned: two-year bonds soared towards 20 percent in the last week of April 2010. Portugal's borrowing costs jumped. Along with Greece and Portugal, Spain's debt was downgraded. Italy also came worryingly close to a failed debt auction. European stock markets plummeted. The euro itself fell to its lowest level in a year against the dollar.

The Greece crisis began in October 2009 when its new government admitted that its predecessor had falsified the national accounts. It was also suffering from a budget deficit of 13.6 percent and a stock of debt equal to 115 percent of GDP. Greece found no way to grow out of trouble because of fiscal retrenchment and also because of its lack of export prowess. It could not devalue since it is in the euro zone. Over and above, its people appeared unwilling to endure the cuts in wages and services needed to make the economy competitive. As a whole, Greece looked bust. During the period, many other European countries scared the investors. Portugal had a high budget deficit and remained chronically uncompetitive. Although, Spain had a low stock of debt, it seemed unable to restructure its economy. Italy was also heavily indebted. Non-euro-zone Britain's budget deficit was also in unnerving level. During this crisis period, world also noticed political indecision or absence of political firmness amongst the leaders of the euro- zone countries. Having concluded by the European leaders in mid-April 2010 that an eventual Greek restructuring was all but inevitable, the whole world presumed that they would quickly get a proposed Euro45 billion (USD60 billion) deal to stave off an imminent and chaotic Greek default, buying time for an ultimate orderly restructuring of Greece and also to begin overdue structural reforms for the other weak economies. However, mainly German leaders appeared scared of upsetting German voters who did not support aiding Greece. Playing for time finally backfired. The mooted rescue plan climbed above Euro100 billion since no private money was available. The longer the euro-zone governments dithered, the more the lenders started to doubt whether the promises to save Greece were worth anything. Euro-zone leaders also initially refused to seek IMF help because it would be humiliating. But eventually, they decided to call in the IMF.

The fear that began in Athens, raced through Europe, shook the stock markets world-wide, and finally affected the broader global economy, from the ability of Asian corporations to raise money to the outlook for money market funds where American savers park their money. What was once a local worry about the debt burden of one of Europe's smallest economies quickly became global. Because of Greek crisis, jittery investors forced Brazil to scale back bond sales as interest rates soared, and also caused currencies in Asia, like the South Korean won, to weaken. Ten companies around the world that had planned to issue stock in the 1st week of May 2010, the most in a single week since October 2008, delayed their plans. The increased global anxiety threatened to slow the recovery in the United States, where job growth finally had just picked up.

The sovereign debt crisis of Greece sent waves of fear through global stock exchanges. A decade ago, it took more than a year for the chain reaction that began with the devaluation of the Thai currency, the baht, to spread beyond Asia to Russia, which defaulted on its debt, and eventually caused the near-collapse of a giant American hedge fund, Long-Term Capital Management. However, this crisis, by contrast seemed to ricochet from country to country in seconds, as traders simultaneously abandoned everything from Portuguese bonds to American blue-chip shares. On 6th May 2010 afternoon on Wall Street, Dow Jones industrial average briefly plunged nearly 1000 points. While the immediate cause of the worries was the ballooning budget deficit in Greece and the risk of default there and in countries like Spain and Portugal, the turmoil also exposed deeper fears that government borrowings in bigger economies like Britain, Germany, Japan, and even the United States might be unsustainable. Worries were also ripe that if Europe would end up in a double-dip recession, that could reduce economic growth in the United States by 0.3 to 0.4 percent as economists predicted. Although the direct exposure of American banks to Greece was small, but there were signs of other cracks below the surface. The strongest banks in Germany and France were having heavy exposure in almost all the troubled economies of the continent; and these big banks in turn were also closely intertwined with their U.S. counterparts. As a whole, American banks had USD3.6 trillion in exposure to European banks as of end-April 2010 as the Bank for International Settlements reported. Such exposure included more than Euro one trillion in loans to France and Germany, and nearly USD200 billion to Spain. Besides, during the period, American money market investors automatically started feeling nervous about hundreds of billions of dollars in short-term loans to big European banks and other financial institutions. In one word, a systematic risk had been prevailing throughout. In this connection, we should remember that uncertainty about the stability of assets in money market funds signaled a tipping point that accelerated the down-ward spiral of the credit crisis in 2008, and ultimately prompted banks to briefly halt lending to one other.

Asian stocks and currencies were also hammered during this crisis period by deepening worries about European sovereign debt and the ability of the local firms to raise capital. On 6th may 2010, China's benchmark Shanghai composite dropped 4.1 percent to an eight month low of 2739.70, while Hong Kong's Hang Seng Index fell 1 percent to 20,133.41. On the same day, Japan's benchmark Nikkei Stock Average of 225 companies shed 3.3 percent to 10695.69 in its first trading day following a three-day holiday. Among other Asian equity markets, South Korea's benchmark ended 2 percent lower at 1684.71, while Australia's lost 2.2 percent to 4573.25. Thailand's SET index fell 1.5 percent to 785.25, and Taiwan's benchmark index slid 1.5 percent to

7579.48. Stocks with exposure to world trade, property and banks were hit especially hard. Asian currency markets were also rattled very much during the period. Investors for months had positioned themselves for Asian currencies to rise against the USD on the back of strong regional economic growth. Many such investors were forced to unwind those trades during this time.

In Europe, the euro fell to a 14-month low, below USD1.27 as the European Central bank failed to offer any substantial new initiatives to address the euro-zone debt crisis. European shares also dropped, with the banking sector skidding after the European Central Bank opted against buying bonds of euro-zone governments as it kept its key rate on hold. European financial companies as big owners of government debt, struggled during the entire first week of May 2010 over worries about euro-zone contagion from Greece's debt crisis. The main stock indexes in Frankfurt and Paris fell more than 3 percent, while the London benchmark dropped nearly 3 percent. Lack of clarity about which European banks were at risk was prompting the banks to avoid making short-term loans to one another, threatening a repeat of the seizure in inter-bank lending that followed the collapse of the American investment bank Lehman Brothers in September 2008. During this period, obviously investors took little notice of the good news that came out on May 7,2010, that the European economy and the American economy were improving overall. German industrial production rose 4 percent in March 2010, reflecting expectations that economy grew modestly in the first quarter of 2010; and stronger than expected U.S. employment figures for April 2010, showing signs of sustained recovery in U.S. economy.

Finally, on 9th May 2010, Euro-zone members and the IMF agreed a euro 110 billion (GBP95 billion; USD146.2 billion) three-year bail-out package to rescue Greece's embattled economy. The emergency meeting, attended by officials from all 27 E.U. states, was called to reach agreement on a so-called European stabilization mechanism. The final rescue package for Greece was nearly three times the level discussed only three weeks ago. The EU agreed to provide euro 80 billion in funding and the rest of euro 30 billion was approved by the International Monetary

Fund to prevent Greece from defaulting on its massive debt. The unprecedented IMF loan, the largest financial commitment the institution had ever made to a single country, included conditions requiring Greece to tighten its fiscal belt and raise taxes. European policy makers and IMF officials, after sanctioning the rescue package, expressed their confidence that the measures were enough to bring the Mediterranean country back from the brink. IMF also forecasted Greece's real GDP to decline 4 percent in 2010 and to grow 1.1 percent in 2012.

In June 2010, Euro-zone nations also started setting up a massive bailout fund of euro 750 billion (USD1 trillion) that could rescue any member of Europe's currency union from default, aiming to soothe market jitters that had sent the euro to a new four-month low against the dollar. Also, the fund from this rescue package could be lent to any indebted Euro-zone nation risking default, and intended to counter investor fears that Spain, Portugal or others could follow Greece in requiring a bailout to meet debt. By end-June 2010, the special purpose vehicle to borrow up to euro 440 billion (USD526 billion) became ready. In a joint statement dated 7th June 2010, Euro-zone nations said that they would draft bigger cuts and tax increases if they require to and would pursue 'structural reforms' to slim state running costs – such as raising retirement ages to curb pension costs. Meanwhile, unemployment in the euro-zone reached a 10-year high of 10.1 percent in April – adding extra welfare costs to governments struggling with higher outgoings, lower tax revenue and debt since they paid out hundreds of billions to shore up the region's banking system.

Although the progress toward global financial stability experienced a setback during April & May 2010, the overall financial situation subsequently again improved all over the world, owing to the forceful response by policymakers which helped to stabilize funding markets and reduce tail risk. More precisely, as of 30th September 2010, in Europe, while coordinated support programs and the announcement of ambitious fiscal reforms in countries facing the greatest funding difficulties helped contain the turmoil in the euro area after its rapid escalation in May 2010, sovereign risks still remained elevated as markets continue to focus on high public debt burdens, unfavorable growth dynamics, increased rollover risks, and linkages to banks. As IMF suggested, continuing forceful policy measures are required to remain firmly on track toward building financial system resilience. In the United States, financial stability has apparently improved. However, pockets of vulnerability still remain in the banking system. Also, weakness in the real estate sector constitutes an additional challenge. While U.S. banks have been able to raise a substantial amount of capital, and also expected demands appear manageable, still raising of some additional capital may be needed to reverse recent de-leveraging trends and presumably to comply with U.S. regulatory reforms. The apparently modest capital needs of the US banks highlight the large scale of government-sponsored enterprises and other government interventions without which those needs would have been substantially higher, and also reflect the extent to which risks have been transferred from private to public balance sheets, as well as the need to address the burden placed on public institutions. As of September 30, 2010, as IMF reported, a near-term disruption in the government bond market of Japan remains unlikely. While the stable domestic savings base and healthy current account surplus of Japan reduce its need to attract external funding sources, the factors presently supporting the Japanese bond market — high private savings, home bias, and the lack of alternatives to yen-denominated assets – are expected to erode over time as the population ages and the workforce declines. Emerging markets have proven so far to be very resilient to sovereign and banking strains in advanced and mature economies. Also, most of the emerging economies have continued to enjoy access to international capital markets. Cross-border spillover effects of euro-zone crisis were mostly confined to regions with significant economic and financial links to the euro-zone. On the other-hand, emerging countries, in general, have become increasingly attractive to investors because of their relatively sound fundamentals and stronger growth potentials. As long as the current slowdown in growth in advanced countries continues, the shift in global asset allocation is likely to increase. However, as IMF also suggested, a potential build-up of macro-financial risks stemming from strong capital inflows, including excess demand in local markets and possible increased future volatility, remains a considerable concern for countries on the receiving end of this ongoing asset reallocation.

EPILOGUE:

When the economic crisis and credit crunch hit in September 2008, many economists predicted a long term global recession. The governments around the globe, central banks and policymakers of almost all the countries of the world initiated several steps and introduced several packages in order to decouple their own country from the crisis and to bolster the world economy. Now the world economy has started to turn the corner. Still, with the worst economic scenario now behind them, policymakers in most of the advanced countries are already needed to confront the interactions created by slow growth, rising sovereign indebtedness, and still fragile financial institutions. Also, policymakers are under increasing pressure to explain how they will reverse course when the time comes. That task is particularly hard when it comes to the public finances. Fragile economies need fiscal support, but it is harder for finance ministries than central bankers to promise credibly to be very strict in future when they are so liberal today.

As of 30th September 2010, confidence in the financial sector has not been fully restored. On the positive side, bank regulatory capital ratios have improved and global write-downs and loan provisions have declined. Banks have also made progress in recognizing those write-downs, with more than three-quarters of them already reported, leaving a residual amount of approximately USD550 billion. However, there has been little progress in dealing with the imminent bank funding pressure. As IMF reported, nearly USD4 trillion of bank debt will be required to be rolled over in the next 24 months. Therefore, exits from extraordinary financial system support, including the removal of government guarantees of bank debt, will be needed to be carefully sequenced and planned. In order to bring the normalcy to the funding markets and also to bring the better health to the banking industry, restructuring and/or resolving weaker financial institutions through re-capitalization, merger, or closure remains a priority.

In order to strengthen the fundamentals of sovereign balance sheets, the countries facing immediate strains will require, in the short term, adequate supranational support. In the medium term, in order to ensure fiscal sustainability, sovereign balance sheets require to follow a credible path. Also, addressing the sovereign refinancing risks through debt management policies that lengthen the average maturity structures as market conditions permit, will be an imminent task. In responding to the global financial crisis, most of the governments used their fiscal resources and balance sheets to support aggregate demand as well as to strengthen private balance sheets, particularly for financial institutions. This surely helped prevent a deep recession, but at the cost of a high-risk level expansion in public balance sheets. The health of the banking system and the respective sovereign country have become closely intertwined as a result of the unprecedented government support for banking systems during the crisis. Now, the governments face the challenge of dealing with the resulting higher debt burdens amid uncertain growth prospects, with even less fiscal room. Against this backdrop, many advanced economies are now urgently requiring to negotiate a delicate balance between fiscal consolidation to reduce debt and rollover risks, on the one-hand, while ensuring sufficient growth to avoid adverse debt dynamics and unsustainable debt burdens, on the other. At the same time, it is noteworthy that there is continued uncertainty about prospective economic growth, with the risk of abrupt setbacks that could undermine fiscal sustainability and financial stability.

With regard to regulatory reform, much of the proposed financial reform agenda still remains unfinished. While international rule-making bodies have made reasonable progress, as IMF reported in its 'global financial stability report – October 2010', to identify the most egregious failings of the global financial system in the run-up to the crisis, the member countries have yet to agree on many of the details of the reforms. The issues like developing the macro-prudential framework, strengthening supervisory incentives and resources are still under discussion. In light of current situation, a sincere willingness to suppress domestic interests in favor of a more stable and better functioning global financial system is essential for any further progress. The sooner the reforms can be clarified, the sooner the financial institutions can formulate their strategic priorities and business models. In the absence of such specific progress, regulatory inadequacies will continue increasing the chances of renewed financial instability. As part of the ongoing regulatory reform efforts, the recent proposals of the Basel Committee on Banking Supervision (BCBS) are being welcome by the IMF as well as banking industry. Such proposals represent a substantial improvement in the quality and quantity of capital in comparison with the pre-crisis situation. As per BCBS proposals, common equity will represent a higher proportion of capital and thus allow for greater loss absorption; also the amount of intangible and qualified assets that can be included in capital will be limited (to 15 percent). These include deferred tax assets, mortgage servicing rights, significant investments in common shares of financial institutions, and other intangible assets. Phase-in arrangements have been suggested to allow banks to move to these higher standards mainly through retention of earnings. Phasing out intangible completely and scaling back the transition period should be considered as the global financial system stabilizes and the world economic recovery becomes firmly entrenched. In the process, banking sector resilience will rise to absorb any future shocks that may lie ahead.

As a whole, policymakers require to continue their efforts to reduce refinancing risks, strengthen balance sheets, and reform regulatory frameworks. Also, while it is needed to develop 'exit strategies' from the stimulus packages introduced to boost economies, with the situation still fragile, some of the government supports that have been given to banks in recent years are still required to be continued. While it is to be ensured that the need for extraordinary support is temporary as it is no substitute for repairing and reforming financial sectors, planned exit strategies from unconventional monetary and financial policies may require to be delayed until the situation is more robust.

The policy challenges for emerging economies are different. Many of them will need to cope with the effects of relative success, where maintaining stability will depend on their ability to deal with surges in portfolio inflows. As IMF suggested, in some cases, traditional macroeconomic policies may need to be supplemented by macro-prudential measures as they may not be fully adequate to meet the macro-financial challenges arising from inflationary pressures or asset bubbles. Emerging economies should also continue to pursue policies aimed at fostering the development of local financial systems in order to have the capacity to absorb and efficiently intermediate higher volumes of capital flows.

CHAPTER – ELEVEN
Concluding observations

More than eight years on of China's joining to WTO, we observe that multilateral trading system is besieged by a number of thorny problems and potential cracks which threaten to derail or at the very least considerably slow down the process of international economic integration.

It is evident that for both world wars, one of the key sparks was economic discrimination and trade warfare. GATT was established with a limited vision as a stopgap organization until a binding international trade body would be established. GATT nonetheless proved quite effective. Through several rounds of negotiations, tariffs on manufactured goods were sliced from an average of 40 percent in 1948 to about 6 percent in 1980 and then to about nil now. WTO came in place of GATT in 1995 and has been working efficiently so far. However, there is a great deal that needs to be done, and can be done, to see that the WTO functions more effectively.

The issues have also now moved beyond the relatively straight forward task of lowering tariffs to encompass various other measures used to restrict trade. Anti-dumping suits and imposing quotas have become a new way to restrict trade.

The developed countries keep their attention focused on liberalizing international exchanges to promote the knowledge economy. The agenda for the developed countries has been quite well established in terms of dealing with agriculture, industry and services as well as on broader areas such as intellectual property rights, environmental standards, investment regimes, competition policies and anti-dumping procedures.

Concluding observations

Developing countries are becoming increasingly serious to have fair competition and market access in those products where they have comparative advantage and also to have adequate access to technology inflows in order to advance towards higher value-added products. Developing countries are most likely to spend more time pushing a positive agenda in the next round of trade negotiations than on blocking proposals for liberalization from developed countries. Some of the key items in the agenda of developing countries are to direct special and generous aid and technical assistance programs to the least-developed countries instead of providing protection on their labor-intensive products. In 1996, the WTO decided to push through an action plan, for tariff and quota-free market access for exports from 49 least-developed countries. It is apparently a sensible policy. However, the results have been disappointing. For example, only about 20 percent of exports from the least-developed countries to the U.S., as of 2008, were duty free. Subsequently, in 2001, the European Union introduced the EBA policy i.e. 'everything but arms' policy that in principle would allow full access for products from the least developed countries. However, since the plan did not include in the initial stage important products such as rice, bananas and sugar etc, agricultural exporting countries cynically termed it the 'everything but firms' policy. It is, so far, evident that preferences also send a wrong message to poor countries that they can only compete with the help of special assistance. Therefore, it will be more encouraging to: (1) provide special and generous aid and technical assistance to the poor as well as less developed countries in order to explore their respective potentials in the world-trade arena; (2) be more flexible in the implementation of WTO-mandated standards including the landmark TRIPS intellectual-property rights measures; (3) implement the principle of special and differential treatment more fully by the developed countries. Free movement of labor from developing to developed countries is an obvious area of interest where there has been little serious negotiation; (4) amend anti-dumping procedures so that they are not used as a guise for protectionism – a practice that usually victimizes developing countries; (5) avoid linkage between trade and social issues. Developing countries cannot accept such a linkage as it would not be the best way of improving the labor standards.

REFORMING WTO TO BE MORE EFFECTIVE:

Here are some of the measures that could make the WTO itself more effective – (1) WTO has, so far, been a phenomenal success in many ways. Fewer than two dozen countries became members when the GATT was founded in1947. There were only about 100 members when WTO was formed in 1995. But in 2009, there were 153 members and 31 observers in the WTO. With the exception of the Holy See, observers must start accession negotiations within five years of becoming observers. Therefore, virtually every one of the world's traders is either in the WTO or would like to join it. However, accession procedures should not take so long. Since WTO is gradually becoming a truly global trade organization, existing members should not use the accession process to squeeze the applicant countries to the maximum. Simply adopting all existing commitments that current members have accepted, should be enough for newcomers to become a member of the world trade body. Remaining least developed countries waiting for accession, should be allowed to join the WTO with a minimum of conditions. (2) Time is ripe to streamline consensus-based decision making in WTO. Practical alternative decision making process is required to run an organization as complex as the WTO. While the World Bank has a Development committee, the IMF has an Interim committee - likewise WTO can have an alternative decision making body. In case of world bank and IMF, those committees first discuss and then decide basic policy issues. In the same manner, there could be some sort of Council with notating membership that would be in-charge of building consensus and narrowing differences on major and controversial issues within WTO. Such a body could assist the General Council in making the decision making process more efficient in WTO. (3) The dispute settlement body which handles trade conflicts between member countries, is the backbone of the WTO. The number of trade disputes has multiplied in recent years, creating a pressure on the panels. Member countries are becoming more sensitive of the Panel's rulings, particularly when they represent interpretations of unclear WTO rules. Therefore, reforming the dispute settlement body could also make the WTO more effective. (4) Informal consultative groups of member countries can be devised as a way of improving internal communication in order

Concluding observations

to eliminate the frustrations of some smaller countries which feel that they are left out of the core discussions. Although there have been reforms and improvements in the internal and external transparency, there is still room for further improvement. (5) Clarification and regular review of rules are required specially when they clash with other agreements in order to prevent trade conflicts and to avoid trade restrictions. For example, anti-dumping procedures can be reviewed, so that they cannot be used as a means to restrict competition, instead they should be used only as a protection against genuine dumping practices. (6) In today's perspective, WTO is required to make sure that the world trade is more consistent with development. WTO is also increasingly required to put in place the integrated framework to work together with other international organizations on specific issues such as globalization, eradication of poverty , assurance of environmental benign-ness and maintaining consistency with social goals, so that WTO can work more efficiently, effectively and in a rewarding manner.

The member countries of the WTO should create a policy atmosphere where the poorer countries must have their agenda represented at the WTO in order to avoid increased polarization between the developed and the developing world. There can be several trade-offs. If the developed countries wants to talk about, say, industrial tariffs, the developing nations could ask for talks on market access for agricultural products. If the developed nations want to discuss information-technology products, the developing world could push for talks on accelerating the phase-out of the restrictions on textiles, the Agreement on textiles and clothing. If the developed world wants to discuss intellectual property rights, the developing countries could push for a wide-ranging discussion of the anti-dumping regime which is frequently used to keep goods out of wealthier countries. Instead of bickering on issues, it is to be agreed by the WTO members that the time is ripe when the needs of the poor must be represented. Access to basic humanitarian needs, such as cheap medicine, minimum food at affordable price must be met. Liberalization commitments by developed and richer countries have, so far, been implemented half-heartedly. In many cases, developed countries have back-loaded their commitments, saving most of the gains for the years just before the deadline expires. In the area of agricultural goods, world trade continues to be distorted by different provisions such as domestic support schemes, tariff escalations, export subsidies and tariff peaks. Also observing of sanitary standards have appeared as new barriers which slow exports and imports of food. It is true that some of these represent legitimate concerns, but others are abruptly trade barriers. However, developing countries also need the institutional capacity in order to take the advantage of developed markets while facing complex and comprehensive technical and sanitary requirements.

CINA AND WTO:

China's accession to the WTO has brought with it the expectation that the views and interests of the developing countries will acquire a greater voice in the multilateral trading system. In the long-term, China will most probably play a role in WTO as a bridge between the developed and developing member countries taking into consideration the dual role it plays as a developing economy as well as an emerging superpower. However, in the short-run, since China is having a voice in any new trade round, it's presence would certainly help shift the balance of power in upcoming trade talks more in favor of developing nations. In other words, it will certainly push for a developing world agenda, perhaps by teaming up with other major developing nations such as India and Brazil. As an implication of China's entry to the WTO, developing countries have already started to gain a stronger presence in WTO to the extent that their interests coincide with China's. Obviously, the question will arise that what are the scopes of this coincidence. Market opening and economic development, anti-dumping, textiles and clothing, and intellectual property are among the core issues involved in this respect.

While the nature of the individual core issue differs across developing countries according to their initial conditions and actual level of development, China's insistence on the principle of prioritizing domestic market development in the context of progressive trade liberalization is entirely in line with the interests of developing countries. This is not only because of economic reasons, there is social aspects too, particularly that of poverty reduction. In the current as well as in the future round of negotiations in the WTO, this issue is certainly to take center point. Obviously, while discussing this issue, it is also having an implication for economic relationships between other developing countries and China. In the short-run, there has been undoubtedly some growing competition between China and other developing countries in terms of labor-intensive manufactures. However, China's export-mix is visibly and rapidly evolving towards increasingly higher technology products and at the same time Chinese market is also being increasingly opened to products where other developing countries, mainly less developing countries have comparative advantages. Therefore, those countries are gradually going to enjoy growing opportunities to expand their exports to the Chinese market.

Developing member countries including China share the concern about the fairness in the application of anti-dumping actions by developed member countries. China is particularly more concerned since it is getting frequently exposed in the recent times in this regard. The actions and practices by industrialized countries towards anti-dumping constitute a major sensitive issue within WTO for the developing member countries. However, like in other cases, the developing countries are also, so far, at a clear disadvantageous position in terms of the ability to prepare and defend an anti-dumping case before the WTO's Dispute Settlement Panel.

Developing member countries including China are also hurt by the back-loading of the process of liberalization through the Agreement on Textiles and Clothing, and are also exposed to additional restrictions. While liberalization of trade in the area of Textiles and Clothing is definitely in the joint interest of China and that of the developing nations at large, bilateral agreements prior to China's joining to WTO show that there is plenty of room for mutual understanding between China and other developing member countries in this field with the idea of doing away with reciprocal trade frictions.

Intellectual property rights is another core issue between developed and developing member countries in WTO. Drawing on foreign technology, in order to mobilize domestic innovation and to accelerate competitiveness, upgrading is certainly a priority for all developing member countries including China. In order to facilitate access to proprietary technological assets, reaching equitable terms through an intellectual property regime which encourages the transfer of technology rather than deterring it and also lending itself to restrictive business practices should be the basic fundamental to overcome continuous and sustained doubts about the implementation of the respective WTO agreement.

A WAY AHEAD:

China is still a developing country. However, it is eminent that China is quickly emerging as a global power. Some analysts forecast that by 2030, China's gross domestic product will be the same as that of the U.S.A. It is also true that China's resurgence forms part of Asia's rise in the 21st. century. To have a worldwide impact, China can no more simply rely on it's economic and technological muscle, it also requires to demonstrate it's aesthetic soft power through institutional strength and the positive influence of ideas and values as a nation as stated by Anthony Cheung Bing-Leung, the Executive Councilor of HKSAR. Such demonstration will be increasingly required in every organization and institution, obviously including WTO, wherever China is involved. Chinese leadership is presumably aware that although China becomes richer after three decades of reform and opening up, the price for such progress has been the growing inequity and entrenched corruption. As Mr.Leung rightly mentioned that in comparison to many developed countries, freedoms in China are still constrained, protests against local mal-administration are on the rise, ethnic minority issues loom large, building the rule of law and other institutional improvements lags behind construction in infrastructure and technology. While China's economic advancement is huge and unparallel, governance still rates poorly. The 2008 World Bank governance indicators put Beijing's effectiveness at 63.5 out of 100, but 'voice and accountability' was rated only 5.8 and the rule of law, control of corruption, regulatory quality and political stability -- all rated below 50-point mark. China's central leadership are apparently sincere and committed to resolve and tackle the issues in connection with the dark-side of the unparallel growth. Premier Wen Jiabao, while addressing the State reception marking the 60th anniversary of the founding of the People's Republic, pointed out clearly the need to move ahead with economic and political restructuring and continuous reforms, uphold social equity and justice, promote a socialist democracy and adhere to the rule of law, and to build a prosperous, democratic, harmonious and culturally advanced China in the next 40 years when the People's Republic will be celebrating it's centenary. The coming years will certainly tell the world to what extent the Chinese Communist Party is capable of delivering such a transformation.

While China stresses its national characteristics, it should also take heed of world trends and the common pursuits of humanity. Moreover, China's pursuit of socialist democracy should not be devoid of some fundamental values embodied in the notion of democracy world-wide. In the world-trade arena, there is no doubt that China will continue it's rapid pace towards catching up with the advanced industrialized world, provided that trade frictions and market disruptions do not swamp the process, in order to setting a new example of how globalization can be consistent with development and dismissing internal disparities. Nine years on, China's WTO accession has been proved to be clear example of pragmatism in the implementation of a shared will to materialize the long-term benefit for all the developing countries as well as for the world at large.

Economic and Financial Tables

Table 1: General Economic and Financial Indicators, 2000 - 2009

(All figures are in billions of RMB or percent unless otherwise indicated)

Main indicators	2000	2001	2002	2003	2004	2005	2006	2007	2008	2009
GDP	9,921.5	10,965.5	12,033.3	13,582.3	15,987.8	18,321.7	21,192.4	25,730.6	30,067.0	33,535.3
Real GDP growth (%)	8.4	8.3	9.1	10.0	10.1	10.4	11.6	13.0	9.0	8.7
Consumer price index	0.4	0.7	-0.8	1.2	3.9	1.8	1.5	4.8	5.9	-0.7
Industrial value-added output*	2,539.5	2,832.9	3,299.5	4,199.0	5,480.5	7,218.7	9,107.6	11,704.8	NA	NA
% growth	17.8	11.6	16.5	27.3	30.5	31.7	26.2	28.5	12.9	11.0
Fixed-asset investment		3,721.3	4,350.0	5,556.7	7,047.7	8,877.4	10,999.8	13,732.4	17,282.8	22,484.6
% growth	10.3	13.0	16.9	27.7	26.8	26.0	23.9	24.8	25.9	30.1

Retail sales	3,910.6	4,305.5	4,813.6	5,251.6	5,950.1	6,717.7	7,641.0	8,921.0	10,848.8	12,534.3
% growth	9.7	10.1	11.8	9.1	13.3	12.9	13.7	16.8	21.6	15.5
Urban per capita disposable income (RMB)	6,280.0	6,859.6	7,702.8	8,472.2	9,421.6	10,493.0	11,759.5	13,785.8	15,780.8	17,175.0
% growth	7.3	9.2	12.3	10.0	11.2	11.4	12.1	17.2	14.5	8.8
Rural per capita net income (RMB)	2,253.4	2,366.4	2,475.6	2,622.2	2,936.4	3,254.9	3,587.0	4,140.4	4,760.6	5,153.0
% growth	1.9	5.0	4.6	5.9	12.0	10.8	10.2	15.4	15.0	8.2
Unemployment rate**	3.1	3.6	4.0	4.3	4.2	4.2	4.1	4.0	4.2	NA

Notes : NA = not available. * All state-owned industrial enterprises and all non-state industrial enterprises with revenue from principal business of more than RMB 5 million. **Registered urban unemployment according to official PRC National Bureau of Statistics (NBS) figures.

Sources: China Statistical Yearbook 2005 and 2009; NBS Website.

Table 2: China's Financial Indicators, 2000 - 2009

Main indicators	2000	2001	2002	2003	2004	2005	2006	2007	2008	2009
M0 supply	1,465.3	1,568.9	1,727.8	1,974.6	2,146.8	2,403.2	2,707.3	3,037.5	3,421.9	3,824.6
% growth	8.9	7.1	10.1	14.3	8.7	11.9	12.7	12.2	12.7	11.8
M1 supply	5,314.7	5,987.2	7,088.2	8,411.9	9,597.0	10,727.9	12,603.5	15,256.0	16,621.7	22,000.0
% growth	16.0	12.7	16.8	18.7	13.6	11.8	17.5	21.0	9.0	32.4
M2 supply	13,461.0	15,830.2	18,500.7	22,122.3	25,410.7	29,875.6	34,560.4	40,344.2	47,516.7	60,600.0
% growth	12.3	17.6	16.8	19.6	14.7	17.6	15.7	16.7	17.8	27.7
Exchange rate (RMB/$)	8.28	8.28	8.28	8.28	8.28	8.07	7.81	7.30	6.83	6.83
Foreign exchange reserves ($ billion)	165.6	212.2	286.4	403.3	609.9	818.8	1,066.3	1,528.2	1,946.0	2,399.2
Foreign debt ($ billion)	145.7	170.1	171.4	193.6	228.6	281.0	323.0	373.6	374.7	NA

Notes : NA = not available.
Sources : China Statistical Yearbook 2005 and 2009; NBS website.

Table 3 : Trade surplus or deficit by country and region, 2000 - 2005
(US$ million)

	2000	2001	2002	2003	2004	2005
World	24,108.8	22,545.3	30,425.9	25,468.0	32,096.8	101,880.7
America	30,926.7	28,929.4	44,541.4	56,812.1	77,669.5	115,318.0
United States	29,781.9	28,137.7	42,789.0	58,682.1	80,401.1	114,173.3
Other America	1,144.9	791.7	1,752.4	-1,870.1	-2,731.6	1,144.7
Canada	-593.2	-682.2	676.6	1,257.7	808.2	4,142.5
Europe	10,019.8	7,607.3	12,401.8	24,177.4	38,481.4	74,163.3
EC(25)	9,587.4	7,937.9	13,132.9	23,943.0	37,153.5	70,116.2
EFTA	-835.0	-1,223.5	-1,795.2	-1,793.8	-2,474.8	-1,728.5
Other Europe	1,267.4	892.8	1,064.1	2,028.2	3,802.7	5,775.7
CIS[a]	-4,184.2	-6,165.2	-5,523.0	-3,846.0	-2,407.2	676.0
Russian Federation	-3,536.5	-5,248.3	-4,885.9	-3,698.1	-3,029.3	-2,678.7
Africa	-546.5	1,169.7	1,492.5	1,767.4	-1,913.4	-2,379.9

Middle East		-3,820.4	-2,070.8	39.0	-1,158.2	-4,686.6	-8,850.7
Asia		-1,109.8	1,840.6	-7,552.0	-27,178.4	-36,354.9	-21,863.3
Japan		144.6	2,153.2	-5,032.2	-14,739.4	-20,817.7	-16,459.5
Six East Asian Traders		-1,631.6	-774.3	-3,798.5	-12,699.2	-13,699.6	-3,138.1
	Chinese Taipei	-20,454.6	-22,337.7	-31,475.3	-40,356.1	-51,214.5	-58,134.8
	Hong Kong, China	35,089.3	37,118.7	47,736.9	65,155.7	89,071.8	112,254.0
	Korea, Rep of	-11,915.0	-10,858.2	-13,033.4	-23,033.3	-34,422.5	-41,712.7
	Malaysia	-2,915.1	-2,982.9	-4,322.1	-7,845.5	-10,088.7	-9,489.3
	Singapore	701.4	662.4	-62.3	-1,621.1	-1,306.9	116.2
	Thailand	-2,137.5	-2,376.7	-2,642.3	-4,998.9	-5,738.9	-6,171.4
Other Asia		377.2	461.7	1,278.7	260.3	-1,837.5	-2,265.7
	Australia	-1,595.1	-1,856.5	-1,265.5	-1,036.5	-2,714.2	-3,299.0
	India	207.3	196.7	397.3	-908.2	-1,742.0	-833.7
	Indonesia	-1,340.1	-1,052.2	-1,081.9	-1,265.1	-959.2	-86.2

Memorandum :

APEC		21,054.7	20,820.9	27,393.4	24,562.9	35,996.3	29,015.0
ASEAN		-4,840.3	-4,838.6	-7,612.3	-16,400.8	-20,068.0	-19,627.8
EC(15)		7,383.4	5,231.3	9,724.2	19,114.3	31,712.7	63,096.6
a	Commonwealth of Independent States (CIS) includes Armenia, Azerbaijan, Belarus, Georgia, Kazakhstan, Kyrgyzstan, Moldova, Russian Federation, Tajikistan, Turkmenistan, Ukraine, and Uzbekistan.						

Sources : UNSD, Comtrade database (SITC Rev.3); and General Administration of Customs (2005), China's Customs Statistics :

Table 4 : Merchandise exports by group of products, 2001 - 2009

	(US$ million and per cent from 2001-2004)				(US$ billion and per cent from 2005-2009)				
	2001	2002	2003	2004	2005	2006	2007	2008	2009
Total exports (US$ million & US$ billion)	266,098.2	325,596.0	438,227.8	593,325.6	762.0	968.9	1,220.1	1,430.7	1,201.7
Processed exports	147,434.0	179,927.0	241,849.0	327,998.0	54.7	52.7	50.6	47.2	48.8
	(Per cent)				(Per cent)				
Total primary products	11.2	9.9	9.2	8.4	7.9	7.3	6.7	6.8	6.3
Agriculture	6.2	5.8	5.1	4.1	3.8	3.4	3.2	3.0	3.4
Food	5.3	5.0	4.4	3.5	3.2	2.9	2.7	2.5	2.9
Agricultural raw material	0.9	0.8	0.7	0.6	0.5	0.5	0.5	0.4	0.5
Mining	4.9	4.2	4.1	4.3	4.1	4.0	3.5	3.9	2.9
Ores and other minerals	0.5	0.4	0.4	0.3	0.4	0.3	0.2	0.3	0.2
Non-ferrous metals	1.3	1.2	1.2	1.6	1.4	1.9	1.6	1.4	1.0
Fuels	3.2	2.6	2.5	2.4	2.3	1.8	1.7	2.2	1.7
Manufactures	88.6	89.9	90.6	91.4	91.9	92.4	93.1	93.1	..
Iron and steel	1.2	1.0	1.1	2.3	2.5	3.4	4.2	5.0	2.0

Chemicals	5.0	4.7	4.5	4.4	4.7	4.6	4.9	5.5	5.2
Other semi-manfuactures	7.7	7.8	7.3	7.4	7.6	7.8	7.7	7.4	7.4
Machinery and transport equipment	35.7	39.0	42.8	45.2	46.2	47.1	47.4	47.1	49.1
Power generating machines	1.0	0.9	0.8	0.8	0.8	0.8	0.9	1.2	..
Other non-electrical machinery	3.9	4.0	4.2	4.5	4.7	5.0	5.6	6.4	6.0
7415 Air conditioning mch, pts	0.5	0.5	0.7	0.7	..	..	..	..	..
Office machines & telecom. equipment	19.6	23.2	26.9	29.0	29.7	29.7	28.5	26.7	..
7599 Parts, data proc.etc. mch	3.1	4.1	4.2	4.1	..	..	..	..	..
7522 Digital computers	0.4	1.1	3.2	3.9	4.3	4.5	5.5	5.2	..
7526 Input or output units	2.6	3.0	3.6	3.8	3.3	2.7	1.8	1.4	..
7649 Parts, telecommun. equipt	2.5	2.8	3.0	3.1	3.3	3.2	3.0	2.9	..
7643 TV, radio transmittrs etc.	1.7	1.9	1.9	2.7	3.1	3.7	3.0	2.7	..
7599 Parts and accessories of 751.1,751.2,751.9 and 752	..	..	..	..	3.8	3.4	2.7	2.2	..
7638 Sound, video recording/reproducing apparatus	1.5	2.0	2.4	2.7	2.7	2.2	1.7	1.6	..
7764 Electronic integrated circuits and microassemblies	0.9	1.3	1.5	1.9	1.9	2.2	2.0	1.8	..
7527 Storage units, data proc.	1.2	1.2	1.3	1.2	..	..	..	..	..
7763 Diodes, transistors, etc.	..	..	..	..	0.4	0.5	0.7	1.1	..
7513 Photo copying apparatus with optical system, thermo-copying	..	..	..	..	0.4	0.5	1.0	0.9	..

7641 Line telephone etc. equip	1.0	0.9	0.9	1.0	1.1	1.3	1.5	1.3	..
7611 Colour television receivers	0.5	0.7	0.7	0.9	1.1	1.3	1.5	1.3	..
Other electrical machines	7.5	7.5	7.2	7.2	7.1	7.4	7.5	7.5	..
7712 Other electrical power machinery, parts of 771	1.0	1.0	1.0	1.0	1.0	1.0	1.0	1.0	..
7758 Electro-thermic appliances, n.e.s.	1.1	1.1	1.1	1.0	1.0	0.9	0.8	0.8	..
7731 Insulated wire, cable etc.; optical fibre cables	..	..	..	..	0.6	0.7	0.8	0.8	..
Automotive products	0.7	0.8	0.8	1.1	1.3	1.5	1.9	2.0	..
7843 Other parts, motor vehicle parts and accessories of 722, 781 to 783	0.5	0.6	0.6	0.7	0.9	0.9	1.0	1.0	..
Other transport equipment	3.0	2.6	2.9	2.7	2.7	2.7	3.0	3.3	..
7863 Transport containers	0.8	0.7	0.9	0.9	0.5	0.8	..	..	..
7932 Ships, boats, etc. (excl. pleasure craft, tugs, etc.)	..	..	..	..	0.5	0.8	0.9	1.2	..
Textiles	6.3	6.3	6.1	5.6	5.4	5.0	4.6	4.6	5.0
Clothing	13.8	12.7	11.9	10.4	9.7	9.8	9.5	8.4	8.9
8453 Jersys, pullovrs, etc.knit	1.8	1.6	1.3	1.1	1.2	1.3	1.3	1.1	..
8442 Suits, dresses, skirts, etc.	0.6	0.7	0.8	0.7	..	..	..	..	..
Other consumer goods	19.0	18.4	16.9	15.9	15.7	14.7	14.9	15.0	..
8719 Liquid crystal devices, n.e.s.; lasers (excl. laser diodes)	0.2	0.3	0.7	1.2	1.5	1.4	1.7	1.6	..
8942 Children's toys	1.9	1.7	1.4	1.1	..	..	..	..	..

8514 Other footwear, lthr. uppers	1.1	1.1	0.9	0.8	..	..	..	..	..
8943 Articles for funfair, table or parlour games	..	..	..	..	0.9	0.9	0.8	..	..
8211 Seats (excl. of 872.4), and parts	..	..	..	..	0.7	0.8	0.8	1.0	..
Other	0.2	0.2	0.2	0.2	0.2	0.2	0.2	0.9	0.1

.. Not available

Sources:
UNSD, Comtrade database (SITC Rev.3); and General Administration of Customs (2005) & (2009), China's Customs Statistics: Monthly Exports & Imports, 12, Series No. 196 & 244.

Table 5 : Merchandise imports by group of products, 2001 - 2009

	(US$ million and per cent from 2001-2004)				(US$ billion and per cent from 2005-2009)				
	2001	2002	2003	2004	2005	2006	2007	2008	2009
Total imports (US$ million & US$ billion)	243,552.9	295,170.1	412,759.8	561,228.7	660.0	791.5	956.1	1,132.6	1,005.6
Processed imports	93,974.0	122,200.0	162,935.0	221,741.0	41.5	40.6	38.5	33.4	32.1
	(Per cent)				(Per cent)				
Total primary products	21.3	19.2	20.1	23.4	25.0	26.5	28.9	34.8	33.4
Agriculture	8.3	7.4	7.4	7.5	6.8	6.5	6.8	7.7	7.6
Food	3.8	3.4	3.6	3.8	3.3	2.9	3.4	4.4	4.5
2222 Soya beans	1.2	0.8	1.3	1.2	1.2	0.9	1.2	1.9	..
Agricultural raw material	4.4	4.1	3.8	3.8	3.6	3.6	3.4	3.3	3.1
Mining	13.1	11.8	12.7	15.9	18.1	20.0	22.0	27.2	24.9
Ores and other minerals	3.3	2.8	3.2	4.8	5.8	5.9	7.6	9.4	8.8
2815 Iron ores and concentrates, not agglomerated	0.9	0.8	1.0	1.9	2.4	2.4	3.2	5.0	..
2813 Copper ores and concentrates	..	..	..	..	0.6	0.8	0.9	0.9	..
2882 Other non-ferrous base metal waste and scrap, n.e.s.	..	..	..	..	0.7	0.8	0.9	0.8	..

Non-ferrous metals	2.5	2.5	2.5	2.5	2.6	2.9	3.4	2.8	3.8
6821 Copper anodes; alloys; unwrought	0.6	0.7	0.7	0.7	0.8	0.8	1.2	1.0	..
Fuels	7.2	6.5	7.1	8.6	9.7	11.2	11.0	14.9	12.3
3341 Motor gasolene, light oil	0.0	0.0	1.4	1.6	..	..	..	..	..
3330 Crude oils of petroleum and bituminous minerals	4.8	4.3	4.8	6.0	7.2	8.4	8.4	11.4	..
Manufactures	78.0	80.2	79.6	76.3	74.7	73.2	70.9	64.8	..
Iron and steel	4.4	4.6	5.3	4.2	4.0	2.7	2.5	2.4	2.6
Chemicals	13.2	13.2	11.9	11.7	11.8	11.0	11.2	10.5	11.2
5138 Polycarboxylic acids, etc	0.7	0.9	0.8	0.9	..	..	..	..	..
5112 Cyclic hydrocarbons	0.5	0.5	0.7	0.8	0.8	0.8	0.9	0.8	..
Other semi-manfuactures	5.1	4.8	4.2	3.8	3.4	3.3	3.1	2.8	2.8
Machinery and transport equipment	43.9	46.4	46.7	45.0	44.0	45.1	43.2	39.0	40.6
Power generating machines	1.6	1.5	1.3	1.2	1.2	1.1	1.0	1.0	..
Other non-electrical machinery	10.6	11.1	10.6	10.3	8.5	8.0	7.5	7.3	7.0
7284 Machinery and appliances for particular industries, n.e.s.	2.2	2.2	2.1	2.2	1.6	1.5	1.6	1.4	..
Office machines & telecom. equipment	20.4	22.5	23.3	22.9	24.3	25.0	23.7	20.5	..
7764 Electronic microcircuits	6.8	8.7	10.0	10.9	12.4	13.4	13.4	11.4	..

Product										
7649 Parts, telecommun. equipt	3.3	2.9	2.9	3.2	3.3	3.2	2.6	2.2	..
7599 Parts and accessories of 751, 751.2, 751.9 and 752	2.8	3.2	2.9	2.6	2.5	2.4	1.8	1.4	..
7527 Storage units, data proc.	0.8	1.0	1.5	1.5	1.7	1.7	1.6	1.5	..
7763 Diodes, transistors, etc.	1.2	1.6	1.4	1.3	1.3	1.3	1.2	1.1	..
Other electrical machines	6.6	6.7	6.5	6.3	6.3	6.6	6.6	6.0	..
7786 Electrical capacitors	0.7	0.8	0.8	0.7	..	..	..	..	..
7722 Printed circuits	0.8	0.8	0.9	0.9	1.0	1.1	1.1	1.0	..
7725 Switch. Apparatus<1000v	0.8	0.8	0.8	0.8	0.9	1.0	1.0	0.9	..
Automotive products	2.0	2.4	3.1	2.6	2.1	2.3	2.5	2.6	..
7812 Pass. Transport vehicles	0.5	0.9	1.1	0.8	0.7	0.9	1.0	1.2	..
7843 Other parts, motor vehicle	1.0	1.0	1.5	1.3	1.0	1.1	1.1	1.0	..
Other transport equipment	2.7	2.2	1.9	1.7	1.6	2.1	1.8	1.7	..
7924 Aircraft etc. ULW>1500kg	1.0	0.9	0.8	0.7	0.8	1.2	0.9	0.7	..
Textiles	5.2	4.4	3.4	2.7	2.3	2.1	1.7	1.4	1.5
Clothing	0.5	0.5	0.3	0.3	0.2	0.2	0.2	0.2	0.2
Other consumer goods	5.7	6.2	7.7	8.7	9.0	8.8	8.9	8.4	..
8719 Liquid crystal devices, n.e.s.; lasers (excl. laser diodes)	0.6	1.5	3.1	4.1	4.6	4.5	4.7	4.3	..
Other	0.7	0.5	0.3	0.3	0.3	0.3	0.3	0.4	..

.. Not available

Sources : UNSD, Comtrade database (SITC Rev.3); and General Administration of Customs (2005) & (2009), China's Customs Statistics : Monthly Exports & Imports, 12, Series No. 196 & 244.

Table 6 : Merchandise imports by origin, 2001 - 2009

	(US$ million and per cent from 2001-2004)				(US$ billion and per cent from 2005-2009)				
	2001	2002	2003	2004	2005	2006	2007	2008	2009
Total imports (US$ million & US$ billion)	243,552.9	295,170.1	412,759.8	561,228.7	660.0	791.5	956.1	1,132.6	1,005.6
	(Per cent)				(Per cent)				
America	15.2	13.3	12.9	13.1	12.6	12.8	13.8	14.6	15.3
United States	10.8	9.2	8.2	8.0	7.4	7.5	7.3	7.2	7.7
Other America	4.4	4.0	4.7	5.2	5.2	5.3	6.5	7.4	7.6
Brazil	1.0	1.0	1.4	1.5	1.5	1.6	1.9	2.6	2.8
Canada	1.7	1.2	1.1	1.3	1.1	1.0	1.1	1.1	1.2
Europe	16.0	14.6	14.3	13.6	12.1	12.3	12.6	12.8	13.9
EC(25)	14.9	13.3	13.2	12.5	..	..	..	..	..
EU(27)	..	..	..	..	11.2	11.5	11.6	11.7	12.7
Germany	5.7	5.6	5.9	5.4	4.7	4.8	4.7	4.9	5.5
France	1.7	1.4	1.5	1.4	1.4	1.4	1.4	1.4	1.3

Italy	1.6	1.5	1.2	1.1	1.0	1.1	1.1	1.0	1.1
United Kingdom	1.4	1.1	0.9	0.8	:	:	:	:	:
EFTA	1.0	1.0	0.9	0.9	0.8	0.7	0.8	0.8	1.0
Other Europe	0.2	0.2	0.3	0.2	0.1	0.1	0.2	0.2	0.2
CIS[a]	4.0	3.6	3.2	2.9	3.1	2.9	2.9	3.0	3.1
Russian Federation	3.3	2.8	2.4	2.2	2.4	2.2	2.1	2.1	2.1
Africa	2.0	1.8	2.0	2.8	3.2	3.6	3.8	4.9	4.3
Angola	0.3	0.4	0.5	0.8	1.0	1.4	1.3	2.0	1.5
Middle East	3.8	3.2	3.5	3.9	4.7	5.2	5.0	7.1	5.6
Saudi Arabia	1.1	1.2	1.3	1.3	1.9	1.9	1.8	2.7	2.3
Iran Islamic Rep.	:	:	:	:	1.0	1.3	1.4	1.7	1.3
Asia	55.5	58.4	58.0	56.8	55.9	54.0	53.0	49.5	49.2
Japan	17.6	18.1	18.0	16.8	15.2	14.6	14.0	13.3	13.0
Six East Asian Traders	31.3	33.6	33.2	32.5	32.5	31.2	30.0	27.0	27.1
Korea, Rep. of	9.6	9.7	10.4	11.1	11.6	11.3	10.9	9.9	10.2
Chinese Taipei	11.2	12.9	12.0	11.5	11.3	11.0	10.6	9.1	8.5
Malaysia	2.5	3.1	3.4	3.2	3.0	3.0	3.0	2.8	3.2

Singapore	2.1	2.4	2.5	2.5	2.5	2.2	1.8	1.8	1.8
Thailand	1.9	1.9	2.1	2.1	2.1	2.3	2.4	2.3	2.5
Hong Kong, China	3.9	3.6	2.7	2.1	1.9	1.4	1.3	1.1	0.9
Other Asia	6.7	6.6	6.9	7.5	8.2	8.2	9.0	9.1	9.1
Australia	2.2	2.0	1.8	2.1	2.5	2.4	2.7	3.3	3.9
Philippines	0.8	1.1	1.5	1.6	2.0	2.2	2.4	1.7	1.2
India	0.7	0.8	1.0	1.4	1.5	1.3	1.5	1.8	1.4
Indonesia	1.6	1.5	1.4	1.3	1.3	1.2	1.3	1.3	1.4
Other	3.6	5.1	6.1	6.9	8.4	9.3	9.0	8.2	8.6
Free zones	3.6	5.1	6.1	6.9	8.4	9.3	9.0	8.2	8.6
Memorandum :									
APEC	71.0	71.6	69.3	67.8	74.8	73.6	72.3	67.5	69.0
ASEAN	9.5	10.6	11.5	11.2	11.4	11.3	11.3	10.3	10.6
EC(15)	14.7	13.1	12.8	12.2	..	..	..	..	..

a Commonwealth of Independent States (CIS) includes Armenia, Azerbaijan, Belarus, Georgia, Kazakhstan, Kyrgyzstan, Moldova, Russian Federation, Tajikistan, Turkmenistan, Ukraine, and Uzbekistan.
Source : UNSD, Comtrade database (SITC Rev.3); and General Administration of Customs (2005) & (2009), China's Customs Statistics : Monthly Exports & Imports, 12, Series No. 196 & 244.

Table7 : Merchandise export by destination, 2001 - 2009

	(US$ million and per cent from 2001-2004)				(US$ billion and per cent from 2005-2009)				
	2001	2002	2003	2004	2005	2006	2007	2008	2009
Total imports (US$ million & US$ billion)	266,098.2	325,596.0	438,227.8	593,325.6	762.0	968.9	1,220.1	1,430.7	1,201.7
	(Per cent)				(Per cent)				
America	24.8	25.7	25.1	25.5	26.0	26.3	24.9	24.2	24.6
United States	20.4	21.5	21.1	21.1	21.4	21.0	19.1	17.7	18.4
Other America	4.3	4.2	4.0	4.4	4.6	5.3	5.8	6.5	6.2
Brazil	..	..	..	..	0.6	0.8	0.9	1.3	1.2
Canada	1.3	1.3	1.3	1.4	1.5	1.6	1.6	1.5	1.5
Mexico	0.7	0.9	0.7	0.8	..	..	..	..	..
Europe	17.5	17.0	19.0	19.3	20.2	20.9	21.6	21.9	21.0
EC(25)	16.6	16.1	17.9	18.1	..	..	..	..	..
EU(27)	..	..	..	..	19.1	19.6	20.1	20.5	19.7
Germany	3.7	3.5	4.0	4.0	4.3	4.2	4.0	4.1	4.2
Netherlands	2.7	2.8	3.1	3.1	3.4	3.2	3.4	3.2	3.1

France	1.4	1.3	1.7	1.7	1.5	1.6	1.7	1.9	1.8
Italy	1.5	1.5	1.5	1.6	1.5	1.4	1.7	1.6	1.7
United Kingdom	2.5	2.5	2.5	2.5	2.5	2.5	2.6	2.5	2.6
Belgium-Luxembourg	1.0	0.9	1.0	1.1	...	...	...	...	...
Spain	0.9	0.8	0.9	0.9	1.1	1.2	1.4	1.5	1.2
EFTA	0.4	0.4	0.4	0.4	0.4	0.4	0.5	0.5	0.4
Other Europe	0.5	0.5	0.7	0.8	0.7	0.9	1.0	0.9	0.8
CIS[a]	1.3	1.6	2.1	2.3	2.8	2.9	3.9	4.5	3.2
Russian Federation	1.0	1.1	1.4	1.5	1.7	1.6	2.3	2.3	1.5
Africa	2.2	2.1	2.3	2.3	2.4	2.7	3.1	3.6	4.0
Middle East	2.7	2.9	3.0	2.9	2.9	3.1	3.6	4.1	4.3
United Arab Emirates	0.9	1.1	1.1	1.2	1.1	1.2	1.4	1.7	1.6
Asia	51.5	50.6	48.4	47.6	45.6	44.0	42.8	41.7	43.0
Japan	16.9	14.9	13.6	12.4	11.0	9.5	8.4	8.1	8.1
Six East Asian Traders	28.3	29.3	28.3	28.4	27.7	27.6	26.6	25.2	25.3
Korea, Rep. of	4.7	4.8	4.6	4.7	4.6	4.6	4.6	5.2	4.5

Chinese Taipei	1.9	2.0	2.1	2.3	2.2	2.1	1.9	1.8	1.7
Malaysia	1.2	1.5	1.4	1.4	1.4	1.4	1.5	1.5	1.6
Singapore	2.2	2.1	2.0	2.1	2.2	2.4	2.5	2.3	2.5
Thailand	0.9	0.9	0.9	1.0	1.0	1.0	1.0	1.1	1.1
Hong Kong, China	17.5	18.0	17.4	17.0	16.3	16.0	15.1	13.3	13.8
Other Asia	6.3	6.4	6.5	6.8	6.8	7.0	7.9	8.4	9.6
Australia	1.3	1.4	1.4	1.5	1.5	1.4	1.5	1.6	1.7
India	0.7	0.8	0.8	1.0	1.2	1.5	2.0	2.2	2.5
Viet Nam	..	..	..	..	0.7	0.8	1.0	1.1	1.4
Indonesia	1.1	1.1	1.0	1.1	1.1	1.0	1.0	1.2	1.2
Memorandum :									
APEC	72.8	73.3	70.9	70.2	68.6	66.6	63.7	61.0	61.6
ASEAN	6.9	7.2	7.1	7.2	7.3	7.4	7.8	8.0	8.8
EC(15)	15.4	14.8	16.5	16.8	..	..	..	..	..

a   Commonwealth of Independent States (CIS) includes Armenia, Azerbaijan, Belarus, Georgia, Kazakhstan, Kyrgyzstan, Moldova, Russian Federation, Tajikistan, Turkmenistan, Ukraine, and Uzbekistan.

Sources : UNSD, Comtrade database (SITC Rev.3); and General Administration of Customs (2005) & (2009), China's Customs Statistics : Monthly Exports & Imports, 12, Series No. 196 & 244.

Table 8 : International trade, processing trade, and shares of FIEs, 2007 - 2009

(US$ billion, unless otherwise indicated)

	2007	2008	2009	Growth rate 2008/07 (%)	Growth rate 2009/08 (%)
Total exports	1,220.5	1,430.7	1,201.0	17.2	-16.0
Processed export	617.6	675.1	587.0	9.3	-13.1
Share of processing trade in total exports (%)	50.6	47.2	48.8	n.a.	n.a.
Exports of FIEs	695.4	790.5	672.2	13.7	-15.0
Share in total exports (%)	57.0	55.3	55.9	n.a.	n.a.
Processed exports in FIEs	521.5	572.2	493.7	9.7	-13.7
Share in FIEs' total exports (%)	75.0	72.4	73.4	n.a.	n.a.
Share of FIEs processed exports in total processed exports (%)	84.4	84.8	84.1	n.a.	n.a.
Total imports	956.1	1,132.6	1,005.6	18.5	-11.2

Processed imports	368.5	378.4	322.3	2.7	-14.8
Share of processing trade in total imports (%)	38.5	33.4	32.1	n.a.	n.a.
Imports of FIEs	559.8	619.4	545.2	10.7	-12.0
Share in total imports (%)	58.5	54.7	54.20	n.a.	n.a.
Processed imports in FIEs	309.7	318.4	270.8	2.8	-15.0
Share in FIEs' total imports (%)	55.3	51.4	49.7	n.a.	n.a.
Share of FIEs processed imports in total processed imports (%)	84.0	84.2	84.0		n.a.

n.a.   Not applicable.

Sources: National Bureau of Statistics of China, Statistical Yearbook 2009; and General Administration of Customs, China's Customs Statistics (various issues).

Table 9 : World imports of commercial services by region and selected economy, 1999 - 2009

(Million dollars)

	1999	2000	2001	2002	2003	2004	2005	2006	2007	2008	2009
World	1367000	1460500	1478600	1564200	1786100	2124100	2364000	2645700	3131700	3555000	3142600
North America	257600	268200	264200	270900	291700	335900	365900	408700	443700	477600	429200
Canada	40060	43597	43236	44455	51771	58023	64906	71841	81723	87953	77579
Mexico	14061	16718	16521	17031	17571	19250	20915	22329	23228	24701	21022
United States	183485	207880	204478	209397	222346	258675	280091	314493	338759	364930	330590
Other North America	-6	5	-35	17	12	-48	-12	37	-10	16	9
South and Central America	50600	54800	55100	48800	51200	58600	71300	81300	99200	120400	110500
Brazil	13357	15574	15825	13496	14350	16111	22409	27149	34700	44396	44074
Other South and Central America	37243	39226	39275	35304	36850	42489	48891	54151	65000	76004	66426
Europe	647700	665500	685200	741600	882800	1031000	1129100	1236500	1471600	1643500	1431200
Denmark	18402	21063	22121	24305	28254	33401	37002	45232	53998	62432	51031
France	62102	64400	66121	72428	86476	98553	105981	112364	128628	140956	126425
Germany	139388	135812	140593	143769	171365	195352	209790	224591	259449	289676	253110

Italy	56240	54632	56087	61110	73107	81673	88364	98107	118685	127861	114581
Netherlands	48121	49941	52166	56492	62954	68565	72413	74678	83762	91918	84708
Norway	15214	14832	15667	17834	20415	23871	28709	31227	38941	43928	37604
Portugal	7064	6810	6573	6906	8022	9372	10089	11725	13941	16230	14094
Spain	31544	32837	34903	38445	47607	58822	66739	78175	96023	104365	86467
Turkey	8449	7624	5633	5528	6690	9188	10311	10739	14547	16637	15607
United Kingdom	93170	96893	97352	107177	122948	145172	158325	170273	195402	196896	160873
European Union (27)	605200	624300	645500	698200	832000	967500	1054600	1156700	1372400	1530500	1329100
Other Europe	-437194	-443644	-457516	-490594	-577038	-660469	-713223	-777311	-904176	-977899	-842400
Commonwealth of Independent States (CIS)	20000	24000	29500	33900	39600	50300	59400	69800	90100	113300	98800
Russian Federation	13351	16230	19819	22852	26487	32216	37795	43679	56768	73616	59388
Other (CIS)	6649	7770	9681	11048	13113	18084	21605	26121	33332	39684	31412
Africa	37400	38600	41200	42300	45500	60100	71800	84800	107900	136700	114200
Algeria	2560	2360	2440	2480	2920	3858	4787	4780	6934	11063	10910
Egypt	5959	7161	6356	6013	6038	7470	9507	10288	13088	16335	12765
Ethiopia	463	479	516	556	689	932	1178	1154	1737	2379	..

Kenya	505	665	712	588	575	803	955	1235	1479	1663		
Mozambique	392	439	607	559	553	511	627	729	819	918	1004	
Nigeria	3311	3144	4420	4688	5715	5973	6384	10667	12364	..	..	
South Africa	5580	5657	5109	5376	7848	10063	11833	13900	16100	16515	14348	
Uganda	419	459	479	521	..	473	593	756	958	1233	1426	
Other Africa	18211	18236	20561	21519	24162	30017	35936	41291	54421	86594	73747	
Middle East	43800	48800	46900	51100	60500	77700	97400	121500	158800	187600	170700	
Iran, Islamic Rep. of	1905	2161	2451	5381	6432	9730	10407	11407	14760	17076	..	
Israel	10047	11703	11644	10701	10978	12611	13498	14424	17322	19629	16921	
Jordan	1485	1463	1520	1627	1690	1972	2465	2854	3356	3926	3657	
Kuwait	3867	4115	4520	4881	5534	6202	7444	8805	10494	12149	11100	
Saudi Arabia	9426	10928	7155	7152	7936	11057	19684	29488	45917	49571	45540	
United Arab Emirates	7757	8275	8893	9934	11440	14655	18891	24322	33372	42773	36799	
Other Middle East	18739	21083	17872	18576	24426	32530	44695	58688	79496	92047	102223	
Asia	329900	360500	356400	375600	411700	510400	569100	644200	759900	875900	796000	
Australia	18385	18555	17020	18023	21476	27377	29909	31600	39197	47613	41360	
China	30967	35858	39032	46080	54852	71602	83173	100327	129254	158004	158200	
Hong Kong, China	23759	24588	24797	25833	25994	30983	33838	36905	42450	46918	44379	

India	17045	18898	19792	20776	24679	35293	46820	58222	70127	87395	79774
Indonesia	12139	15381	15596	16770	17171	20620	21836	21175	24075	27994	27626
Japan	103151	105230	98762	97865	99906	119925	122369	133900	148685	163270	146903
Korea, Republic of	26773	32957	32473	36132	39928	49373	58055	68023	82108	92915	74978
New Zealand	4482	4429	4265	4715	5667	7130	8151	7795	9078	9553	7703
Thailand	13464	15329	14475	16572	17999	22909	26881	32841	38173	46029	37823
Other Asia	79735	89275	90188	92834	104028	125188	138068	153412	176753	196209	177254
Memorandum items :											
World excluding											
intra-EU (27) imports	-	-	-	-	-	1543500	1730900	1950900	2306900	2646100	2356400
intra-EU (15) imports	1049500	1135300	1140500	1189100	1338100	1612500	1813200	:	:	:	:
Europe excluding											
intra-EU (27) imports	-	-	-	-	-	450400	496000	541700	646800	734600	645000
intra-EU (15) imports	330200	340300	347100	366500	434800	519400	578300	:	:	:	:

Note : Due to frequent revisions to the services data, there are numerous breaks in the continuity of the data series at the country and regional levels.

Sources : UNSD, Comtrade database (SITC Rev.3); and General Administration of Customs (2005) & (2009), China's Customs Statistics : Monthly Exports & Imports, 12, Series No. 196 & 244.

Table 10 : Merchandise trade by region and seleted economies, 2001 - 2009 - China
(Billion dollars)

	2001	2002	2003	2004	2005	2006	2007	2008	2009
Exports									
World	266.1	325.6	438.2	593.3	762.0	969.0	1220.5	1430.7	1201.5
North America	77.5	100.4	130.4	176.2	226.0	284.2	326.2	350.2	304.8
United States	71.1	91.4	119.2	159.7	204.9	255.0	289.4	308.3	269.3
Other North America	6.4	9.0	11.2	16.4	21.1	29.2	36.9	41.8	35.5
South and Central America	6.3	6.5	8.4	13.0	17.7	26.6	39.5	56.9	42.9
Brazil	1.3	1.5	2.1	3.7	4.8	7.4	11.4	18.8	14.1
Other South and Central America	5.0	5.0	6.3	9.3	12.9	19.3	28.1	38.0	28.8
Europe	55.4	67.2	100.8	140.5	186.8	244.3	317.8	371.8	301.5
European Union (27)	53.4	64.7	96.5	134.4	178.3	231.4	299.3	351.9	285.9
Other Europe	2.0	2.5	4.2	6.0	8.5	12.9	18.6	19.9	15.7
Commonwealth of Independent States (CIS)	3.5	5.1	9.3	13.8	21.4	28.0	48.1	64.7	39.0
Russian Federation	2.7	3.5	6.0	9.1	13.2	15.8	28.5	33.1	17.5
Other (CIS)	0.8	1.6	3.3	4.7	8.2	12.2	19.6	31.6	21.5

Africa	5.9	6.9	10.1	13.6	18.5	26.2	36.8	50.5	46.3
South Africa	1.0	1.3	2.0	3.0	3.8	5.8	7.4	8.6	7.4
Other Africa	4.8	5.6	8.1	10.7	14.7	20.4	29.3	41.9	39.0
Middle East	7.1	9.5	13.3	16.9	22.2	29.6	44.3	58.8	51.1
Asia	110.3	130.0	165.9	219.1	269.2	329.5	406.6	476.8	413.3
Japan	49.1	55.3	70.8	89.6	102.4	112.0	124.9	138.8	118.1
Six East Asian Traders	43.6	52.4	64.6	86.5	111.7	145.8	181.1	212.2	175.2
Other Asia	17.7	22.2	30.5	43.0	55.2	71.6	100.6	125.9	120.0

Imports

World	243.6	295.2	412.8	561.2	660.0	791.5	956.1	1132.6	1005.7
North America	31.0	32.0	40.0	54.2	58.5	69.6	83.8	97.9	93.7
United States	26.2	27.3	33.9	44.8	48.7	59.3	69.5	81.6	77.8
Other North America	4.8	4.7	6.1	9.5	9.7	10.3	14.2	16.4	15.9
South and Central America	5.9	7.2	13.2	19.5	24.4	31.5	47.7	67.7	60.2
Brazil	2.3	3.0	5.8	8.7	10.0	12.9	18.3	29.9	28.3
Other South and Central America	3.6	4.2	7.3	10.9	14.4	18.6	29.4	37.8	32.0

Region										
Europe	39.0	43.1	59.1	76.2	79.9	97.2	120.0	144.4	139.8
European Union (27)	36.4	39.8	55.0	70.5	74.0	90.6	111.0	132.6	127.8
Other Europe	2.6	3.3	4.2	5.7	5.9	6.6	9.0	11.8	12.0
Commonwealth of Independent States (CIS)	9.6	10.6	13.1	16.2	20.7	22.8	28.0	33.9	31.0
Russian Federation	8.0	8.4	9.7	12.1	15.9	17.6	19.7	23.8	21.3
Other (CIS)	1.7	2.2	3.4	4.1	4.8	5.2	8.3	10.1	9.8
Africa	4.8	5.4	8.4	15.6	21.1	28.8	36.4	56.0	43.3
South Africa	1.2	1.3	1.8	3.0	3.4	4.1	6.6	9.2	8.7
Other Africa	3.6	4.2	6.5	12.7	17.6	24.7	29.7	46.7	34.6
Middle East	9.2	9.5	14.4	21.6	31.0	40.8	47.9	79.9	56.2
Asia	144.0	187.3	264.5	357.7	424.3	500.8	592.3	652.7	581.2
China	8.8	15.0	25.1	38.7	55.2	73.3	85.8	92.5	86.4
Japan	42.8	53.5	74.1	94.3	100.4	115.7	134.0	150.6	130.9
Six East Asian Traders	76.2	99.3	136.9	182.5	214.3	246.8	286.5	306.3	272.0
Other Asia	16.3	19.6	28.4	42.2	54.4	65.0	86.1	103.3	91.9

Sources: UNSD, Comtrade database (SITC Rev.3); and General Administration of Customs (2005) & (2009), China's Customs Statistics: Monthly Exports & Imports, 12, Series No. 196 & 244.

Bibliography

1. Acharya, Rohini and Daly, Michael. 2004. "Selected Issues Concerning the Multilateral Trading System." Discussion Paper No.7, The World Trade Organization.
2. Anderson, Jonathan. 2005. "How to think about China (Part 3): Which Way Out for the Banking System?" Asian Economic Perspectives, UBS Investment Research, May 9.
3. Antkiewicz, Agara and Whalley, John. 2005. "China's New Regional Trade Agreements." Journal of World Trade, no.10 : 1539-57.
4. ASEAN Secretariat. 2001. "Forging closer ASEAN-China Economic Relations in the Twenty-first Century." Report submitted by the ASEAN-China Expert Group on Economic Co-operation.
5. Asian Development Bank. 2000-2009. "Country Economic Review - People's Republic of China."
6. Barnett, Steven. 2004. "Banking Sector Development." In Eswar Prasad, ed., China's Growth and Integration into the World Economy : Prospects and Challenges. International Monetary Fund.Washington, D.C.
7. Bhagwati, Jagdish and Panagariya, Arvind. 1999. "Preferential Trading Areas and Multilateralism - Strangers, Friends, or Foes?" In Trading Blocs : Alternative Approaches to Analyzing Preferential Trade Agreement, edited by Bhagwati, Jagdish. The MIT Press. Cambridge, Massachusetts.
8. Burch, D. and Goss, J. 2005. "Regionalisation, Globalisation and Multinational Agribusiness : A Comparative Perspective from Southeast Asia." In Multinational Agribusiness, edited by R. Rama, Haworth Press : New York.
9. Buszynski, Leszek. 2004. "Asia Pacific Security - Values and Identity." Routledge : London.
10. Cai, Kevin G. 1999. "Outward Foreign Direct Investment : A Novel Dimension of China's Integration into the Regional and Global Economy." The China Quarterly, December edition.

Bibliography

11. Cass, Deborah Z; Williams, Brett G.; and Barker, George. 2003. "China and the World Trading System." Cambridge University Press, Cambridge.
12. Chen, Lingying. 2002. "China-ASEAN Free Trade Area : Background, Significance and Future." All-round southeast Asia, no.8.
13. Chen, Shaohua; and Ravallion, Martin. 2004. "Welfare Impacts of China's Accession to the WTO." In D. Bhattasali, S.Li, and W. Martin, eds., China and the WTO : Accession, Policy Reform, and Poverty Reduction Strategies; World Bank and Oxford University Press, Washington, D.C.
14. Chen, Wen and Shaolian, Liao. 2005. "China-ASEAN Trade Relations : A Discussion on Complementarity and Competition." ISEAS : Singapore.
15. Chen, Xiwen. 2006. "China's Agricultural Development and Policy Readjustment after its WTO accession."
16. Chen, Yuan. 2003. "Financial System Reform and Economic Development." Speech given at the Seminar on Development and Reform in India and China, New Delhi, November 15.
17. China Statistical Abstract. 2001-2010. Beijing.
18. Chirathivat, S. 2002. "ASEAN-China Economic Partnership in an Integrating World Economy." Chulalongkorn Review 14.
19. Cooper George. 2008. "The Origin of Financial crisis." Vintage Books, New York.
20. Cordenillo, Raul L. 2005. "The Economic Benefits to ASEAN of the ASEAN-China Free Trade Area (ACFTA)." The Studies Unit of the Bureau for Economic Integration, ASEAN Secretariat.
21. Cui, Ning. 2001. " Technology-a Growth Engine to Economy." China Daily, June 18.
22. Das, Bhagirath Lal. 2003. "The WTO and the Multilateral Trading System : Past, Present and Future." Third World Network, Malaysia.
23. Das, Bhagirath Lal. 2003. "WTO : The Doha Agenda - The New Negotiations on World Trade." Third World Network : Malaysia & Zed Books : London & New York.
24. Davidson, Paul J. 2002. "The Evolving Legal Framework for Economic Co-operation." Times Academic Press, Singapore.
25. Dicken, P. 1998. "Global Shift : Transforming the World Economy." Paul Chapman Publishing Company, London.
26. Fan, Y. 2002. "Questioning Guanxi : Definition, Classification and Implications." International Business Review, 11: 543-61.

27. Fishman, Ted. 2004. "The Chinese Century," New York Times Magazine, July 4.
28. Frost, Stephen. 2004. "Chinese Outward Direct Investment in Southeast Asia : How much and what are the Regional Implications?" SEARC Working Papers Series No. 67.
29. Gao, Sheldon. 2002. "China Stock Market in a Global Perspective." Dow Jones Research Report, New York.
30. Gomez, E.T. 2002. "Political Business in East Asia : Introduction." In Political Business in East Asia, edited by Gomez, E.T., Routledge : London.
31. Gomez, E.T. and Hsiao, H.H.M. 2004. "Chinese Business Research in Southeast Asia." In Chinese Business in Southeast Asia : Contesting Cultural Explanations, Researching Entrepreneurship, edited by Gomez, E.T. and Hsiao, H.H.M. Routledge-Curzon : London.
32. Gong, Zhankui. 2003. "China and ASEAN Economic Integration : Model Comparative and Policy Choice." China Foreign Economic Relations and Trade Publishing House, Beijing.
33. Green, Stephen. 2003. "China's Stock Market : Eight Myths and Some Reasons to be Optimistic." Royal Institute of International Affairs. London.
34. Gruthrie, Doug. 2001. "The Emergence of Market Practices in China's Economic Transition : Price Setting in Shanghai's Industrial Firms." In Managing Organizational Change in Transition Economics, edited by Daniel Denison, Mahwah, NJ : Lawrence Erlbaum.
35. Gruthrie, Doug. 2003. "The Quiet Revolution : The Emergence of Capitalism in China." Harvard International Review 25(2) : 48-53.
36. Gruthrie, Doug. 2005. "Organizational Learning and Productivity : State Structure and Foreign Investment in the Rise of the Chinese Corporation." Management and Organization Review.
37. Gruthrie, Doug. 2006. "China and Globalization : The Social, Economic and Political Transformation of Chinese Society." Routledge, Taylor & Francis Group: New York, London.
38. Haggard, S. 1995. "Developing Nations and the Politics of Global Integration." Brookings Institution, Washinton, DC.
39. He, Xiaoqin. 2003. "Analysis on the Goal, Process and Benfits of China-ASEAN Free Trade Area." World Economy Study, no.6.
40. Hew, Denis. 2005. "Roadmap to an ASEAN Economic Community." Institute of Southeast Asian Studies : Singapore.

Bibliography

41. Ho, Khai Leong and Ku, C.Y. Samuel. 2005. "China and Southeast Asia - Global Changes and Regional Changes." Institute of Southeast Asian Studies : Singapore.
42. Hsu, Immanuel C.Y. 1999. "The Rise of Modern China." Oxford University Press, New York.
43. Huang, Jikun; Rozelle, Scott; and Chang, Min. 2007. "The Nature of Distortions to Agricultural Incentives in China and Implications of WTO accession."
44. Huang, Yasheng. 2003. "Selling China : Foreign Direct Investment during the Reform Era." Cambridge University Press, New York.
45. Imam, Michael. 2005. "The Chinese Interbank Markets : Cornerstone of Financial Liberalization." China and World Economy 12(5) : 17-33.
46. IMF. 2001-2010. World Economic Outlook.
47. Jands, Richard and Jing, Men. 2002. "China and Long March to Global Trade." Routledge : London.
48. Jomo, K.S. 2003. "Chinese Capitalism in Southeast Asia." In Ethnic Business : Chinese Capitalism in Southeast Asia, edited by Jomo, K.S. and Folk, B.C., Routledge Curzon : London.
49. Kansas, Dave. 2009. "The End of Wall Street As We Know It." Guide to The Wall Street Journal, Collins Business.
50. Keith, Ronald C. 2005. "China as a Rising World Power and its Response to Globalization." Routledge, London.
51. Khor, M. 2002. "The WTO, the Post-Doha Agenda and the Future of the Trade System : A Development Perspective." Third World Network, Penang, Malaysia.
52. Khor, Martin. 2003. "The WTO Agriculture Agreement: Features, Effects, Negotiations, and Suggested Changes." Third World Network, Malaysia.
53. Kingsbury, Damien. 2001. "South-East Asia - A Political Profile." Oxford University Press, Oxford.
54. Kuijs, Louis. 2005. "Investment and Saving in China." World Bank Policy Research Working Paper No. 3633, June.
55. Lardy, Nicholas R. 2002. "Integrating China into Global economy." Brookings Institution Press, Washington D.C.
56. Lall, S. 2001. "Competitiveness, Technology and Skills." Edward Elgar, Cheltenham.
57. Liang, Zhiming. 2003. "The Significance and Prospect of China-ASEAN Free Trade Area." Peace and Development, no.2.
58. Lieberthal, K. 1995. "Governing China : From Revolution through Reform." W.W. Norton, New York.

59. Liu, Ling. 2005. "China's Industrial Policies and the Global Business Revolution." Routledge, London.
60. Low, Linda. 2004. "The Political Economy of East Asia : A Business Model." Nova Science Publishers : New York. Manual on Statistics of International Trade Statistics.
61. Lubman, S.B. 1991. "Studying Contemporary Chinese Law : Limits, Possibilities and Strategy." American Journal of Comparative Law; Vol. 39.
62. Mahbubani, Kishore. 2005. "Understanding China." Foreign Affairs, September - October, pp. 49-60.
63. McCargo, D. and Pathmanand, Ukrist. 2005. "The Thaksinization of Thailand." Nordic Institute of Asian Studies Press : Copenhagen.
64. Meyer, Marshall. 2005. "Is China for Sale?" Management and Organization Review 1(2) : 303-07
65. Mingmaneenakin, Wanrak, et al. 2006. "China's Economy : The Eleven Provinces of Potential Significance to Thailand." Manager Publishing House : Bangkok.
66. Ministry of Agriculture, 2001-2010. "China Statistical Year Book." Agriculture Press, Beijing.
67. Mirati, Riyana and Hew, Denis. 2004. "APEC in the 21st Centrury." Institute of Southeast Asian Studies : Singapore.
68. MOFCOM. 2001-2010. China Foreign Investment Report.
69. National Bureau of Statistics, 2001-2010. "Statistical Yearbook of China." China Statistics Press, Beijing.
70. Newman, Richard. 2005. "The Rise of a New Power." U.S. News and World Report, June 20.
71. Nolan, Peter. 2004. "Transforming China : Globalization, Transition and Development." Anthem Press : London.
72. Nyberg, A.and Rozelle, S. 1999. "Accelerating China's Rural Transformation." World Bank, Washington, D.C.
73. Ogden, Suzanne. 2004. "Global Studies : China." Dushkin/Mc Graw-Hiu : New York.
74. Ostry, Sylvia. 1998. "China and the WTO : The Transparency Issue." Spring 3 UCLA Journal of International Law and Foreign Affairs.
75. Ostry, Sylvia, Alan S., Alexandroff, and Gomez Rafael. 2002. "China and the Long March to Global Trade - The accession of China to the World Trade Organization."
76. Panitchpakdi, Supachai and Clifford, Mark L. 2002. "China and the WTO; Changing China Changing World Trade." John Wiley & Sons (Asia) Pte Ltd, Singapore.

77. Peng, Mike and York, Anne. 2001. "Behind Intermediary Performance in Export Trade : Transactions, Agents, and Resources." Journal of International Business Studies 32(2) : 327-46.
78. Phongpaichit, Pasuk and Baker, C. 2004. "Thaksin : The Business of Politics in Thailand." Silkworm Books : Chiangmai.
79. Potter, P.B. 1994. "Riding the Tiger : Legitimacy and Legal Culture in Post-Mao China." The China Quarterly; Vol.138
80. Putatunda, Pradip and MacPherson, Stewart. 2001. "China Perspectives." Sterling Publishers Private Ltd. : New Delhi.
81. Rawski, Thomas G. 1999. "Reforming China's Economy : What Have We Learned?" The China Journal 41 : 139-56
82. Riedel, James; Jin, Jing; and Gao, Jian. 2007. "How China Grows : Investment , Finance, and Reform." Princeton University Press, New Jersey.
83. Roach, Stephen S. 2006. "The Untold China Story." Newsweek (8th May).
84. Saich, Tony. 2008. "China : Socio-Political Issues." In Hoffmann, John. W and Enright, Michael J. (eds), China into the Future : Making sense of the World's most Dynamic Economy. John Wiley & Sons (Asia) Pte. Ltd., Singapore.
85. Santoro, Michael. 1999. "Profits and Principles. "Cornell University Press : Ithaca, N.Y.
86. Saw, S.H. 2005. "ASEAN-China Relations : Realities and Prospects." Institute of Southeast Asian Studies, Singapore.
87. Segal, Adam. 2003. "Digital Dragon : High-Technology Enterprises in China." Cornell University Press : Ithaca, N.Y.
88. Sen, Rahul. 2004. "Free Trade Agreements in Southeast Asia. "Institute of Southeast Asian Studies, Singapore.
89. Sheng, Lijun. 2005. "An overiew of ASEAN-China Relations." In ASEAN-China Relations : Realities and Prospects, edited by Saw Swee Hork, Sheng Lijun and Chin Kin Wah. Institute of Southeast Asia Studies, Singapore.
90. Shenkar Oded. 2006. "The Chinese Century - The Rising Chinese economy and its impact on the global economy, the Balance of Power, and your Job." Wharton School Publishing, New Jersey, USA.
91. Shenkar, Oded. 2006. "The Chinese Century." Wharton School Publishing, Philadelphia, P.A.
92. Solomon, Richard H. 1999. "Chinese Negotiating Behavior : Pursuing Interests through Old Friends." United States Institute of Peace Press : Washington D.C.

93. Spence, Jonathan. 1999. "The Search for Modern China." W.W. Norton : New York.
94. Suehiro, A. 2003. "Determinants of Business Capability in Thailand." In Ethnic Business : Chinese Capitalism in Southeast Asia, edited by Jomo, K.S., and Folk, B.C., Routledge Curzon : London.
95. The World Bank, 1997. "China 2020. Development Challenges in the New Century." Wahsington, D.C.
96. Third World Network. 2001. "The Multilateral Trading System: A Development Perspective." United Nations Development Programme : New York.
97. Trebilcock, Michael J. and Howse, Robert. 2005. "Regulation of International Trade." Routledge : London.
98. United Nations Conference on Trade and Development (UNCTAD). 2003. "Trade and Development Report." United Nations : New York and Geneva.
99. United Nations Conference on Trade and Development. 2004. "World Investment Report : The shift towards services." United Nations : New York and Geneva.
100. United Nations Development Programme (UNDP). 2003. "Making Global Trade Work for People." Earthscan Publications : London & Virginia.
101. Walder, Andrew. 2004. "The Party Elite and China's Trajectory of Change." China : An International Journal 2(2) : 189-209.
102. Wang, Jisi. 2005. "China's Search for Stability with America." Foreign Affairs, September - October, pp.39-48
103. Wang, Tao. 2004. "China : Sources of Real Exchange Rate Fluctuations." International Monetary Fund Working Paper No. WP/04/18.
104. Wank, David. 2002. "Business - State Clientelism in China : Decline or Evolution?" In Social Connections in China : Institutions, Culture, and the Changing Nature of Guanxi, edited by Thomas Gold, Doug Guthrie, and David Wank. Cambridge University Press : New York.
105. Weatherbee, Donald E. 2005. "International Relations in Southeast Asia." Rowman & Littlefield Publishing Group, Inc.
106. WHO/WTO. 2002. "WTO Agreements and Public Health. A Joint Guide by the WHO and the WTO Secretariat." Geneva.
107. William, Ian, 2004. "China - U.S. : Double Bubbles in Danger of Colliding." Asia Times, January 23.

108. World Bank. 2000-2010. "World Development Report." Oxford University Press, New York.
109. UNIDO. 2000-2010. "World Industrial Development Reports."
110. WTO. 2000-2010. "International Trade Statistics." World Trade Organization : Geneva.
111. WTO. 2000-2010. "World Trade Report. "World Trade Organization : Geneva.
112. Yeung, H.W.C. 2004. "Chinese Capitalism in a Global Era." Routledge : London.
113. Yu An. 1999. "Several Basic Questions about my Country's Administrative Review Law." Fazhi Ribao, Legal Daily, 6th May.
114. Yu, V. (2002) : "WTO Agenda : Moving Forward?." Geneva Update, IATP, Geneva.
115. Zhang, Chunsheng. 1998. "The Development and Prospect of Administrative Procedure Law of China." Unpublished paper given at the International Symposium of Administrative Procedure Law, Shanghai, 16th November.
116. Zhang, Le-Yin. 2004. "The Roles of Corporatization and Stock Market Listing in Reforming China's State Industry." World Development 32(12) : 2031-47.
117. Zhang, Zhen. 2002. "Analysis on the constraints for China-ASEAN Free Trade Area." World Economy Study, no.6.
118. Zheng, Bijian. 2005. "Peacefully Rising to Great Power Status." Foreign Affairs, September - October, pp.18-24.

Abbreviations

AA	-	Agreement on Agriculture
AB	-	Appellate Body
ABC	-	Agriculture Bank of China
ABTC	-	APEC Business Travel Card
ACP	-	African, Caribbean and Pacific Group
ADR	-	American Depository Receipt
AEC	-	African Economic Community
ALL	-	Administrative Litigation Law
AMC	-	Asset Management Company
APTA	-	Asia Pacific Trade Agreement
ARL	-	Administrative Review Law
ASEAN	-	Association of South-East Asian Nations
ASEM	-	Asia Europe Meeting
ASG	-	Agreement on Safeguards
ATC	-	Agreement on Textiles and Clothing
AU	-	African Union
AVE	-	Ad-Valorem Equivalent
BCBS	-	Basel Committee on Banking Supervision
BCI	-	Business Competitive Index
BOD	-	Board of Directors
BOP	-	Balance of Payments
BOS	-	Board of Supervisors
CAFTA	-	China-Asean Free Trade Area
CAR	-	Capital Adequacy Ratio
CCAMC	-	Changcheng Assets Management Co. Ltd
CCB	-	China Construction Bank
CCCEWC	-	CCP Central Committee Enterprises Works Commission
CDO	-	Collateralized Debt Obligation
CDS	-	Credit Default Swaps

Abbreviations

CEPA	-	Closer Economic Partnership Agreement
CMIM	-	Chiang Mai Initiative Multilateralization Agreement
CMO	-	Collateralized Mortgage Obligation
COSTIND	-	Commission of Science, Technology, and Industry for National Defense
CPC	-	Communist Party of China
CPI	-	Consumer Price Index
CPSB	-	China Postal Savings Bank
CRR	-	Cash Reserve Ratio
CSDCC	-	China Securities Depositing and Clearing Corporation
CSRC	-	China Securities Regulatory Commission
DFAMC	-	Dong Fang Assets Management Company Ltd.
DSB	-	Dispute Settlement Body
DSU	-	Dispute Settlement Understanding
EC	-	European Commission
ECB	-	External Commercial Borrowing
EEC	-	European Economic Community
EU	-	European Union
EME	-	Emerging Market Economy
ERP	-	Effective Rate of Protection
ETDZ	-	Economic and Technological Development Zones
FAO	-	Food and Agriculture Organization
FDI	-	Foreign Direct Investment
FFE	-	Foreign Funded Enterprise
FIE	-	Foreign Invested Enterprise
FII	-	Foreign Institutional Investment
FOCAC	-	Forum on China-Africa Co-operation
FTA	-	Free-Trade Agreement
GATS	-	General Agreement on Trade in Services
GATT	-	General Agreement on Tariffs and Trade
GCI	-	Growth Competitiveness Index
GDI	-	Gross Domestic Investment
GMS	-	The Great Mekong Sub-regional Co-operation
GNP	-	Gross National Product
HRAMC	-	Hua Rong Assets Management Company Limited
IAP	-	Individual Action Plan
IASB	-	International Accounting Standards Board
IATP	-	Institute for Agriculture and Trade Policy

IBC	-	Investment Bank of China
ICBC	-	Industrial and Commercial Bank of China
ICITO	-	Interim Commission for the International Trade Organization
IEB	-	Import-Export Bank
IL	-	Import License
IMF	-	International Monetary Fund
IPO	-	Initial Public Offering
IPR	-	Intellectual Property Rights
LDC	-	Least Developed Country
LTA	-	Long-Term Agreement
LTC	-	Long-Term Care
MES	-	Modern Enterprise System
MFA	-	Multi-Fibre Agreement
MFN	-	Most Favored Nation
MHRSS	-	Ministry of Human Resources and Social Security
MIIT	-	Ministry of Industry and Information Technology
MOFCOM	-	Ministry of Commerce
MOFTEC	-	Ministry of Foreign Trade and Economic Co-operation
MOLSS	-	Ministry of Labor and Social Security
MTN	-	Multilateral Trade Negotiation
MVA	-	Manufacturing Value Added
NAFTA	-	North American Free-Trade Agreement
NAMA	-	Non-Agricultural Market Access
NDRC	-	National Development and Reform Commission
NEDL	-	National Essential Drug List
NPA	-	Non-Performing Asset
NPC	-	National Peoples' Congress
NPL	-	Non-Performing Loan
NTM	-	Non-Tariff Measure
OECD	-	Organization for Economic Co-operation and Development
OTC	-	Over the Counter
PBOC	-	Peoples' Bank of China
PCBC	-	Peoples' Construction Bank of China
POE	-	Privately Owned Enterprise
PRC	-	Peoples' Republic of China
PSE	-	Producer Subsidy Equivalent
PSI	-	Pre-Shipment Inspection

Abbreviations

PSU	-	Public Service Unit
PTA	-	Preferential Trade Agreement
RBI	-	Reserve Bank of India
RCC	-	Rural Credit Co-operative
RMCC	-	Rural Mutual Credit Co-operatives
ROO	-	Rules of Origin
SAC	-	Sino-African Co-operation
SAR	-	Special Administrative Region
SASAC	-	State-owned Asset Supervision and Administration Commission
SCM	-	Subsidies and Countervailing Measures
SCO	-	Shanghai Co-operation Organization
SCRES	-	State Commission for Restructuring the Economic System
SCSC	-	State Council Securities Committee
SCT	-	Single Commodity Transfer
SDB	-	State Development Bank
SDPC	-	State Development and Planning Commission
SETC	-	State Economic and Trade Commission
SOB	-	State-owned Banks
SOCB	-	State-owned Commercial Banks
SOE	-	State-owned Enterprises
SPS	-	Sanitary and Phytosanitary Measures
SSE	-	Shanghai Stock Exchange
SSG	-	Special Safe Guard
STE	-	State Trading Enterprises
SZSE	-	Shenzhen Stock Exchange
TBT	-	Technical Barriers to Trade
TFAP	-	Trade Facilitation Action Plan
TFP	-	Total Factor Productivity
TNC	-	Trade Negotiations Committee
TRIMS	-	Trade Related Investment Measures
TRIPS	-	Trade Related Intellectual Property Rights
TRQ	-	Tariff Rate Quota
TSE	-	Total Support Estimate
TVE	-	Township and Village Enterprise
UNCTAD	-	United Nations Conference on Trade and Development
USTR	-	United States Trade Representative
VAT	-	Value Added Tax

VER	-	Voluntary Export Restraint
VTB	-	Village / Township Banks
WDI	-	World Development Indicators
WTO	-	World Trade Organization
XDAMC	-	Xinda Assets Management Co. Ltd.